Nationalism in a Global World

Nationalism in a Global World

Sam Pryke

Liverpool Hope University, Liverpool, UK

palgrave
macmillan

First published 2009 by
PALGRAVE MACMILLAN

Palgrave Macmillan in the UK is an imprint of Macmillan Publishers Limited,
registered in England, company number 785998, of Houndmills, Basingstoke,
Hampshire RG21 6XS.

Palgrave Macmillan in the US is a division of St Martin's Press LLC,
175 Fifth Avenue, New York, NY 10010.

Palgrave Macmillan is the global academic imprint of the above companies
and has companies and representatives throughout the world.

Palgrave® and Macmillan® are registered trademarks in the United States,
the United Kingdom, Europe and other countries.

ISBN-13: 978–0–230–52730–0   hardback
ISBN-13: 978–0–230–52736–2   paperback

This book is printed on paper suitable for recycling and made from fully
managed and sustained forest sources. Logging, pulping and manufacturing
processes are expected to conform to the environmental regulations of the
country of origin.

A catalogue record for this book is available from the British Library.

A catalog record for this book is available from the Library of Congress.

10 9 8 7 6 5 4 3 2 1
18 17 16 15 14 13 12 11 10 09

Printed in China

Contents

Acknowledgements

I would like to acknowledge and thank Liverpool Hope University for granting me research leave for the first term of the academic year 2007–8 when I was able to really get into the writing of this book. During that time, storm clouds were gathering over the global economy. The subsequent recession we are now in is obviously not something I was able to incorporate into the discussion, but I don't think that detracts seriously from the various chapters, including the one on economic nationalism. My thanks to the following people who read and provided feedback on drafts of chapters: Charles Jones, Neil Ferguson and Richard Pryke and the two anonymous Palgrave Macmillan referees. As always, I am very grateful to Jo Pryke for proofreadings the texts for me. Thanks to Emily Salz and then Anna Reeve at Palgrave Macmillan, who have been tolerant over schedules and enthusiastic about the project. Thanks also to Maggie Lythgoe, the copyeditor with the gimlet eye, who made the final stages relatively pain free. Finally, thanks to my son George Susil Pryke, who, over two years, put up with my reply 'I've been writing my book' when he asked what I'd been doing during the day. I dedicate this book to him.

Introduction

This book concerns the paradox of the general and the particular. The general is the worldwide process known as 'globalization', the particular is a form of division termed 'nationalism'. It is about interconnectedness wrought by globalization and at the same time the separations of nationalism. The interconnections and separations are not uniform to all groups. They differ profoundly according to the particular nation and class. But qualifications should not be used to obscure the extent of globalization as measured by, among other things, the growth of trade, the volume of international financial shifts, the transfer of culture and the reach of communication. This is something not difficult to document. Trade grew fifteenfold between 1950 and 2000 and it now accounts for over 30% of world economic output (Gomes, 2003, pp. 309–12). By April 2007, over $3,210bn of foreign exchange were traded on international markets each day, an increase of more than double in three years (Garnham, 2007). Hollywood's latest blockbusters reach a global audience through a variety of media – cinemas, DVDs, websites, games and so on. Communication systems that enable forms of contact across time and space that would have seemed fantastic even 10 years ago are now routine. Ever greater numbers of migrants (of all categories) shift and settle across national borders. Their numbers are dwarfed by tourists whose movement within and between continents is temporary. One of the arguments of this book is that 'globalization lasts a long time'. With that in mind, it is worth stating that with some adjustments – both up and down – the same sort of claims could have been made 100 years ago. Indeed, one could argue, for example, that the leaps in technological advance of the telephone and its influence on interactions were greater than, say, the internet. However, while I argue that globalization is a process that has been with us for a while, it is also the case that it is now a more extensive and profound feature across human societies than at any point in history. Therefore the relationship of the general to the particular, of globalization to nationalism, demands particular attention. It is with this that the book is concerned – a relationship, not something that should be considered a necessary contradiction.

However, as indicated, try as we might, binaries, oppositions, perceived contradictions, call them what you will, are difficult things to escape from as they organize our thoughts and allow us to think through complex problems. It is for this reason that the question of globalization and nationalism is often posed by commentators in this fashion, specifically through discussion of whether globalization equals the accentuation or attenuation of nationalism.

This kind of approach is, for example, common to the consideration of culture: is globalization leading to cultural homogenization or is it providing the potential for greater diversity between and within national cultures – 'glocalization' as it is sometimes referred to? The general answer to this question about culture and other things is that both are true.

The real problem with the globalization versus nationalism dichotomy is that it can too easily be used by those who are sceptical about globalization. That is because it is easy enough to show that globalization has little significant impact on the resilience of nationalism. Certainly, as an ideology of mass mobilization, it remains central to mass politics and culture. It continues to fire national liberation struggles across a world beset by manifold territorial disputes and injustices. More than 60 years after the advent of the United Nations, various national wars smoulder and flare – although now the hostile parties can potentially contact each other by mobile phone and internet while watching coverage of the fighting on international television channels. Even within the one area of the world where something like a post-national, more specifically post-nation-state, organization exists, the European Union, the centrifugal nationalist forces it comprises make political federalism highly unlikely. Furthermore, there are good reasons for thinking that the very inequalities wrought by globalization sharpen national (and ethnic) divisions and its communication forms enable the further reach of the 'imagined community'. The demarcated national patches of the world might be porous to ever greater migration flows, but this hardly means that governments are relaxed about the matter. Fearful of rising public resentment of foreigners, they spend ever greater sums trying to keep out the unwanted, and monitor those they are prepared to tolerate for economic purposes. Whatever liberalization there has been of national economies over recent decades, it is hardly as if economic protectionism is a thing of the past. It is an irony that the term given to the hegemony of neoliberal economics, 'the Washington consensus', derives its name from a city where a national government, the US Congress and the presidency, oversees entrenched protection of American markets. So rather than posing the relationship between globalization and nationalism as one of straight opposition and trying to assess which force, nationalism or globalization, is coming out on top, for the most part it is more profitable to set out to assess their relationship at this present conjuncture. This will involve accentuation and attenuation questions, strengthening and weakening. However, it is not a case of a crude polarity of who is 'winning'.

If the division of nationalism versus globalization is overplayed, we might go further and suggest that the very terms are questionable. In particular, there is a danger of treating the term 'nationalism' both as an analytic magic talisman and/or a blanket description that covers just about everything that somehow smacks of the national as opposed to the global. For example, as certain forms of economic protection are in some instances attributable to complex alliances of state and business lobbies, the term 'nationalism' is not particularly helpful in conveying their motivation. Simultaneously, globalization has become one of those words that are useful because it conveys a vague reality without being tied down by a specific definition. When one asks a user for an explanation, they receive either further generalities like 'the world is getting smaller', 'the global village' or actual examples like a well-known multinational company. However, while I provide initial definitions in this chapter and try to be attentive to the meaning of the key terms at issue as they are found throughout the book, to some extent we simply have to accept that nationalism and globalization are inevitable catch-alls.

With this in mind, this chapter examines how and why writers, from within the study of globalization and the study of nationalism, have suggested that the heyday of nationalism has passed and that it faces an inevitable decline in its role and relevance with the globalized contraction of the world's polity and economy. In Chapter 2, we look at theorists, again from within the study of both subjects, who have suggested the opposite, that is, they argue that globalization only serves to heighten nationalist antagonism. Chapter 3 examines the relationship between globalization and economic nationalism. Chapter 4 looks at the case that minority nations within larger states are able to flourish in a globalized world. Chapter 5 considers the relationship between national cultures and globalization. Finally, Chapter 6 discusses whether or not a globalized religion, specifically neofundamentalist Islam, is overcoming national divisions among Muslims.

The list of chapters is not exhaustive. For example, although I deal with migration in the chapter on culture, the subject could arguably command a whole separate consideration, given its importance in undermining stable zones of culture, that is, national cultures. And while for the sake of clarity I have tried to steer away from the nation-state as distinct from nations and nationalism, a complete consideration of the subject would inevitably merge into a fuller examination of the changed role of the state in a global world. But that is the subject of another book.

This book relies very much, not wholly, on the work of others, rather than providing any empirical examination of the issues. It is intended to provide an overview of the work of published authors for students studying courses on globalization and nationalism. The publications of others provide crucial intellectual stepping stones through the relatively diverse issues that I cover. I am aware that there may, at times, appear to be a certain arbitrariness to the discussion: why, the reader might ask, include consideration of a particular writer when another is only mentioned in passing or omitted altogether? To some degree this is inevitable as the book presents a series of case studies; it is not intended to be an encyclopedia. However, I have tried to hone in on key authors in the field. For better or worse, it is certainly the case that the writers discussed in Chapters 1 and 2 have been highly influential in the study of nationalism and globalization. Similarly, those dealt with in Chapter 4 on small nations have made key contributions to their academic study. Arjun Appadurai and Olivier Roy in Chapters 5 and 6 on culture and religion respectively have, I think, made influential contributions, and they also present useful arguments to work discussion around. The choice of inclusions in Chapter 3 on economic nationalism is perhaps the most questionable. Possibly key authorities have been left out. However, in contrast to the other parts of the book, my discussion here is constructed through a historical examination of the fortunes of economic nationalism, rather than an overview of key contributors. This is because I think that the subject of economic nationalism has been somewhat overlooked in the literatures on nationalism and globalization. Whatever the shortcomings of the book, I think it does, at least, cover a fairly wide set of readings and debates. It remains in this chapter to provide definitions of the terms at issue and say something about the nature of the discussion about them.

Definitions

Nations and Nationalism

Definitions of nationalism and nations are far from straightforward. The same can be said of globalization. That is because there is fundamental disagreement about the nature of the two phenomena among scholars. In the vast academic literature on nationalism, questions of definition of what nations and nationalism are cannot be neatly separated from understandings of how and when they arose. Different understandings of the development of nations and nationalism rest on and shape the different definitions of what they are. Key within the debate is the relationship between ethnicity and nation. Although in this debate, as many others, there is a temptation to exaggerate the scale of the disagreement between the various accounts and to neatly group them together to face off against each other, it is permissible to draw a definite distinction between ethnosymbolist and modernist accounts of nations and nationalism. The term 'ethnosymbolism' is one taken from the later writings of Anthony D. Smith. The emphasis in this approach is with the historical gestation of nations and nationalism from earlier sociological formations: ethnicities. Nations have, in the title of Smith's (1986) best-known book, 'ethnic origins', a thesis he has subsequently reiterated on numerous occasions. The modernist account of nations and nationalism denies, by contrast, that there is any intrinsic relationship between ethnicity and nationalism. Instead, the various writers associated with this approach argue that nations and nationalism are of far more recent vintage, the product of social, economic and political transformations of the past 250 years of human history.

We can see how issues of definition are handled by writers from within the opposing positions. For example, Geoffrey Hastings, a strong critic of the modernist account of nations and nationalism, is concerned to differentiate a nation from an ethnicity in an account that emphasizes the full formation of the former in early medieval Europe. Hastings (1997, p. 10) suggests that:

> A nation is a far more self-conscious community than an ethnicity. Formed from one or more ethnicities it possesses or claims the right to political identity and autonomy as a people, together with the control of specific territory'.

This definition, like the slightly different variant on nations and nationalism of Anthony D. Smith, indicates a historical growth of nations from one or more ethnicity. In this kind of account, the nation, certainly some European nations at least, is thought to have had a proper existence prior to what modernists consider the coming of the modern age of nationalism, the nineteenth century. As Hastings (1997, p. 9) continues:

> If nationalism became theoretically central to western political thinking in the nineteenth century, it existed as a powerful reality in some places long before that. As something which can empower large numbers of ordinary people, nationalism is a movement which seeks to provide a state for a given 'nation' or further to advance the supposed interests of its own 'nation-state' regardless of other considerations.

So nations give rise to nationalism and nationalisms demand nation-states to further their interests. Chronologically, he claims that English nationalism 'of a sort was already present in the fourteenth century in the long wars with France' (p. 4). More generally, nations and nationalism are not the social constructions of a particular historical conjuncture, but have a genuine lineage. So the order of definitions and academic enquiry should fit the order of development: nations are followed by nationalism.

The approach of modernist writers, especially (notwithstanding important differences of emphasis) Breuilly (1985), Gellner (1983) and Hobsbawm (1992), reverses this ordering, and simultaneously suggests a more limited definition of nation: the principle that the polity and culture of a group should be coterminous, that is, state boundaries should reflect cultural ones. The doctrine of nationalism insists that the political responsibilities of the citizen to their nation override all others. There is no necessary ethnic precursor in this. On the contrary, such writers are generally sceptical of the notion that there is an indispensable link to an earlier ethnicity, an 'ethnic origin' (Smith, 1986). Modernists concede that there may be such a link – there are obvious examples – but such a forerunner is not inevitable, and the presence or absence of an ethnic link does not in itself bestow any particular characteristics (a point made by Gellner (1996) in a debate with Smith). There are, for example, no grounds for thinking that a historic ethnicity makes for an essentially unchanging continuity of composition; nations, no matter how formed, are not unchanging social entities. Such writers have emphasized the 'creation' of nations. As Hobsbawm (1992, p. 10) puts it:

> I would stress the element of artifact, invention and social engineering which enters into the making of nations. Nations as a natural, God-given way of classifying men, as an inherent . . . political destiny, are a myth; nationalism, which sometimes takes pre-existing cultures and turns them into nations, sometimes invents them, and often obliterates pre-existing cultures: that is a reality. In short, for the purposes of analysis nationalism comes before nations.

These then are the well-worn questions that preoccupied students of nations and nationalism over recent years: are nations the creations of the political, social and economic transformations of the nineteenth century in which the 'invention of tradition' was central, or are they entities that have deeper and more profound historic roots and/or an ethnic core? I do not intend to pursue this ethnosymbolist versus modernist debate in itself further here, certainly not at a historical level. Suffice it to say that the debate does enter directly into questions of the future of nationalism discussed in this book, for plainly those less inclined to view nations as comparatively recent and arbitrary will be less receptive to projections of their demise.

It remains to say that I think that Umut Özkirimli (2005, pp. 61–2) is correct in saying that there is now something of a consensus that, at least on one level, it is pointless to try to pin down with any precision quite what a nation is. Rather, it is better to let its meaning emerge in actual historical or contemporary discussion. However, we need some kind of framework to square with the manifold references one finds to nations and nationalism. Simply to give up on definitions altogether and conclude that they are positively unhelpful would allow the nationalist, the journalist or anybody else free rein to assert that a nation is whatever they assume it to be. In framing the parameters of a conceptual framework of what a nation is about, the following four-part explication of Miroslav Hroch (1993), a Czech historian, is useful. No doubt Hroch's approach has a central European ring to it. Without wishing to open up another time-honoured debate – the distinction between Western (republican) and Eastern (ethnic) conceptions of nation – an alternative definition to that of Hroch would play down the notion of common ancestry. It should also be noted that in using the definition of Hroch below, we are not so much concerned with the actual reality of nation – which is not, of course, to suggest that nations do not have objective features as clearly they do – as with the issue of what a people have in mind when they think and talk about a nation.

According to Hroch (1993, p. 5), a nation hinges on:

1   A collective memory of a common past.
2   A myth of common descent.
3   A density of cultural ties that enable a greater degree of communication within the group than outside it.
4   A conception of an essential equality within civil society that rests on a horizontal unity.

Straightaway one can begin to see how globalization both extends and undermines 'the nation' as set out in this way. For example, modern communication systems allow a national citizen of a given country greater facility to communicate both within the zone of their nation and with those outside it. The key point is that the above can act as a framework that, without constantly trying to evaluate and re-evaluate in an age of globalization, will be useful to refer to as a point of reference.

Globalization

As with nations and nationalism, so with globalization: definitions quickly run into analytical tangles, yet are necessary. They are necessary because although the lustre of the term 'globalization' has now worn off, it still exists as a journalistic and political cliché that approximates to general perceptions about the extent of world markets, the ubiquity of multinational companies, and the reach of information technology. In the face of this, we cannot lapse into an 'anything goes' approach and defer to fragments of experience and knowledge that are expressed though references to technological and social innovation – the 'Google generation', for example, to take one among many passing shibboleths, in this instance a reference to the globalized younger age group. However, in trying to move beyond mere description to establish what globalization is, one enters into the realm of theoretical explanation and political opinion. The various definitions that writers have made about globalization reflect the intellectual purpose of their discussion.

   A clear example is found in the influential case made by Paul Hirst and Grahame Thompson in their text *Globalization in Question* (1999). We are not concerned here with the validity of their account, but to see how they go about affixing a definition of globalization. Hirst and Thompson (1999, pp. 7–13) claim that globalization should be taken to mean 'the development of a new economic structure, and not just the conjunctural change towards greater international trade and investment within an existing set of economic relations'. They thus emphasize that the term should mean the culmination of existing trends to produce something quite new, a qualitatively different economic world system from that which existed in previous historical eras. Therefore, it should not be evoked to characterize more of the same, a mere ramping up of international economic activity. This is because they were highly sceptical of a casual acceptance in the mid-1990s by academic and media commentators alike of the originality of the latest phase of the economic developments, something the very term 'globalization' took for granted.

In this light, one can see how they set, as it were, a high bar for the term 'globalization' to be justified in their further definitional clarification. Hirst and Thompson (1999, pp. 7–13) say that in a global 'system distinct national economies are subsumed and rearticulated into the system by international processes and transactions'. The consequences of such a system, should it be proved to exist, would be that:

1   governance would be 'fundamentally problematic'
2   multinational companies would be 'footloose' 'transnational companies'
3   the bargaining power of labour would further decline
4   the emergence of a 'fundamental multipolarity in the international politi-cal system' as 'the hitherto hegemonic national power would no longer be able to impose its own distinct regulatory objectives in either its own terri-tories or elsewhere'.

The authors counterpoise this global model to 'a simple and extreme' inter-national model, in which 'the principal entities are national economies' with trade serving to integrate world market relationships.

Now this definition of Hirst and Thompson is not an exaggeration for the sake of polemic. On the contrary, it is rigorous. At the same time, the defini-tion – and that of an international model – are, in the words of the authors, 'ideal types' designed to specify the difference by putting, as it were, clear water 'between a new global economy and merely an extensive and intensi-fying international economic relations'. Hirst and Thompson (1999, pp. 7–13) argue that 'too often evidence compatible with the latter is used as though it substantiated the former'. The burden of their book is devoted to substanti-ating what Held et al. (1999, pp. 2–14) describe as a 'sceptical' account of glob-alization through examining the extent of global, as opposed to international, economic activity.

The late Pierre Bourdieu (1930–2002), and others, suggests – in a reflection of a leftward political turn towards the end of his life – that the very term 'globalization' is a saccharine conceit of politicians, media pundits and academics to foster the illusion of the general involvement of populations. What is really taking place, Bourdieu (2002) argued, is an ever greater market penetration of societies for profit. In this account, the extent of economic glob-alization is not denied; at issue is the ideological camouflage it provides for neoliberalism. There is some similarity between this radical understanding of globalization and Justin Rosenberg's (2001) scathing critiques of the general sloppiness of so much writing on the subject. Rosenberg (2005, p. 65) suggests that such is the 'conceptual bankruptcy' of the word, something that has only been underlined by general national retrenchment since 9/11, that the only valid conclusion to draw is that '"globalization" did not even exist' (for further coverage of these issues, see Held and McGrew, 2007).

By contrast, writing at about the same time as Hirst and Thompson in the mid-1990s, Martin Albrow (1996), a writer whose account is included under the heading 'hyperglobalist' by Held and McGrew, suggested that such is the epochal shift that globalization involves, the term itself is inadequate because it implies continuities with the vectors and theories of modernity and post-modernity. Instead, he suggests the term 'globality' is a more appropriate one to capture the 'comprehensive social transformation' that it involves. Rejecting suggestions that what is afoot is principally to be understood as an economic phenomenon, Albrow (1996, pp. 4–6) suggests that: 'The Global Age involves the supplanting of modernity with globality and this means an overall change in the basis of action and social organization.' The overall changes are in respect of the environment, security, communication, the economy and reflexivity. The latter has implications for the co-subject of this book, nationalism, as it involves 'people and groups of all kinds referring to the globe as their frame of reference'. It is also the latter that seems to stimulate Albrow's excitement about what globality involves. He encourages the reader to 'escape the stifling hold of modern on the imagination' as 'we live in our own time and the Global Age opens worlds up to us in unprecedented ways'.

To pursue this discussion any further will anticipate later coverage of theories of globalization as they relate to nationalism that we will shortly consider. Our problem remains trying to affix a definition. In doing this, the point should by now be clear: it is impossible to avoid theoretical anticipation if the definition is to have any analytic purchase. Therefore, while Held et al.'s definition is both in line with their 'transformationalist' perspective on globalization and clearly does not seek to assign priority to any particular variable, their definition as set out below has a number of benefits:

> Globalization can best be understood as a process or set of processes rather than a singular condition. It does not reflect a simple linear developmental logic, nor does it prefigure a world society or a world community. Rather, it refers to the emergence of interregional networks and systems of interaction and exchange. In this respect, the enmeshment of national and societal systems in wider global processes has to be distinguished from any notion of global integration. (Held et al., 1999, p. 27)

From this the authors emphasize the complex transnational networks that arise between communities, states, international institutions, nongovernmental organizations (NGOs) and multinational corporations; the penetration of globalization into most areas of social life; the stretching of space away from a territorial principle as the site of political and economic activity; and, relatedly, the expanding scale of power.

There are four points in particular that deserve emphasis and extension within this definition:

1   It is vital to see globalization as a process, and not as a point we have or have not reached. Seeing it in this way logically allows us to track globalization backwards and recognize that there have been key stages in its development. Although some disagree, notably Hirst and Thompson (1999) in relation to some indices, there is good, indeed obvious, reason to think that the current phase of globalization has resulted in the most intensive and extensive level. The statistics given at the beginning of the chapter on trade and finance are obviously not the whole story, but they give some measure of this.

2   The ability of states, peoples and classes to shape global flows according to their interests reflects differentials of wealth and power. Having said that, it is also the case that aspects of globalization have a momentum that is virtually impossible for even the most powerful actors, states, to control. Financial markets would be one example, migration another.

3   Globalization should not be considered a juggernaut that proceeds along all axes (trade, communication and so on) at uniform speed and reaches all societies and all parts of a society simultaneously. There has been much debate over whether globalization is of general benefit to humanity as a whole. What is in less doubt is that world inequalities have increased while some societies have been largely cut off and marginalized from globalization. There have, in fact, been attempts to measure how globalized various societies are. The *Foreign Policy* website (www.foreignpolicy. com.index.php) produces an annual league table measuring both economic and cultural indicators. The results are interesting but we should note that the shorthand of referring to a society as a whole as being 'globalized' or not is an oversimplification. Within all societies there are profound differences of exposure and access to global finance, communication, travel and so on, according to class, particular geographic location and age.

4   Given the inequalities referred to, globalization should not be considered something that means mutual interdependence, cultural homogeneity or universalism. The relationship between economies and societies is not generally one of mutual interdependence. It is logically possible to conceive of globalization as giving rise to greater disparities of dependence between economies and states, cultural diversity and political disharmony. The binaries of homogeneity versus heterogeneity are, as indicated, in themselves misleading, although inevitable. The point is that both features are observable.

One could go on endlessly refining the above definition. But, as stated, definitions are always only provisional and are outstripped by the messiness of reality. Key for our purposes in the consideration of globalization and nationalism is how previously isolated groups are connected in time and space. Held (2005, pp. 1–2) refers to this in a more recent publication:

> We no longer inhabit, if we ever did, a world of circumscribed communities. Instead we live in a world of what I like to call 'overlapping communities of fate' where trajectories are enmeshed with each other. In our world, it is not only the violent exception that links people together across borders; the very nature of everyday living – of work and money and beliefs, as well as trade, communications and finance, not to speak of the earth's environment – connects us all in multiple ways with increasing intensity.

It is worth noting that the term 'communities of fate' is how Max Weber referred to nations over 100 years ago. With these provisional definitions in mind, we conclude with an overview of how writers have dealt with the relationship between globalization and nationalism.

Accounts of Globalization and Nationalism

How, then, have writers on the subjects of globalization and nationalism considered the relationship between the two things? No total answer can be made to this kind of question and, given the specificity of the question, the reflections made have often been brief. Moreover, in trying to identify intellectual trajectories that suggest that the power of nationalisms will decline with the advance of globalization in Chapter 1, writers are grouped together who have approached the relationship from contrasting disciplinary starting points. Some writers I have identified as contributing to the industrial convergence school have been primarily concerned with the study of nationalism and some with globalization. The same is true of the so-called 'hyperglobalist' position. Here I make some general remarks about the study of the subjects.

The first thing to be said about the study of nations and nationalism is that it is obviously far older than that expressly of globalization as a named term, and is vast. Most serious accounts of nationalism have been undertaken by professional historians. Insofar as that subject's influence is possible to discern, Anthony D. Smith (1992) suggests that they have tended to view nationalism with a certain scepticism as its advocates – nationalists – generally rely upon myths to embellish their nations' pasts. Inasmuch as the professionalism of historians obliges them to objectively assess the past, rather than selectively cull, air brush and fabricate for present purposes like the nationalist – to 'invent tradition' as Hobsbawn and Ranger's (1983) book is entitled – this is no doubt true. However, Paul Lawrence (2004, p. 60), who has assiduously tracked the study of nationalism in Europe, identifies many historians whose gaze has been distorted by their national perspective, particularly when their study has been that of narrative national histories not the general phenomenon.

So far as nationalism and globalization is concerned, Lawrence identifies a tradition stretching back to the First World War – it is a feature of intellectual history that projections of the demise of something are often made towards the end of a period when the contrary tendency is most apparent – which forecasts the wane of the former with, broadly, the rise of the latter. He does not include the writers on war and nationalism in this period (approximately 1916–21), who suggested that their power will recede with greater internationalism, under the heading of 'modernism', and thereby indicate the emergence of a coherent school of thought. However, Lawrence suggests that for the first time in this era, scholars offered accounts of nationalism that did not claim, or at least assume, that nations and nationalism are constant features of human history. He points out, logically enough, that in order to be able even to think of the demise of nationalism, it is necessary to periodize its rise. If a phenomenon has always existed in some form as an essential human force, it follows that it will never fade. The periodization of nationalism – when and in what circumstances it arose – is one of the principal concerns of the modernist approach to the subject as it has developed over the past 30 years.

For the most part, nineteenth-century historiography either suggested that nations and nationalism were indeed a permanent features of all societies or were so vague on the matter that the writer appeared to have taken their existence as a given. Notwithstanding the accounts written towards the end of the First World War noted by Lawrence, writing on nationalism in the 1920s and 30s tended to suggest its antiquity. For example, the American historian and diplomat Carlton Hayes (1931, p. 1) attempted to define a five-point typology of nationalism of varying degrees of intensity, while insisting that it was a timeless force. 'It becomes clear to us that the prehistoric world was peopled with nationalists', he claimed. The more influential work of Hans Kohn in the 1930s and after suggests a rise in nationalist consciousness in Europe after the French Revolution (Kohn, 1937), but the assumption in his work was that nationalism was a force in waiting.

Speculation about the decline of nationalism in the face of what might broadly be described as the 'internationalization' of the postwar era – the birth of the United Nations and so on – is evident and culminates in a spate of influential modernist accounts in the 1980s and early 90s. Among these writers, Gellner and Hobsbawm were prepared to venture furthest in anticipating a definite erosion of nationalism in the face of, broadly, globalization. We will examine Gellner's account later within what I have termed the 'industrial convergence' approach. The high tide of the modernist position on the future of nationalism also requires its own section below.

The period when Hobsbawm made his most trenchant statements on the future of nationalism, the early 1990s, was one when the academic study of nationalism was, naturally enough given the historical backdrop, making something of a comeback. Despite the profile of the modernist accounts of the previous era – above all Benedict Anderson's *Imagined Communities* (1983) – the subject had not been a mainstream academic activity. Shortly after the Eastern European revolutions of 1989, events motivated at least in part by the desire for national liberation, the subject became relatively fashionable, with a plethora of books and journals devoted to the myriad aspects of the phenomenon. Once again, generalizations are difficult but it is probably true that over the past 20 years, analyses that in some way spell the weakening of nationalism in the face of globalization have, to say the least, not been prominent. Instead, the analysis of nationalism has moved away somewhat from the strict modernist approach of Hobsbawm and Gellner.

Few serious scholars have taken up primordialism – the assertion that nations have existed since time immemorial – in its place. But is likely that Anthony Smith's (1986) thesis that nations have 'ethnic origins', more recently that they have a historic 'ethnosymbolic' dimension, has grown in intellectual influence. Without wishing to rehearse in detail Smith's arguments, which we examine in Chapter 2, his voluminous critiques of modernism hinge on the contention that contemporary nations and nationalism are not, as Hobsbawm suggests, social constructs that in current circumstances provide people with simplistic solutions to complex problems. Rather, they are cultural entities that have genuine and deep-seated connections to identity and belonging. Thus, while the violence of national independence campaigns may be reprehensible, the aspiration for a 'national state' (Smith's preferred term) is not. Rather, as an expression of national identity, it is intrinsic to humanity; such identities correspond with collective histories and thus bestow meaning to human life (Smith, 1995). So while there is the important and influential position of modernism within the study of nationalism that suggests the likely waning of its power due, broadly conceived, to globalization, such a form of analysis has at least been partially replaced by a school of thought that suggests that such a stance misconceives the way in which nations are rooted within humanity.

Within the academic and wider public debate over globalization since the early 1990s, there has in fact been relatively little discussion of nationalism. Instead, discussion has tended to revolve around two things. The first has centred around its alleged general benefit to humanity, principally but not exclusively its economic benefit. It has certainly had a 'nationalist' dimension, as in part it has been about whether or not globalization – identical products, media forms and so on – is trampling over local cultures, traditions and national identities. The arguments have been both heightened and offset by the usual approach of governments, exemplified by the New Labour admin- istration in Britain, that as globalization is an established fact, the options of governments are limited and that all they can realistically hope to do is to provide minimum safeguards – educational, economic, cultural and environ- mental – for people from the uncertainties it brings. In other words, govern- ments have generally attempted to make a political virtue out of what they suggest is the reality of economic neoliberalism.

The debate on whether globalization leads to general prosperity has been played out in different countries between various commentators. The exchange between the *Financial Times* writer Martin Wolf (2001) and the Cambridge academic Noreena Hertz (2001) would be one instance in Britain. Perhaps the most famous contribution in this charged discussion was that of former World Bank economist Joseph Stiglitz. His *Globalization and its Discontents* (2000), written in part as a critique of the bank's policies vis-à-vis the 1997 Asia financial crash, prompted a flurry of responses, not least from his former colleagues in Washington (see, for example, Dabrowski et al., 2000). A more recent and restrained instance of the debate over 'who benefits', perhaps because none of the distinguished commentators are overtly critical of capitalism per se, is a recent collection of pieces in *Debating Globalisation* (Barnett et al., 2005).

A second strand of debate, more within its academic study, has been over the extent of globalization. Central to it is the fate of the nation-state as the forces of globalization – finance, commodities, images, people – wash over their reduced barriers. An important early contribution here was that of Hirst and Thompson's *Globalization in Question* (1996), mentioned above. The book attracted some attention outside academia because it provided a formidable critique of the notion that globalization is an all-consuming, modern-day leviathan that national governments were fools to try to check. The authors choose to do this through a thorough-going examination of contemporary political economy that questioned key assumptions in the economic global- ization literature. However, in the Preface to the second edition of the book, Hirst and Thompson (1999) state that although their book discusses issues like trade, foreign direct investment and so on, their principal objective in *Globalization in Question* is to undermine the easy assumptions of global trans- formation in cultural and social studies. Hirst and Thompson (1999, p. xiii) aimed to puncture a glib academic consensus, a new grand narrative in the social sciences, which 'treats global processes and the local response to them as part of a long-run tendency towards the dissolution of local and national "societies" in which causes within cultural or political borders predominantly determine social outcomes'.

Such an assumption – a profound transformation of the world through globalization – is found in the recent work of, among others, the British sociologist John Urry. In his book *Sociology Beyond Societies* (2000) – notable for an opening chapter devoted to defending Margaret Thatcher's infamous claim that 'there is no such thing as society' – there is no extended discussion of globalization as such, certainly there is no attempt to empirically prove its existence. However, Urry argues that social science should shift its frame of reference away from society, almost unconsciously the national society, to a widened realm of social phenomena. Subsequently, this sort of discussion within the rarefied higher echelons of academic sociology has shifted to considerations of 'cosmopolitanism'. Within the recent work of Ulrich Beck, for example, there is less emphasis on globalization as an burgeoning crisis of the nation-state than as a phase in a trajectory that has existed at least since the Enlightenment that imbues individuals with a sense and orientation towards cosmopolitanism from within – a positive 'reflexive cosmopolitanism' (Beck and Sznaider, 2006).

This second debate – the extent of globalization – has obviously had rather more to say about nationalism than the first. However, it has not been nationalism as such that has been of central importance to the debate. Rather, it has been more about the nation-state. Clearly there is a connection, as the nation-state is, by its very name, that organization that embodies and acts on behalf of a nation. But the discussion among writers – within various academic subjects, such as sociology, economics and international relations, which generally make little reference to each other – has been more about the independence of national governments as economic actors and sovereign polities. Discussion has not generally been about the effect of globalization on nationalism as a means of state legitimization, popular ideology and means of mass mobilization. It has not therefore directly tended to engage with the underpinnings of nation as set out above. This said, hyperglobalist accounts form a part of the discussion of accounts of the globalization-induced decline of nationalism considered in Chapter 1.

Conclusion

It remains to attempt to pull together the strands of the subject matter of the book as they have emerged in this chapter. Our subject, nationalism in a global world, is one that looks at the general and the specific. It tries to assess what impact global flows of commodities, currencies, images, peoples and faiths are having on an ideology, nationalism, that is concerned with the particular, the nation. Although there is contradiction here, the relationship between globalization and nationalism should not be taken to be a kind of struggle for supremacy, as the matter is too complex, too multivariate, too dialectical to be understood in this fashion. However, much of the discussion that has taken place on globalization and nationalism over the past 20 years has framed the issue in terms of which force is the greater. Perhaps it is inevitable that the matter has been posed in this way. Such an approach is evident in sections of my discussion. For example, Chapter 5 on global culture examines issues of cultural homogenization besides the possibility that national difference is being accentuated.

The subjects at the heart of the book are difficult to define with precision as the definitions authors attach to them stem from contrasting accounts of their nature and development. Here I define nationalism as an ideology that insists that certain groups of people have a primary right to occupy a territory by virtue of a common ancestry, history and culture. A nation involves the presence of memory, descent, a capacity for communication and a conception of equality. Globalization should be understood as a historical process that links peoples together through the sort of flows mentioned above. It is profoundly uneven in intensity and impact, there are vast inequalities in material outcomes and it can be reversed.

The claim that nationalism belongs to a certain historical period and will fade with a generalized change in circumstances is one that emerges relatively early in the history of the study of nationalism. However, it only becomes explicit, as we will shortly examine in detail, after 1945, with the approach generally known as 'modernism'. Although modernist writers are still influential, their emphasis on the temporal nature of nationalism has been replaced more recently by an emphasis on the deeper historical roots and therefore the cultural resonance of nationalism. Within the study of globalization, nationalism – indeed the nation-state – has been considered. However, the principal debates have been on the extent of globalization and whether it has produced general improvements in wealth. Therefore, although the literatures I pick through are extensive, the following discussion lies outside the well-worn tracks of academic debate.

Summary Points

- This book concerns the relationship between nationalism and globalization.
- Although there is an implicit contradiction in their relationship – as nationalism is concerned with the particular and globalization the general – it is unhelpful to see them as playing out a sort of struggle for dominance.

- 'Who is winning?' is, however, the way in which commentators have characterized the relationship between nationalism and globalization.
- In fact, while we cannot escape binaries, we should be attentive to the fact that globalization may stimulate nationalism and vice versa.
- Definitions of nations, nationalism and globalization reflect the way in which they are understood – how writers explain their origin, causes and so on.
- The definition in this book is that nationalism is an ideology that insists that different groups of people, that is, nations, inhabit the world as defined by their common culture and historical inhabitation of discrete patches of land.
- Globalization is a historical process that links people together through ties of trade, finance, travel, culture, media and communication.
- Within the academic study of nationalism, writers within what is known as the 'modernist' approach have suggested that is not a permanent feature of history but is likely to weaken as the conditions that gave rise to its emergence begin to disappear.
- Debates in the study of globalization have not generally been concerned with nationalism, but one can find within what has been termed 'hyper-globalist' accounts, the claim that they are fading in importance.

1

The Weakening of Nationalism?

The Introduction provided definitions of nations, nationalism and globalization. It suggested that one can identify accounts within the study of nationalism, principally in what is known as the 'modernist' approach, that suggest it is a passing force. Such accounts should be set against the theoretical understandings we examine in Chapter 2, which suggest that as nations are built on older and more durable foundations, they are unlikely to fade. The study of globalization has, in part, been concerned with the fate of the nation-state. Contributions that have claimed that the nation-state is a declining organizational form as globalization sweeps all before it have subsequently been dubbed 'the hyperglobalist' approach in an influential account by Held et al. (1999).

In this chapter, we examine the ways in which modernists and hyperglobalists understand our subject, nationalism and globalization. In addition, we examine an older school of thought, that of 'industrial convergence'. Examination of these two strands of thought involves bringing together a number of writers in a given intellectual discourse. This type of exercise is always somewhat arbitrary and at times misleading, as it can have the effect of flattening differences between authors. Nevertheless, the positions do have key intellectual coordinates. With the first, the modernist approach to nationalism, the coherence of the position is enhanced by taking the highly influential case of Eric Hobsbawm. The hyperglobalist case is examined through the work of Karl Marx, Kenichi Ohmae, Nigel Harris, and Michael Hardt and Antonio Negri. The final section on industrial convergence theory deals chiefly with the writings on nationalism of Ernest Gellner. Gellner's approach to nationalism is generally regarded as that of a modernist, but, for reasons I make clear, his case falls within a tradition stretching back to the writings of Herbert Spencer in the nineteenth century. The chapter concludes by pulling the strands of the various authors together and suggesting possible shortcomings.

The Modernism of Nationalism

As suggested in the Introduction, the modernist approach to nations and nationalism is one that suggests that the subject is confined to a particular historical time frame. It argues that nations, as we can observe them in their present form, are the product of modernity, that is, the creations of the economic, political and social transformations of the past 250 years. Nationalism as a means of mass identification and mobilization is a relatively recent phenomenon, something that exists in a definite form from the end of the eighteenth century. Intimations of the modernist approach are found in some discussions of war and nationalism in the period 1916–20. Crucially, for the first time such accounts periodized the existence of nationalism, rather than directly suggesting that it is a force that emanates from the timeless cultural entities known as nations or simply assuming that this is the case. This was the tendency in most nineteenth-century and much twentieth-century historiography. The modernist approach did not emerge as a systematic understanding of nationalism until the postwar period. The most important works by writers such as Eric Hobsbawm, John Breuilly, Ernest Gellner and (with some qualifications) Benedict Anderson were written between 1975 and 1990.

Each has made a distinctive contribution to this general approach. Breuilly's work drew attention to the role of the state as the agency that nationalists have created and used to structure nationalisms. Anderson's account looked at the intellectual process by which a zone of imagination was constructed by nationalists, in which groups – nations – assumed and nurtured a cultural togetherness. Gellner's work on the rise of nations, examined shortly, considered what function nationalism plays within industrialization. I have placed Gellner's understanding of the weakening of nationalism within a postwar Anglo-American school of thought called 'industrial convergence theory'. Hobsbawm's writings on nationalism have, in keeping with his Marxism, considered the class basis of nationalism as an ideology. He provides the most substantial and direct modernist consideration of the reduced power of nationalism, so for this reason we consider him as a representative of this approach. It should be mentioned in connection with this that although there are important differences in the work of Breuilly, Anderson and Hobsbawm, all were influenced by Marxism more directly than was the case with Gellner. Therefore it makes sense to set them apart within related, but distinct approaches.

Hobsbawm's direct interest in nationalism is contained in, among other places, his well-known trilogy of books on the 'long nineteenth century' (Hobsbawm, 1962, 1975, 1987). His position, expounded in writings over 60 years, is that nationalism politically arose in the late eighteenth century and subsequently gained momentum in the long nineteenth century (until 1914) because of social and economic transformations. From this period to the mid-twentieth century, it played a crucial role in state building, as it supplied the ideological cement to establish polities, national economies, armed forces, educational and broadcasting systems and civil services. Simultaneously, certainly from the end of the nineteenth century onwards, nationalism became contaminated by the politics of race, open to all claimants whether large or small and inclined to the political Right. In such a way, it was a constituent of the age of extremes, the name of the book that completes Hobsbawm's history of the world over the past 200 years (Hobsbawm, 1994).

As regards the debate over the origination of nations and nationalism, Hobsbawm acknowledges that the construction of some nationalisms drew on pre-existing national sentiments – they had a 'proto-nationalism'. However, in his view, there is no necessary precursor of this type and, in general terms, modern nationalisms should not be understood as the product of older existing nations or group ethnicities. Therefore, whatever its contemporary fires, the fact that it is of recent origin reveals that it is not necessarily a permanent feature of human societies. Hobsbawm set out such an account most comprehensibly in a series of lectures in 1985 given at Queen's University, Belfast, which formed the basis of his widely read book, *Nations and Nationalism since 1780*, published in 1990. Published two years later, the second edition of the book devoted a chapter to the present and future of nationalism. In it, Hobsbawm (1992) denies that the contemporary and continuing resurgence of nationalism is comparable to its historic arc from the nineteenth century to the decades immediately after the Second World War. In that period, the unificatory nationalisms of the advanced world first pulled together disparate and hitherto fragmented peoples under the wing of the nation-state. Subsequently, this unificatory model provided the impetus for national liberation movements in Africa and Asia that sought to unite the various ethnicities first packaged together into states by European imperialists.

In relation to the 1990s, Hobsbawm rejected the widely held belief that the fall of Communism in Eastern Europe was brought about by nationalism. Instead, he suggested that the crucial factor was the implosion of Communist parties through the demise of their own regimes. More generally, Hobsbawm (1992, p. 191) argued that today nationalism is 'historically less important' than its nation-building phase: 'It is no longer, as it were, a global political programme, as it may have been said to have been in the nineteenth and twentieth centuries.' This is because the viability of the nation-state has been much reduced. Once it was the practical organizational form for bounding and protecting national economies and the conduct of international diplomacy. Today, in a 'transnational' economic world – the term 'globalization' had not become commonplace in 1992, if it had Hobsbawm would undoubtedly have used it and does so in later writings (Hobsbawm, 2007) – the capture and promotion of a distinctly national economy is no more feasible than the pursuit of outright political independence, given the systemic limitations imposed by regional and international organizations. The historic connection between nationalism and the creation of viable nation-states has thus been undermined, with the result that 'the idea of "the nation", once extracted, like a mollusk, from the apparently hard shell of the "nation-state", emerges in distinctly wobbly shape' (Hobsbawm, 2007, p. 190).

The current wave of 'essentially separatist and divisive "ethnic" group assertion' that aims to break up existing nation states 'has no positive programme or prospect' (p. 170). Instead, it should be understood as an expression of a general wave of insecurity and confusion felt by people who look for a ready target, a scapegoat, to blame – the foreigner, immigrant, ethnic insider or troublesome national neighbour. Contemporary ethnic nationalism is part of the wider rise of identity politics, something that Hobsbawm is generally sceptical and sometimes frankly contemptuous of:

> The anguish and disorientation which finds expression in this hunger to belong, and hence the 'politics of identity' – not necessarily national identity – is no more a moving force of history than the hunger for 'law and order' which is an equally understandable response to another aspect of social disorganization. Both are symptoms of sickness rather than diagnoses, let alone therapy. Nevertheless, they create an illusion of nations and nationalism as an irresistibly rising force ready for the third millennium. This force is exaggerated by the semantic illusion which today turns all states into 'nations' (and members of the United Nations), even when they patently are not. Consequently, all movements seeking territorial autonomy tend to think of themselves as establishing 'nations' even when this is plainly not the case; and all movements for regional, local or even sectional interests against central power and state bureaucracy will, if they possibly can, put on the national costume, preferably in its ethnic linguistic styles. (Hobsbawm, 2007, p. 177)

Hobsbawm concludes his argument with a memorable and much quoted – usually in critique – flourish: 'The owl of Minerva which brings wisdom, said Hegel, flies out at dusk. It is a good sign that it is now circling round nations and nationalism' (p. 192).

There has been scepticism about these claims, even among those sympathetic to Hobsbawm's general long-term case. Marxist critics pointed to the uneven nature of development and the injustices of imperialism as stimulating national conflict across the globe for the foreseeable future. Some of these issues are examined in subsequent chapters. More fundamental criticism of Hobsbawm's position is provided in Chapter 2.

Hyperglobalism

Hyperglobalism is the name given by Held et al. (1999) to a number of thinkers from the early to mid-1990s who hailed globalization as a new epoch of human history. They did not seek to stress the continuities and connections with long-term historical economic trends, but emphasized the quantum leap in capitalism. The economic, specifically the transformative power of the market was the orientation of their analysis. As Held et al. (1999, p. 3) say of this approach: 'Such a view of globalization generally privileges an economic logic and, in its neoliberal variant, celebrates the emergence of a single global market and the principle of competition as the harbinger of human progress.' They further comment that such an approach has been adopted by both neoliberals and neo-Marxists; the difference being that the former celebrate the market as the triumph of individual freedom and consumer choice over state power, the latter see it as the completion of capitalist domination. The term 'hyperglobalist' is placed beside two others: 'sceptics' and 'transformationalists'. Sceptics, like Hirst and Thompson (1999), stress the constrained and limited nature of world markets and are highly doubtful that the state has been made obsolescent. Transformationalists, who include the authors of *Global Transformations* and other widely read works, seek a sort of 'halfway house', in which allowance is made for the historical continuities of the growth in trade and so on, but suggest that the role that governments can play has been substantially altered by markets.

As concerns our subject, the emphasis within the hyperglobalist approach is on how globalization impacts upon the nation-state, nationalism and national identity. The analysis proceeds in that order: an integrating and therefore constricting global market system systematically reduces the scope of the nation-state as an institution, nationalism as an ideology and national identity as an individual and collective sense of self. The essential argument is that demarcated territories, the stuff of the nation-state and nationalism with their original insistence that culture and political boundaries should be coterminous, are increasingly being circumvented by the flow of currencies, commodities, products, words, images and people that cut across the poorly fenced geographic partitions. Naturally enough, the interest of the writers reflects this given trajectory, that is, they come in on the issue of the particular, nationalism, from the view point of the general, globalization. On occasions, therefore, nations and nationalism are not really considered in their own right such is the preoccupation with the tremendous power of the global. Some writers considered below do, however, combine this angle of analysis with careful theoretical and historical consideration of nationalism.

Marx and Engels

Marx and Engels are obviously not recent theorists of globalization. In fact, their thoughts pertinent to this section were not even made late in their lives as Victorian capitalism matured. Rather, they are reflective of their revolutionary optimism in the mid-nineteenth century. I have included them here as some of their insights into the consequences of the expansion of world markets anticipate the writings of more recent analysts. Substantively, therefore, as a noted contemporary observer has pointed out, the early writings of Marx and Engels are very much those of a hyperglobalist (Callinicos, 2002, p. 249). Theoretically, Marx is perhaps a natural and a slightly curious choice for this label – natural because Marx was obviously a proponent of the Enlightenment, with its emphasis on a general shift in historical progress and scientific reasoning. He drew on the classical political economy of Adam Smith and David Ricardo who emphasized the universal character of the market, something that was autonomous of governments. The period when Marx seemed most optimistic that national governments as expressions of human difference would fade was 'the golden age' of laissez faire, the 1840s and 50s – the age when Adam Smith seemed most relevant. As contemporaries pointed out and is considered in greater detail in Chapter 3, British advocacy of free trade and its ability to hold it up as a universal standard in the mid-nineteenth century had less to do with the principle itself than self-interest, given its industrial supremacy. However, the role of government, the nation-state, was generally thought to be of limited importance – that of an 'executive committee of the bourgeoisie', as he referred to it in *The Communist Manifesto* (Marx and Engels, 1998: 19) – in accounting for the phenomenal growth in overseas trade in the preceding 50-year period. The subsequent 50 years were more clearly characterized by the expansion of Britain's empire and the international rise of economic protectionism. Simultaneously, Marx is a curious selection because the history of Marxism is hardly that of the victory of proletarian internationalism, derived from capitalist globalization, over nationalism. By and large, the opposite is the case as Marxism as a political movement entrenched and extended states in the twentieth century, albeit in the name of the world working class. Within Marx's writings, the claim that nationalism will inevitably fade with the spread of the market is relatively rare. Nevertheless, the points below are very much in line with his general historical framework and were never repudiated in later writings. For these reasons his inclusion in this section is legitimate.

It would be too much to say that Marx prophesied the end of nations. To have done so would have involved a theoretical conception of their existence. Rather, as numerous commentators have made clear, Marx and Engels failed to address nations and nationalism in any systematic fashion (see, for example, Munck, 1985). Insofar as they did refer to nations, it was in the context of thoughts about progress and modernity. Here the prejudices of Engels, in particular, against small 'non-historic peoples' (a phrase of Hegel) – entities that were likely to disappear with historical development both inside and outside Europe – were given full vent (see Chapter 4). Other than that they did so through comments on the 'national question' as it was termed, that is, as a matter of contemporary political concerns. Thus they were concerned with key political changes like Polish liberation from the oppression of the tsarist autocracy, the unification of Italy, the independence of Ireland from the British; all developments they thought would set the scene for proletarian internationalism. The well-known remarks of Marx and Engels about nationality as an aspect of diminishing difference that we now outline are most notably made in *The Communist Manifesto* (1998).

It is not just the brevity and brilliance of its language that have made the *Manifesto* the best known and most widely read Marxist work since its publication in early 1848. The prescience and vitality of the text make it a work whose ongoing relevance is periodically stressed. That in itself does not mean that the *Manifesto* should be treated as a theoretical exposition, so much as a series of brilliant insights set within a clarion call to arms that 'The working men have no country'. That said, the work does convey Marx's thoughts on capitalism and nationality effectively. It is not as if there is a *Capital*, his most substantial work, on nationality that we can turn to get a fuller sense of Marx's thinking, as there is with economic history and so on. However, the emphasis on the internationalization of capital without respect for the impediment of states found in the *Manifesto* continues throughout his work. In the *Grundrisse*, for example, Marx (1973, p. 408) notes: 'The tendency to create the world market is directly given in the concept of capital itself.' In *Capital* (1976, p. 727), he concedes that he abstracts from the existence of national differences and in doing so 'treat[s] the whole world of trade as if it was one nation'.

There are a number of features of the *Manifesto* relevant for our purposes:

1   Most obviously, the pre-eminent role given by Marx and Engels to the expansion of capitalist markets. In the latter stages of the *Manifesto*, and this is a point taken up in other works, most famously in *Capital*, Marx talks of how capitalism first succeeds in national unification through drawing neighbouring provinces together. Central to this account is the way in which it subsequently transforms and pulls the world together as the need of the 'constantly expanding market for its products chases the bourgeoisie over the entire surface of the globe', as 'it must nestle everywhere, settle everywhere, establish connections everywhere' (Marx and Engels, 1998, p. 39).

2   Capitalism has a cosmopolitan character through the variety of raw materials and commodities it draws into world markets, in contrast to limited locally derived resources.

3 Capitalism ends national self-sufficiency by bringing about economic interdependence.
4 Through market homogenization, 'national one-sidedness and narrow-mindedness become more and more impossible, and from the numerous national and local literatures, there arises a world literature' (p. 39).

So a single world market undermines cultural difference. This gives rise to the attenuation of nationalism and, more specifically, national identity. Marx claimed:

> National differences and antagonism between peoples are daily more and more vanishing, owing to the development of the bourgeoisie, to freedom of commerce, to the world market, to uniformity in the mode of production and in the conditions of life corresponding thereto. (p. 58)

Marx further notes that capitalism robs workers of historic senses of national character as capitalism levels cultural difference. Here, speaking of the worker, for a moment the tone is almost nostalgic: 'Modern industrial labor, modern subjection to capital, the same in England as in France, in America as in Germany, has stripped him of every trace of national character' (p. 48). However, for Marx, there is no place for sentiment as all this sets the scene in the *Manifesto* for class struggle, something Marx thought would be conducted first on a national and then an international scale.

It is important to note that Marx does not in the *Manifesto* or elsewhere predict the end of nations as such either under capitalism or Communism. He thinks that such is the power and reach of the market that national differences will be systematically undermined. Moreover, this general and theoretical projection did not, as indicated, prevent him from addressing the reality of political struggles over national issues.

Far from nationalism fading with the development of capitalism in the subsequent period, its importance grew. Within the Marxist movement, the national question was central to the most important debates in the Second International prior to the First World War. At issue was whether social democratic (that is, Marxist parties) should further national liberation movements within European empires (Habsburg and Romanov) by supporting them, not whether nationalism was a force to be taken seriously. It was not until a very different era, that following the fall of the Berlin Wall approximately 100 years later, that the Marx of the *Manifesto*, in which the state is conceived as something of an irrelevance as the global market sweeps all before it, was taken up again. Neoliberals, bankers and financiers proceeded to hail Marx as the long-lost prophet of globalization (for a discussion of this, see Wheen, 2000, pp. 5–6). At about this time, and in this instance without any reference to Marx, descriptions of a new world economic order had appeared in the writings of Kenichi Ohmae. We now examine his case.

Ohmae

Ohmae's two books on globalization, *The Borderless World* (1990) and *The End of the Nation State* (1996), seem to have been written in part to attract the attention of executives with some intellectual aspirations, perhaps browsing in airport bookstores before a business class flight. Certainly they contain striking assertions that can be easily refuted. For this reason they have been used by critics of the hyperglobalist case as they provide a good illustration of the exaggeration of this position. But despite some of the wilder claims he makes, Ohmae's books are not only well argued but have the subtlety of qualification. Ohmae (1996, pp. 11–12) claims that, despite the proliferation of nation-states in the 1990s and the daily prominence of nationalist politics:

> What we are witnessing is the cumulative effect of fundamental changes in the currents of economic activity around the globe. So powerful have these currents become that they have carved out entirely new channels for themselves – channels that owe nothing to lines of demarcation on traditional political maps. Put simply, in terms of real flows of economic activity, nation states have *already* lost their role as meaningful units of participation in the global economy in today's borderless world . . . The uncomfortable truth is that, in terms of the global economy, nation-states have become little more than bit part actors.

According to Ohmae (1996, pp. 2–5), states no longer perform the functions vital to capitalism they once did. He thinks that the relationship has been transformed in respect of what he terms the 'four Is':

1 *Financial investment* is no longer geographically constrained.
2 *Industry* is more global in orientation as firms are less inclined to strike deals with governments.
3 *Information technology* allows companies to operate in various parts of the globe.
4 *Informed consumers* buy products and services from across the world.

It is not that globalization has made all forms of organization obsolete. Nor has the cultural significance of geography been erased as the world has become a bland one-dimensional place. What has happened instead is that humanity, through the guidance of capitalism, is increasingly orienting itself towards regions of economic activity. Such wider regions link business activity between key areas or zones of nation-states. The success of such areas within states is determined by their comparative economic advantage, resulting dynamic growth rates, and their product innovation and relationship to external markets, rather than by their location within a wider and enclosed national economy. Therefore, the economic map of the world is at once larger and smaller than the one it has replaced.

There is, Ohmae (1996) says, nothing new in regions as opposed to states acting as the principal environments for economic activity. Nor is there any novelty in dynamic smaller areas within stagnant contexts. He mentions Tallin, Riga and Danzig as examples from the medieval era of hubs of commercial activity as well as the Italian city-states. Their contemporary equivalents are Kansia in Japan, and a number of Chinese coastal cities and their hinterlands – Dalian, Zhejiang, Shanghai, Guangzhou – that have acted as the engines of growth in China over the past 25 years through their links to key enterprise areas in South Korea, Taiwain, Japan and elsewhere in Asia. As a result, their per capita income is five times more than the Chinese national average. The trading connections within such zones are little influenced by the general economic relationships between the nation-states they span. Business proceeds as if this is an irrelevance. Neither does the business class place much store by its original national identities as executives flit between business hubs within economic zones. Although Ohmae's tone is different from that of the sociologist Manuel Castells, the references to nodes and networks in the global economy are similar.

Ohmae does not directly tackle nationalism. Instead, he refers to it in passing, treating it, like the nation-state that is central to his account, as something of an anachronism. This is not true of the work over the past 25 years of the development economist Nigel Harris that we now consider.

Harris

Although through a string of influential books Harris's work has been widely read internationally, it is safe to say that he has had a more strictly academic audience than Ohmae, whose work has reached a general readership. Harris's political path, which can be clearly discerned in the chronology of his writings, has taken him from the Marxist Left to an enthusiast for global capitalism. However, this has not been prefaced by a rejection of Marxism like so many others in the past 25 years, probably because his particular strand of Marxism identified the Soviet Union and the so-called Communist countries as 'state capitalist' rather than socialist. Therefore, he did not conceive the revolutions of 1989 as a defeat for Marxism as such. However, he did, like so many others, come to the view that there is no credible alternative to market capitalism, because the various intellectual models on hand, all involving some degree of national economic control, have suffered profound political defeat as the economic ground beneath them has shifted. In Harris's most recent book, *The Return of Cosmopolitan Capital* (2003), he pays tribute to Marx as providing the single greatest influence on his work, even if he has ultimately come to disagree with him. This is not just in respect to Harris's enthrallment with the transformative powers of capitalism so strikingly set out by Marx in *The Communist Manifesto*, as he employs an analysis that is explicitly historical materialist in orientation. In the final analysis, it is the long international march of the productive forces that will drag the political superstructure away from states and nations.

Like Ohmae, Harris's essential approach is to examine the influence of globalization on the relationship between state and capital. However, he is far more explicit in linking nationalism to the state as he thinks it is principally about the aspiration to establish a state. At the outset of *National Liberation* (1990), Harris acknowledges Breuilly's (1985) *Nationalism and the State* as being especially influential to his thinking. Without going into an exposition of Breuilly's general account, his book lays primary emphasis on the development of national sentiment as provincial elites within multiethnic empires sought political independence through separate statehood. Thereafter, the state acts as the forum for the emergence of an overriding national identity from hitherto disparate allegiances. No doubt this analysis was particularly appealing to Harris because it can be readily transferred from a historic central European context – the Austro-Hungarian Empire as the nursery of nationality – to his own area specialism of the post-1945 Third World, as indeed Breuilly does himself.

In *National Liberation* (1990), Harris confines direct comments about the future of nationalism until the final chapter of the book, although the issue surfaces at earlier points, suggesting a preoccupation with the matter. He states that: 'The role of the state is being re-shaped. It is less and less the leadership of a discrete national segment of the world's capital, relating to a relatively autonomous domestic market and currency area' (p. 281). In earlier writings, Harris (1986, p. 202) had talked of the 'disassociation' of the state and capital with the acceleration of economic internationalization. As the state ceases to be a central economic player and business activity is not located in, and therefore defined by, rival national blocks, so the logic becomes more pressing for ever greater international migration to fill labour shortages. In such a situation, the myth of stable populations, of 'national-states', becomes less tenable. Drawing on the work of Charles Jones (1987), Harris cites historical evidence of the emergence of a cosmopolitan trading bourgeoisie in the nineteenth century. The evidence of a more generalized contemporary trend towards the ethnic diversity of populations is something that Harris (1990, p. 284) welcomes:

> With increased international migration, quantity can become quality. To the panic of ruling orders, increasingly cosmopolitan labour forces increase the heterogeneity within, and decrease it between countries. Migration subverts the artificial cultural homogeneity which States have instilled in their citizens.

In *The Return of Cosmopolitan Capital* (2003), these sorts of argument are taken a stage further. Here, despite some acknowledgement that the state historically played a key role in the mercantilist stage of production, Harris posits a fundamental contradiction between states and capitalists: the interests of the two groups of people are fundamentally different. The imperative of capitalists is to do business of one type or another to obtain profits. By contrast, the imperative of states is akin to warriors, their aim to protect and extend the territory they have acquired. The personnel of the capitalist class and state may sometimes merge, for example a politician may run a company. More generally, bourgeoisies – at least fractions of them – have historically been happy enough to accept guaranteed monopoly markets granted by governments, and the spoils of war captured by their armed forces. However, this does not alter the fact that their primary motivations are fundamentally different. Given this, a thorough-going bourgeoisie revolution in the nineteenth century would, presumably, have required an incipient international bourgeoisie to re-orient the warrior impulse of states, and replace it with one conducive only to business.

One of the many possible criticisms of *The Return of Cosmopolitan Capital* is that Harris fails to mention the rise of modern states as educational and welfare agencies – and by extension any mention of liberal and socialist reform – from the end of the nineteenth century on, except insofar as this is part of an insidious attempt to 'nationalize' peoples, the better to involve them in making war. According to Harris (2003, p. 210), what happened in the twentieth century is that emergent business classes were either co-opted or subsumed by the state into 'national capital projects'. This process was taken to its extreme by Fascist and Communist regimes where the market was completely subdued. In a milder form, as typified by the Western postwar era as set out in the Bretton Woods agreement of 1944 with fixed currency rates, it characterized much of the twentieth century as a whole – the century when state war and genocide reached their zenith.

In Harris's view, the accelerating pace of economic globalization over the past 50 years has, as indicated, succeeding in breaking open the state's control of capital. Indeed, so internationalized has it become that capital as a financial form, as distinct from the lingering sentimental attachments of individual capitalists, now has no logical loyalty to a particular nation-state as it seeks markets. Wherever it locates, it will look to the local state to secure its investments through various forms of legal protection, business incentives – subsidies, tax breaks and so on – and the guarantee of educated labour and infrastructural capability. However, as it is now globally footloose, it no longer has an overriding national allegiance to a particular nation-state: it is cosmopolitan.

In these circumstances, nation-states remain as immensely powerful relics of a bygone age. But as they are no longer the dominant players through enforced mergers with capital, they lack the impulse to pursue economic objectives through war, as happened in the age of imperialism. The American-led invasion of Iraq in 2003 would, however, seem to question this claim. The response of Harris to this kind of event is that the states that invaded Iraq did so through their own volition without direct regard to the interests of their business class. Whether the CEOs of American multinationals supported the invasions of Iraq or not was largely irrelevant to the Bush administrations (this was the line Harris took with the first Gulf War in 1991, see Harris, 1991). From a quite different intellectual trajectory, this kind of argument is similar to realist understandings of the autonomy of the state in international relations theory.

Although it is a subject he has written widely about in recent years (Harris, 1996), he does not pursue the issue of migration at length in *The Return of Cosmopolitan Capital*. In fact, in contrast with his earlier writing, he does not seem to hold out much hope for the attenuation of nationalism through cultural globalization – the mixing and merging of populations. He comments on the need to reformulate democracy – one example of the historic concern of nationalist movements within national states – at a global level, in a fashion that is redolent of Held's conception of cosmopolitan democracy. According to Held (1995), globalization now necessitates governance that transcends the confines of particular states.

Hardt and Negri

Harris's writings are characterized by the influence of Marx and an impressive use of statistical detail. Marxism is also one of the intellectual influences to be found in *Empire* by Michael Hardt and Antonio Negri, published in 2000. However, their work is more that of non-empirical continental philosophy. As such, it attempts to generate a picture of the world through the plausibility of its discourse, without recourse to substantiation. The theoretical point of departure of Hardt and Negri, based in legal-theoretical considerations of state sovereignty, is actually derived from the philosophy of the seventeenth-century rationalist thinker Spinoza. While Harris's account of contemporary capitalism is almost a celebration, Hardt and Negri have been important intellectual figures in what has become known in recent years as the 'anti-globalization movement', although the tag is particularly misleading in their case as their new politics of liberation is predicated on the emergence of 'the multitude' as the flip side of capitalist globalization.

Hardt and Negri first attempt to redefine the legal territorial basis of sovereignty in the light of globalization. As suggested, globalization is taken as a given. There is no attempt to prove its existence through facts and figures beyond the mention of the general flows of commodities, currencies and populations that cut across nation-states. This has, the writers claim, led to a decisive diminution in the sovereignty of nation-states as they lack the ability to control what happens within their purview. However, this should not be understood as a weakening of territorial sovereignty per se. Instead the global order signals the transference of sovereignty from nation-states to new global forms of sovereignty and authority they refer to as 'empire'. Considering the claim that there is a crucial continuity with an earlier phase of nation-state domination, Hardt and Negri (2000, p. 9) assert that:

> Without underestimating these real and important lines of continuity, we think it is important to note that what used to be conflict or competition among several impe-rialist powers has in important respects been replaced by the idea of a single power that over determines them all, structures them in a unitary way, and treats them under one common notion or right that is postcolonial and postimperialist.

Empire is characterized by a 'a new notion of right, a new inscription of authority and a new design of the production of norms and legal instruments of coercion that guarantee contracts and resolve conflicts' (p. 9).

This is not akin to a return to an age of European imperialism or the birth of a new era of American domination. European empires in the nineteenth and twentieth centuries were nation-states writ large, inasmuch as they were characterized by territorial centres of administration and control that set the limits of power within geographical boundaries. By contrast, the global empire is characterized by the 'decentered and deterritorializing apparatus of rule that progressively incorporates the entire global realm within its open expanding frontiers' (Hardt and Negri, 2000, pp. xii–xiii). This concept is elaborated as

- spatial totality
- a world form that suspends history
- something that extends down to all levels of the social.

Moreover, as later discussion of nationalism makes clear, imperialism depended upon hierarchies of racial domination. Such demarcations of authority are now less clear: 'Empire manages hybrid identities, flexible hier-archies and plural exchanges through modulating networks of command. The distinct national colours of the imperialist map of the world have merged and blended into an imperial global rainbow' (p. xii). Hardt and Negri (2000) pay little specific attention to the emergence of the USA as the unchallenged superpower since the end of the Cold War. But they are sure that whatever dominance it can exercise upon a global stage is postimperialist: 'Imperialism is over. No nation will be world leader in the way modern European nations were' (p. 136).

Direct consideration of nationalism in *Empire* is set within a discussion of sovereignty and liberation. Negri and Hardt (2000, pp. 101–2) understand nationalism as a means of sovereign legitimation that conceals its own ideological construction; it is a hoax that rests on a spurious antiquity:

> Just as the concept of nation completes the notion of sovereignty by claiming to precede it, so too the concept of the people completes that of the nation through another feigned logical regression. Each logical step back functions to solidify the power of sovereignty by mystifying its basis, that is, by resting on the naturalness of the concept. The identity of the nation and even more so the identity of the people must appear natural and originary.

Within this historical schema, the traditional distinction between German and French forms of nationalism are dissolved. According to Hardt and Negri (2000), all nationalisms have played the same essential role in securing an identity between nation and people based on culture, history and language. There is nothing natural or neutral in this process. On the contrary, Hardt and Negri (2000, p. 106) identify the bourgeois origin of nationalism as a means to secure a 'class victory, a stable market, the potential for economic expansion, and new spaces to invest and civilize'.

While the nation often rests on racial exclusivity, the agent of liberation within empire, 'the multitude' – the disenfranchised rabble that has replaced the industrial working class as the agency of liberation – proclaims its diversity, according to Hardt and Negri. If this were to happen, this would constitute an important development in the history of left-wing politics as the reality has been one of the issues of nations taking precedence over the issues of class. In particular, Communist parties in the twentieth century played the role of leading national liberation struggles under the banner of 'the people'. Hardt and Negri reject this legacy and suggest instead that the enforced cultural homogeneity and exclusivity of a people contained within a geographical area are directly contrary to the 'nomadism and miscegenation' of the multitude. Indeed, Hardt and Negri (2000, p. 361) equate the multitude's rejection of national identities as a struggle against bondage: 'The struggle against the slavery of belonging to a nation, an identity, and a people, and thus the desertion from the sovereignty and the limits it places on subjectivity is entirely positive.'

Industrial Convergence

Both the hyperglobalist and industrial convergence schools of thought have roots in Enlightenment conceptions of progress (for a discussion of this point, see Weinberg, 1969). The hyperglobalist position emphasizes the power of market relationships to reach out and pull together peoples regardless of geography, state or culture. The industrial progress, or, as it is often referred to, the industrial convergence, thesis does not discount the reach and role of the market. In part, the argument rests on the notion that the spread of the market is responsible for greater parity of incomes and cultures between industrial societies, but the emphasis in this school of thought is on how this has been achieved through the development of societies as autonomous, self-contained units, which subsequently merge into each other as they lose their distinctive and antagonistic features. Therefore, the approach, as I want to discuss it here, is more a sociological than economic one. The essential case is that as societies enter modernity by dint of industry and education, their common standard of living rises and equalizes. Simultaneously, such a mature level of civilization reduces the propensity for national conflict, a feature of earlier stages of industrialization.

Intellectual intimations of this conception of social change are found in the work of Herbert Spencer (1820–1903), one of the acknowledged founders of the discipline of sociology in the nineteenth century. Spencer thought that the free markets of his time were enabling industrial societies to supercede militant societies. Militant societies were primitive entities in which the population was permanently on a war footing, prone to feuds and bloody revenge. There were no individual rights worth speaking of and consequently little liberty within them. Although Spencer did not use the reference, the depiction seems akin to Hobbes' (1962, p. 97) state of nature where there is a 'continual fear and danger of violent death; and the life of man ... [is] solitary, poor, nasty, brutish, and short'. By contrast, industrial society is characterized by 'cooperation, industry and contract and happiness' (Spencer, 1885, pp. 28–9). In such societies, the individual is supreme and dissent is tolerated. It is important to note that Spencer was not concerned with the lessening of violence between nations so much as violence within societies. However, it seems reasonable to assume that he would not have discounted the pacific effects of industry and commerce on violence between societies as a whole.

Spencer's approach, like that of Marx, reflects the optimism of the mid-nineteenth century. In the final decades of the nineteenth century, Spencer was to become somewhat disillusioned with perceived state intrusion in the workings of the free market. Among other things he thought that this blocked the spontaneous evolution to industrial society. Insofar as he influenced intellectual developments in his time, it was through the transference of ideas taken by social Darwinism, not least his notorious phrase 'the survival of the fittest'.

In the period before 1914, there are no real traces of the attempt to identify the type of societies that are prone to aggressive excess – nationalist or otherwise. During the war itself, there were numerous commentators, French and British, who speculated about the causes of the exceptional virulence and cruelty of German nationalism. This strain of writing on Germans and Germany, with the aim of identifying an authoritarian national character, ran throughout the twentieth century. This discourse, however, did not generally consist of delineating types of society, aggressive or pacific, and placing Germany in the former. More usually they were based on historical sketches of Germany's particular historical path – its late development, geographical vulnerability, lack of a self-confident bourgeoisie, militaristic mindset and so on.

However, as noted in the Introduction, in a detailed consideration of writings on nationalism in this period, Lawrence (2004, p. 60) comments, speaking of the final years of the First World War: 'Many investigations into nationalism began to consider the possibility of the growth of internationalism and the notion that, far from being an eternal phenomenon, nationalism was fixed to a particular set of historical circumstances and could, hence, perhaps one day fade away.' For example, the British historian John Holland Rose (1916) claimed that nationalism was a modern phenomenon that, with historical progress, might fade as a active force, having 'exhausted its strength' in advanced societies, remaining a relic only among backward peoples. There were scholars during First World War who augmented such analysis with more general theoretical speculation. For example, Israel Zangwill, generally noted as a passionate Zionist, proposed in various speeches and writings to place some intellectual and political order on nationalism. Zangwill (1917, p. 38) claimed that it is a definable phenomenon with 'regular laws of origin, development and decay' and, to this end, drew up a typology of the evolving internal complexity of nations.

For the most part, considerations of nationalism in the interwar period did not seek to periodize nationalism – a precondition we earlier saw for a projection of its demise. It is not until the postwar era that there are any discernible developments in this trajectory. On one level, the 1940s and 50s are not decades that would seem to provide any kind of impetus to considerations of the attenuation of nationalism. The period saw the most dramatic historical wave of national liberation struggles as colonial peoples won independence from the imperial powers that had controlled them with varying degrees of brutality since the nineteenth century. Such emergent 'Third World' states – the term was coined in 1952 and first popularized by the 1955 meeting in Bandung, Indonesia of non-aligned countries – erected state nationalisms within the arbitrary borders and ethnic internal complexity bequeathed by the European power.

The subsequent period of elite-led nation-building in Africa and Asia made the state the central economic agency of development and planning, often with some ideological and actual material reliance on the Soviet Union. Even in Asia where state governments were ideologically anti-Communist and backed by the American government in the context of the emerging Cold War with the Soviet Union, there is no reason to think that the state was any less interventionist in the economy or society. In Western Europe, John Maynard Keynes was the most important economic authority in the emerging consensus that governments must act to stimulate demand, if necessary, through investment and taking over failing chunks of domestic industry. In the Communist world, which by the late 1940s had expanded to take in China and Eastern and Central Europe, planning, generally encapsulated in grandiose five-year plans, was of course central.

At some level of intellectual remove, this is the post-1945 context for industrial convergence theory. As is often the case, this label – which might include 'structural functionalism' and modernization theory – is something of a retrospective catch-all for a variety of positions. For our purposes, two aspects of it are particularly important. First, there is the assertion that historical development takes place through a sequence of universal normative stages. The most influential version of this was Walt Rostow's (1960) five-point typology ascending from traditional society, to preconditions for take-off, to take-off, through the drive for maturity, to finally reach an age of high mass consumption. Rostow himself had relatively little to say about nationalism, the burden of his account being concerned with informing 'backward' countries how they might successfully navigate the take-off stage. Other social scientists of the day who tried to define the historical stepping stones of development did deal with nationalism. For example, Daniel Lerner (1958) identified it as a byproduct of a formative, secondary stage of development within a three-point typology. Here it has the function, according to Lerner, of informing individuals attempting to build educational systems and national cultures.

Such analysis is similar to that Lerner's more famous contemporary Karl Deutsche (1966), generally referred to as a communication theorist. He similarly located the most disruptive stage of nationalism within transitional periods of development within a modernization paradigm. For Deutsch, and it is worth noting that he was personally aware of nationalist excess, having fled his native Prague for the USA in 1938, nationalism is a product of the mass transition from the countryside to towns and cities, with their industries and means of mass communication. As traditional networks are fractured by this transition, people cleave to truculent forms of national identity.

Second, industrial convergence theory conceived development taking place within a common historical continuum. As the name suggests, the theory, conceived in a period of Cold War tensions, held that advanced industrial societies – especially the USA and USSR – were increasingly coming to resemble each other. They were characterized by rising levels of affluence, health and education, based upon industrial planning and the diffusion of technology under the supervision of experts.

The influence of both modernization and industrial convergence theory is evident in the work on nationalism of Gellner. Gellner's modernism (modernism in relation to the study of nationalism) was revealed in his first substantial piece of writing on the subject *Thought and Change* (1964, p. 168), in which Gellner declared: 'Nationalism is not the awakening of nations to self consciousness: it invents them where they do not exist.' Although he conceded that some differentiating markers are necessary for their creation, even if they are purely negative, he was clear that the age of nationalism, the age of the fruition of nations, was relatively recent: 'As an ideology and a language nationalism is relatively modern, emerging in the late Eighteenth Century' (p. 71). Gellner thought that there was nothing inevitable or natural about nationalism. Rather he considered it a functional sociological form of organization – that polity and culture should be one and the same thing – as it imparted a zone of communication for the horizontal integration of industrial society. Previously, in the agrarian age, it was not much of a problem that peasant and master had lived in separate communities, both geographical and cultural. By contrast, Gellner suggested that nationalism is functional to an industrial society by legitimizing a demarcated state where a common culture allows for collective integration. Vertical social division within modern national societies, that is, inequality, is not assumed to be the natural outcome of God's ordering of the world, but, at least in principle, is understood as a matter of merit within a wider and complex division of labour. While the shift to nationalism as a principle of organization was a general social move, Gellner made allowance for a pronounced political role in the process of particular class groups.

As early as *Thought and Change* (1964), there is some intimation of Gellner's thoughts on the end of nationalism in his discussion of whether or not world government is desirable. But his remarks are heavily qualified by an acknowledgement of the continuing reality of massive economic inequality between nations. There are further reflections on these matters in various articles published over the next two decades. For example, in an essay entitled 'Scale and nation', Gellner (1973) speculates about how a greater degree of international cultural homogeneity may be attainable than has hitherto existed through modern educational systems. He quickly points out that modern education is accompanied by an ever greater division of labour both within and between societies. So in that sense, nations are less, not more, similar. However, the intent is clear: Gellner was trying to discern the way in which nationalism may attenuate in the long term by dint of the advancement of the forces that brought it into being in the first place.

Ten years later, in his one book exclusively dedicated to the subject, *Nations and Nationalism* (1983), Gellner devoted an entire chapter to the future of nationalism. This chapter notes, and the point is made elsewhere in his account, that the most violent phase of nationalism is 'that which accompanies early industrialism and the diffusion of industrialism' (p. 111). During that period, 'the social chasms created by early industrialism, and by the unevenness of its diffusion, made it acute'. In feudal societies, inequality and dislocation may have been greater, but in them time-honoured customs serve to legitimate them and thus soften a sense of collective grievance. This is not the case in early capitalist conditions where Gellner refers to the 'class' nature of national conflict. The implication is that the given context is empire where economic exploitation takes a national form, that is, one nation, the imperial master, acts as a class to oppresses another. As a result, the subjugated nation becomes, in more Marxist language, a conscious 'nation for itself'. With the transition from early industrialism to greater affluence and stability, 'the sharpness of nationalist conflict may be expected to diminish' (p. 121).

There are two ways in which this may happen. First, international inequality may diminish with the spread of industrialism. Gellner was well aware that this was not a reality. In fact, in the early 1980s when *Nations and Nationalism* was written, global inequality was rising. However, he argued that it is possible that although objective economic differences between nations may not narrow, the fact that historically poorer peoples have risen out of dire poverty may mean that their perception of difference may be dulled – and presumably therefore their commensurate resentment against richer peoples may fall. The second possible way is through the probable emergence of a transnational intellectual class. Gellner (1997) thought that intellectuals provided the cultural raw materials for the creation (or outright invention) of nations during industrialism.[1] Now, however, that segmented culture has been eroded by greater cultural homogeneity. Although Gellner does not give one, one possible example of this is that English is the language used by an increasing number of universities throughout the world, regardless of the indigenous national language spoken. Therefore, possessing a particular national language does not direct an academic – sometimes an intellectual – to 'their nation' with the compulsion it once did, while simultaneously debarring others. Having mastered English, an academic is free to work elsewhere. Gellner was actually sceptical of this sort of development as he said that the actual career trajectory of professionals orients them towards domestic employment. More widely, he recognized the power of the state to largely preserve labour markets for its own citizens and thus enforce national ties that bind.

Gellner (1991) returned to this theme in an article on nationalism in Eastern Europe. For many, 1991 would not have seemed a good moment to speculate about the dimming of nationalism, given that it had largely succeeded in bringing down the Soviet Union – he actually wrote the article in Moscow – and its satellite states, was currently splitting his native Czechoslovakia in two and was tearing Yugoslavia limb from limb. However, one of the features of Gellner's theory of nationalism is that while he acknowledged its empirical problems, he retained absolute confidence in its theoretical kernel. For example, he responded to the observation that nationalism arose in parts of Europe in the nineteenth century where industrialization had hardly begun not by retracting the claim, but by enlarging his definition of the term to that of modernization in general, that is, not just the advent of manufacturing industry. In relation to our subject, Gellner (1991, p. 131) was to go further by now referring to 'the standardization of industrial cultures'. Having immediately accepted that such standardization in Eastern Europe was not an 'established fact', he proceeded to sketch the 'benign' form of 'advanced industrialism':

> It is marked by the greater and better diffused affluence of later industrialism. This means that hostility between culturally distinct groups is not exacerbated so much by jealousy and by the humiliation of a poverty visibly and consciously associated with ethnic status and treated as 'backwardness'. More advanced industrialism also more effectively modifies the occupational structure and standardizes cultures, so that mutual differences become, at least in some measure, merely phonetic rather than semantic: they do similar things and have similar concepts, even if they use different words. (Gellner, 1991, p. 131)

The emphasis on the homogenization of culture here differs in emphasis with that in earlier writings. What is clearly consistent is the claim that whatever cultural difference there is between neighbouring nations, it no longer corresponds with different entry points into industrialism and levels of affluence. Gellner immediately pointed out that the thesis was far from fully established, but thought that it applied largely to Western Europe where there is little prospect of a war between neighbours. In such circumstances, federalization beckons as national groups in this region are content with cultural preservation alone, and no longer seek a political severance from others through isolation or secession: 'Economic and cultural convergence jointly diminish ethnic hostilities'. He added, with a unusually wistful sentence: 'This, at any rate, is the desirable end point of the development which, under industrialism, has transformed the relationship between culture and polity. After the storm, a relative calm' (Gellner, 1991, p. 131).

Conclusion

This chapter has discussed a number of writers who have suggested that nationalism is a transitory phenomenon, something that has, as it were, played a leading role on the stage of modern history. On a global level, it does not exit the stage completely, but shifts to the side while other forces move towards the centre. Its voice can still be heard from the fringes and, in certain circumstances, it returns to the fore, but if it does so, it lacks the strength of character to dictate events given the constrictions on it. If this captures the conception of the historical trajectory of the different accounts, it remains to try to pull together what they have in common. Analytically, this is a more difficult task as there are clearly major differences between the manner in which, for example, Gellner constructed his account compared to the approach of Hardt and Negri. Nevertheless, there are sufficient commonalities to draw together to make the attempt a worthwhile one.

First, to underline the point made above and first raised in the Introduction, all the writers share a temporal understanding of nationalism. In the case of modernist and industrial convergence writers on nationalism, this is explicit. In the case of hyperglobalists, this view is sometimes expressed directly, and on occasions the conception is implicit. Therefore all the authors discussed above do not take the view that nations and nationalism have either permanently existed or, more importantly in the context of academic debate, have roots and precursors that run back a considerable period of time before modernity. What has not existed will not always remain. Or as Marx famously put it referring to the acceleration of the historical process with capitalism:

> All fixed, fast-frozen relations, with their train of ancient and venerable prejudices and opinions, are swept away, all new-formed ones become antiquated before they can ossify. All that is solid melts into air, all that is holy is profaned. (Marx and Engels, 1998, p. 10)

Only Marx was sufficiently bold, or perhaps foolish, to predict that national sentiment will fade away – although he did seem to accept a residual role for the existence of nations – but all the above accounts suggest that its power will be reduced. This is because nationalism plays a definite functional part in development. It was not, as some contemporary economic liberals believe (see Chapter 3), a wrong turn that led peoples away from peace and prosperity in the nineteenth century. Rather, nationalism was central to the formation of the modern organizational forms of humanity, that is, nation-states. Only Gellner was comfortable with the term 'functional' in describing the development process, but shorn of its teleological intimations, it would apply to all the writers considered in this chapter. With the growth of economic, political and cultural forces that are, in the broadest sense, not marked by any national peculiarity and are to a greater or lesser extent outside state control, the nation-state loses its central historical role.

Second, it is clearly the case that all the writers emphasize not simply the current extent of globalization, but the propensity of capitalism (or 'industrialization' as Gellner termed it) to continue to move remorselessly in such a direction. This is most marked in the theoretical discourse of Hardt and Negri, where the authors seem confident not that capitalism is moving to a world of empire, beyond the age of nations and nationalism, but that such a stage has already been reached. The underlying assumption is that economic activity is now more global than national. This fundamental issue is dealt with at length in Chapter 3. I do not intend to rehearse the arguments here, suffice it to mention that the assumption seriously exaggerates the proportion of GDP composed of trade for larger national economies, overlooks that service industries are still predominantly domestic and neglects the economic role that states continue to play – something dramatically underlined by the present recession. There is good reason for thinking that there is no turning back to the autarchy – economic isolation – of the 1930s or the Keynesian economic management of the postwar period, but this is a much lesser claim than the above writers are apt to make.

Third, all the above accounts are of sufficient abstraction to accommodate definite evidence to the contrary. In the writings of Hobsbawm, Harris and Gellner in particular, it is acknowledged that nationalist struggles show no sign of abating with the onset of globalization or late industrialization. On the contrary, there is recognition that nationalism appears as vital and vibrant as at any time in recent history. However, they suggest that trends are maturing that in the longer term will dim its powers. With the first two authors, this is clearly because they think that a global market is undermining the ability of the state to play a central economic role. With Gellner, he thought that the longer term spread of consumer affluence is smoothing the jagged edges of development that gave rise to nationalist strife in earlier periods.

Ultimately, any theoretical projection must concur with reality if it is to have any value. However, it is unwise to think that just by citing contemporary examples to the contrary, a theory is fatally flawed. This is, for instance, something that Castells (2004) does in discussing Hobsbawm's understanding of nationalism. A wider approach needs to be taken. As suggested, this is something that Chapter 3 on the extent of economic globalization will try to do. Some issues pertinent to Gellner's account on the diffusion of a common lifestyle will be looked at in Chapter 4 on global culture and nationalism. Finally, in conclusion, it is worth mentioning a somewhat different type of observation. It is one made by Perry Anderson in relation to Gellner, but applies equally to other writers who predict the attenuation of nationalism.

Perry Anderson (1992) notes, in an essay comparing Weber and Gellner, that while some scholars had overemphasized nationalism's 'destructively irrational, atavistic forces', Gellner went to the opposite extreme in conceiving it as a 'wholesomely constructive and forward-looking principle'. We saw above that Gellner thought that the excesses of nationalism were the by-products of a particular stage of development that it itself was functional to. Once its work has been done, it begins to leave the historical stage. This, Anderson (1992, pp. 205–6) suggests:

> plainly neglects the overpowering dimension of collective *meaning* that modern nationalism has always involved: that is, not its functionality for industry, but its fulfillment of identity. Here, in effect, only the rational is real: the irrational . . . is set aside – economy and psyche do not join. The result is that, in his tour of reenchantments, Gellner has paradoxically missed by far the most important of all in the twentieth century . . . Where Weber was so bewitched by its spell that he was never able to theorize nationalism, Gellner has theorized nationalism without detecting the spell. What was the tragic fate for the one becomes prosaic function for the other. Here the difference between idealist and utilitarian background tells. Gellner's view of nationalism focuses . . . calmly – at times blithely – on cause at the expense of meaning.

Gellner noted in reply to this criticism and others in a colloquium on his work near to the end of his life that he well understands the emotional power of nationalism. He confessed that Czech folk music is one of the few things that can move him to tears, although one detects a slightly flippant tone to his remarks. Gellner's main point was that his theory takes account of the power of national identity through its recognition that it is most apparent when the state and cultural unit are out of synch with each other. Therefore, when, as in an imperial age, a people are subject to a daily dose of humiliation when they feel that the institutions they have to encounter – the school, post office, policemen – are not their own, their national identities will come to be most keenly felt (Gellner, 1997, pp. 82–7). This may well be true and is in line with his wider account. It can logically be extended to the global age where he might have argued that the anonymity of global forms offends the sense that what we experience should, in some way, be 'ours'. However, it is more difficult to see how it explains the 'normal', everyday love of country in this account of the acuity of national identity. We will now consider accounts that think they do this by looking at writers who suggest that such are the deep cultural roots of nationalism, there is little likelihood that globalization will dim its power.

Summary Points

- The claim that nations and nationalism are becoming less important is found within the work of writers who suggest that they arose fairly recently in human history.

- As nations and nationalism have not always existed, they claim that there is no reason to think they will always remain.
- Although there are different reasons given by those who suggest that nations and nationalism are less important, they all tend to stress the following tendencies:
  - The nation-state does not play the central economic and political role that it once did
  - The direction of capitalism is away from economic activity within the boundaries of the nation towards ever greater globalization
  - This will mean that national differences are less marked as societies become culturally more similar.
- As such arguments are abstract and concerned with long-term developments, they cannot be dismissed simply by pointing to evidence of the continuing power of nationalism.
- That said, several of the writers do appear to have underestimated the continuing role of the nation-state and exaggerated the globalization of economic activity.
- It has also been suggested that theories of post-nationalism overlook the emotional hold that nations exert over peoples, that is, the vitality of national identities.

2
The Resilience of Nations and Nationalism

The previous chapter examined accounts of nationalism and globalization that predict the former will inexorably weaken with the rise of the latter. They hardly seem to square with the reality of the continuing power of nationalism, but that in itself is not fatal to a theoretical projection based on historical analysis. Instead we need to turn to alternative accounts to counterbalance the claims made by modernists and hyperglobalists. Here I take two such approaches. The first one I term 'primordialism and ethnosymbolism'. Specifically, I look at the account of nations and nationalism of the eighteenth-century philosopher Johann Herder and the contemporary scholars Anthony D. Smith and John Hutchinson. The second approach I examine is not a specific account of nations and nationalism, but one from within the influential writings on globalization of Castells.

Primordialism and Ethnosymbolism

Primordialism is a term generally used by those critical of its crude approach. For modernists, it is the intellectually lazy and politically convenient rationalization of the chauvinists that nations, certainly their nation, have always been; certainly they go back far enough for its sentiments to be ingrained in a people. The importance that a people attach to their nation is thought to be indicative of a deep cultural bond. The approach is above question; nations just 'are' and will continue to be. If this basic fact about humanity has been acknowledged, there is little point in discussing the matter, and considerations of their demise are a pointless intellectual exercise. Once we can put aside visions of cavemen running around with national flags on their bear skins, however, primordialism does have a more formidable intellectual history. There is a school of thought going back to the late eighteenth century that rejects the notion that nations will form and dissolve and fade away as the material ground underneath subsides.

43

In this, the romantic reaction to the Enlightenment, the quintessential figure was the philosopher Johann Gottfried von Herder (1744–1803). His forthright assertion of the centrality of nations to humanity would seem to indicate that he was reacting against the orthodoxy that they are bound to wither in the long run. In fact, it is more accurate to say that Herder's real concern was not the view that nations are sure to wax and wane,[1] but that nationality was not being taken seriously enough. Certainly he thought this was true across German states. Insofar as one can discern in his diffuse writings a partial reaction to the Enlightenment, it is in his rejection of general conceptions of linear progress in historiography that did not tend to make nations crucial to the historical process – as opposed to an implicit assumption of the pre-eminent role of a particular nation in the forward march of humanity. Connected to this last point, he was generally vehemently against the presumption of the emerging European imperial states that peoples might be melded together in artificial unions. As he put it: 'Whom nature separated by language, custom and character, let no man artificially join together by chemistry.' Multinational empires were, he felt, 'a wild mingling of various tribes and peoples under one spectre. They rest on force, have feet of clay and must collapse' (Herder, quoted in Berlin, 1976, p. 159).[2] Indeed, the national motivation in his writings was against his countrymen who were in his eyes almost wilfully unaware of the longevity of nations in general and Germany in particular. He saw, for example, the education of young middle-class Germans in French as a form of national suicide, given that language – and this indicates the convergence of intellectual interest in philology and folklore, his love of poetry and political concerns besides a wider eighteenth-century assumption that the particular geography and climate of a people give rise to a peculiar national character – conveyed the soul of a people. He urged them 'not to make themselves ridiculous or contemptible by imitating foreign nationalities' (Herder, quoted in Ergang, 1931, p. 154).

Approximately 200 years later there were those who evoked Herder in explaining the revolutions of 1989. No less a figure than Professor Isaiah Berlin, the doyen of the liberal intelligentsia, hailed him as his 'hero' in 1991. He claimed that his writings were unsurpassed in explaining the tumultuous events of the previous two years (Berlin, 1991). But as suggested, notwithstanding the praise of Isaiah Berlin, few scholars of nationalism would accept Herder's claims. His central contention that a national language captures the history of people does not easily square with the way in which national languages are in some instances relatively recent constructs, dropped and adopted by countless numbers of migrants and modified as much by external influences as by internal ones. There is more to be said on this subject and we will return to some of the issues in the later discussion of culture in Chapter 5. The point is that in the work and legacy of Herder there is an approach to the study of nationalism that rejects in principle the proposition that as it is a temporal phenomenon, it is vulnerable to globalization.

The writings on nationalism of Anthony D. Smith do not rely on a Herderian evocation of the deep cultural and emotional resonances of nationalism, but are based on rational academic analysis through history and sociology. Much of Smith's work since the early 1970s when he was a graduate student of Gellner at the London School of Economics has been devoted to scholarly critiques of modernist accounts of nationalism. This reached its culmination in Smith's book *Nationalism and Modernism* (1998), which drew together and extended numerous critiques of writers like Hobsbawm and Gellner he had made over the previous 15 years. To reiterate, his understanding of nationalism should not be neatly pigeonholed as primordialist. Indeed, in important respects his account incorporates key contentions of the modernist approach. For example, he accepts that nationalism did not become a mass popular ideology until after the French Revolution when, among other things, elites sought to disseminate notions of common national identity. Smith (1991, p. 71) states: 'As an ideology and a language nationalism is relatively modern, emerging into the period of the late eighteenth century'. However, he similarly rejects the contention that nationalism is a strictly modern phenomenon. Nations are not, as Hobsbawm (1992) suggests, social constructs that in current circumstances provide people with simplistic solutions to complex problems. Instead they are cultural entities that have genuine and deep-seated connections to identity and belonging. National traditions may have been invented by intellectuals and others, but in order to strike a chord and be adopted and incorporated into an identity of a people, they must concur with older, pre-existing cultural sentiments that were found among the ethnic forerunners of the nation. Therefore, the attempt to protect a national identity is, as much as the aspiration for national independence, historically quite legitimate. Of course, the ensuing politics may involve problems, and the violence of nationalism – its dark side – is reprehensible. But this does not mean, according to Smith, that the aspiration for identity and/or state sovereignty is illegitimate, as nationalism is intrinsic to humanity.

In Smith's (1995) view, national identities correspond to collective histories and thus bestow meaning to human life. Nations are not temporal artefacts that are subject to erosion. On the contrary, they are rooted in humanity. The images, words, currencies and commodities that spin around our world are superficial phenomena, given the hold of nations over humanity. Such issues take us into the realm of culture and globalization, a subject for Chapter 5. Here discussion of the ethnosymbolist understanding of globalization and nationalism is substantiated through consideration of the work of John Hutchinson, an intellectual fellow traveller and sometime academic collaborator with Anthony Smith.

John Hutchinson's (2005) essay, 'Nationalism and the clash of civilizations', is notable for taking the long view of nationalism and globalization. It can be considered as an exercise in historical sociology that applies the ethnic origins of nations thesis of Anthony Smith to a world stage. Insofar as ethnic groups and nations are treated as phenomena, it is only in respect to their periodization, not the essentials of their character. Hutchinson argues that historically, as at the present time, globalization is incoherent in character. In relation to his principal concerns, ethnicity and nationalism, he thinks that in certain respects it serves to blur their divisions. However, in general terms, if it is realized that there has been interplay between globalization and nationalism over the long term, then there must be acknowledgement that globalization has 'gone hand in hand with ethnic differentiation of populations' (Hutchinson, 2005, p. 166). As he puts it: 'If globalisation has been in process for a millennium or more, then claims that it will result in the supersession of nations becomes problematic' (p. 161). In accordance with this, Hutchinson suggests that every wave of globalization has been shot through with the influence of ethnicity and nationality. More than that, nationality has frequently had an internationalist agenda. Initially the key model upon which nationalists drew was the French republican one. This was replaced by a romantic current of thought derived from German thinkers. But whatever the particular influence, it is crucial that there was a global diffusion of the notion of nationality. Hutchinson does not make the connection but this is something that Benedict Anderson (1998a) has referred to as the 'logic of seriality'. This principle is so entrenched in the contemporary world that participation in virtually all its forms for a group is predicated on having a nation-state, and for an individual upon possessing a nationality.

Globalization, according to Hutchinson (2005), should not be considered as primarily the rise to economic and political dominance of the West. Crucial factors in its gestation involved the spread of Islam and the rise of overlapping imperial circuits of power. As regards ethnicity, it has involved and furthered globalization in the following specific ways:

1 Ethnicity was often the organizational form and means of identification in conquest and expansion. War was obviously integral to this. The memory of wars has subsequently been one of the key memories that ethnicities/nations use in commemorating themselves. Hutchinson points out that the message derived from this and other happenings within a group's past are multiple and sometimes contradictory. He does not make the point, but nations will invariably have both defeats and victories in their past on which they draw to identify and re-identify themselves.
2 Ethnicities have acted as the harbingers of world religions.
3 Ethnicities have spread trade through their control of commercial routes and/or their association with particular markets and commodities.

Although Hutchinson does not use the word, his conception of the process might be described as 'dialectical', as he points out that all these processes serve to simultaneously blur ethnicity and strengthen it. For example, again to extrapolate from his argument, one can see how trade has historically led to miscegenation – sexual mixing – between ethnicities as it has drawn members of a group away from the area of original habitation and into contact with other groups. At the same time, business can reinforce ethnicity as it acts as a trustworthy medium through which supply routes are established, credit is given and customer bases are built. However, despite the admission of contradictory tendencies, something that serves to make Hutchinson's argument more sophisticated rather than weaken it, it is clearly the reinforcement of ethnicity that is key. Globalization has served to crystallize ethnicity as the forerunner of nations. An ethnic past is crucial to the stability of a nation in the global era. This contention, together with the wider ethnosymbolist account, is conveyed in the following quote:

> The validity of national projects in the contemporary world depends on whether . . . [a group] can draw on the ethnic crystallisations of early globalisations. Without such heritages, establishing a cohesive community that can act as the base of modernisation will be difficult and long drawn out. (Hutchinson, 2005, p. 194)

As concerns contemporary writings on globalization, Hutchinson (2005) suggests – he does not refer to writers who might be termed 'hyperglobalist', but the inference is clear – that coverage tends to overstate the historic independence of the state. Rather, states have always pooled sovereignty so the notion that formerly governments could act as they liked is mistaken. At the present time, they may seed sovereignty more directly through international organizations, but such institutions are charged with the responsibility of furthering their interests rather than subverting them. The colouring of globalization reflects, as in the past, the predominant power of a particular global player. Therefore, while it is legitimate to claim that globalization is in a sense Americanization, there is nothing new in a particular state and culture having a leading role in a given historical period. Britain did so in the nineteenth century, for example. Simultaneously, American influence may trigger defensive nationalist reactions.

From these points, Hutchinson moves to consideration of how regional organizations, namely the European Union (EU), might act as an organization and means of identity that will serve to sap the power of nationalism. His arguments are persuasive but appear a little trite as he does not identify an author who has suggested that a collective European identity capable of replacing national identities is likely to emerge. Instead, as we will examine in Chapter 3, a number of writers have suggested that the EU can act as an incubator for stateless nations. That aside, he points out that the EU is an elite not a collective project like nations, that a wider European identity among the people of Continental Europe is currently weak and that any suggestion that the EU will eclipse national identities conflates nationality and nation-states. More interestingly, and in line with his thoughts on how globalization is furthered by a particularly nationality, Hutchinson points out that visions of European unity have historically taken a national guise. Over recent years, prominent members of the French and German establishment have been most vocal in promoting a federal organization that reflects their political inclinations. Inevitably, such European visions have clashed with those of others, in part because they are perceived as an expression of French and German self-interest.

Meanwhile, the banality of everyday nationalisms – the flags, the traditions, the sporting events – trundle on. Hutchinson suggests that the only thing really capable of giving rise to a European identity is a perceived collective threat from outside. This takes him to consideration of Samuel Huntingdon's clash of civilizations thesis, something touched on in Chapter 6. For now I consider some possible criticisms of the case Hutchinson has presented.

First, while his assessment of hyperglobalist-type propositions over the collapse of the state and the remit of regional organizations are apposite, there is no consideration of whether the latest phase of globalization is qualitatively different from that which preceded it. One need not assume that such has been the intensification of the flows of finance, commodities and communication that, *pace* authors like Hardt and Negri (2000), miraculously yet mysteriously we live in a global world in which all has changed utterly. But Hutchinson makes no real attempt to engage with the position of a writer like Held that the latest phase of globalization has led to a transformation of the relationship between politics and economics. For ethnosymbolist understandings of nationalism, the intensification of global flows will not serve to diminish the resilience of national attachments as nations are rooted in the historic experience of peoples. Criticisms of this understanding involve, as implied in the Introduction, some restatement of the well-known modernist criticisms of this position.[3] Among them are that much nationalist history has been distorted, even fabricated, to present a particular image of the nation's past. Such histories may well come to be fervently believed by nationals, but this does not mean that they are actually true.

However, rather than be drawn into the well-worn debate between ethnosymbolists and modernists, I will simply draw attention to a second possible criticism of Hutchinson's case, one that is especially pertinent to globalization. It is that his claim that nations are ethnic entities – and those contemporary national projects must rest on earlier 'ethnic crystallization' – overlooks the massive migration flows that are central to globalization. This observation – that migration disturbs the stable composition of an ethnicity –

is true historically. At the present time, population movements across the world are more intensive and extensive, something that makes for ever greater ethnic heterogeneity.

A third possible criticism of Hutchinson's account is that his argument appears at times to be couched at a level of abstraction that imparts sophistication yet makes it difficult to apply to concrete phenomena. It has the strength of recognizing how globalization incipiently undermines nationalism and simultaneously propels it across the world. However, there is a difficulty in knowing quite what the terms 'nationalism' and 'globalization' come to refer to in his discussion. By contrast, the recent writings of Castells, who we now consider, on globalization and identity are rather more concrete. Before doing so, it is worth briefly mentioning the similarity of Hutchinson's case to that of Tom Nairn, a long-time authority on nationalism, advocate of Scottish independence and formerly a Marxist.

The Global Nation for Tom Nairn

Nairn, writing in collaboration with Paul James in their book *Global Matrix* (2005), also suggests that the long view of globalization indicates that it will not weaken nationalism. The focus in their account is not so much on the role of ethnicity as the forerunner of modern nations, but how the two things buttressed each other in the late nineteenth and early twentieth centuries, by common consent a critical historical period in the deepening and widening of national allegiances. They accept, as Hutchinson does, that there is, in part, a contradictory relationship between nationalism and globalization. Nairn and James's contention is that the notion that national peculiarities will be swept away by the levelling force of global markets, a claim of Marx and Engels discussed in Chapter 1, seriously underestimates the conservative resilience of peoples. If the tenacity of peoples in retaining their culture and identity has been a strangely overlooked long-term historical trend, then the most recent phase of globalization has actually strengthened the most overt forms of nationalism. Nairn and James (2005) claim that the unabashed imperial nationalism of the Bush administration has, since 2000, legitimized the pursuit of naked self-interest. Previously the leaders of the civilized world could pretend that nationalism was the property of Balkan and Arab dictators. Since George W. Bush became president of the USA in 2000, they suggest that such a conceit looks increasingly ridiculous. In fact, the continuity is patently obvious to all. As Nairn and James (2005, p. 91) put it, 'From Milosevic in 1991 to Bush in 2001, the word is out: we are all nationalists now'.

Castells on Globalization and Nationalism

The structural sociology of Castells would appear to place him closer to Gellner and, in particular, Hobsbawm, given the common influence of Marxism. However, Castells is strongly critical of Hobsbawm while approving of Anthony Smith's understanding of national identity. Smith's approach is endorsed in *The Power of Identity* (2004), the second volume of Castells' trilogy, *The Information Age*. He is also mentioned in the third volume, *The End of Millennium* (2000). Nationalism is not of any special intellectual interest to Castells, his background being in urban and economic sociology. To some extent this shows, as it is clear that he has not really endeavoured to understand Hobsbawm's contemporary analysis of nationalism as, although their conclusions are clearly quite different, their actual analyses of a globalized world, specifically the way in which it triggers local revolts, are similar. But although not a major academic concern, his reflections on his own national identity in a recent collection of interviews (Castells and Ince, 2003, pp. 7–8) reveal that national identity – born in Spain, raised in Barcelona under Franco, exiled to France before taking his academic career to California – has been a preoccupying feature of his own life.

For Castells, in the first instance, globalization is the ability of capitalism to work in real time as an extended single market. His key contribution to the debate is his analysis of the role of 'networks' to globalization, a concept with which he is now synonymous. He argues that the power and flexibility of their organizational form is integral to globalization. His initial writings on networks were published in the early 1990s before the full impact of the internet had occurred. More recent work on the 'flow of flows' integrates this phase of the communication revolution (Castells, 2002a). According to Castells (1996, pp. 470–1), a network-based social structure is:

> A highly dynamic, open system, susceptible to innovation without threatening its balance. Networks are appropriate instruments for a capitalist economy based on innovation, globalization and decentralized concentration; for work, workers and firms based on flexibility and adaptability, for a culture of endless deconstruction and reconstruction ... Observations and analyses seem to indicate that the new economy is organized around global networks of capital management and information whose access to technology know-how is at the roots of productivity and competiveness.

From the point of view of understanding an ideology like nationalism, it is important that this definition allows for the existence of both economic inequality and the marginalization of population groups who are excluded from the power and influence of networks. Simultaneously, networks may bypass the traditional agglomerations of capital within nation-states, having implications for the formation of regional identities within older established structures.

Castells' actual analysis of the construction of identity is fairly straightforward. He suggests that it is the process in which groups and individuals generate meaning in life through the prioritization of certain cultural attributes. Castells delineates identity from a role, the latter typically being a task or set of tasks within the division of labour, although he suggests that in reality they can meld. Prioritization of cultural attributes obviously entails making choices, one over another, for example placing store by a particular flag, but identity is multiple not singular. The incongruence between the different identities that an individual may have may be reconciled through their confinement to different spheres of life. However, in contrast to some postmodernist understandings of identity, he suggests that multiple identities can give rise to confusion and distress.

Drawing on the work of Craig Calhoun, Castells (2004, pp. 6–12) provides the following typology of identity. It is one that tilts towards understanding contemporary national identity and nationalism rather than other forms of identity, for example gender. He posits that:

1 Identity can be a 'legitimizing' type, which is one fostered by elites among the mass of the population.
2 It can be based on 'resistance', where actors whose positions/conditions are devalued and/or stigmatized by the logic of domination 'build trenches of resistance and survival of principles different from, or opposed to, those permeating the institutions of society'.
3 There can be a 'project' identity, where actors build a new identity on the basis of whatever cultural attributes are available to them, which seeks to redefine their position in society and thus transform the overall social structure.

The second and third types of identity, resistance and project, account for the power of identity politics in the networked world.

From this, Castells proceeds to an understanding of nationalism. In the face of two contrasting understandings of nationalism, modernism as opposed to some variant of primordialism, he suggests a sort of intermediate stance. In fact, his position is not incompatible with Anthony Smith, an authority whom he cites on particular nations. Castells (1996, p. 31) suggests that:

> The explosion of nationalisms at the turn of millennium, in close relationship to the weakening of the existing nation-states, does not fit well this [modernist] model that assimilates nations and nationalism to the emergence and consolidation of the modern nation-state after the French Revolution, which operated in much of the world as its founding mold.

He comments, sardonically, 'Never mind' of this given discrepancy between modernist accounts and the explosive reality of nationalism, before incorrectly suggesting that Hobsbawm dismisses the glaring evidence that contradicts his account by referring to unresolved territorial national problems created by the restructuring after the First World War.

By contrast, Castells (2004, p. 31) says that the:

> incongruence between social theory and contemporary practice comes from the fact that nationalism and nations have a life of their own, independent of statehood, albeit embedded in cultural constructs and political projects.

This is taken a step further through discussion, one might say, advocacy, of Cataluña. He claims, in contrast to the depiction of nations by writers influenced by Anderson, that it is a:

> Cultural community, organized around language and a shared history. Cataluña is not an imagined entity, but a constantly renewed historical product, even if nationalist movements construct/reconstruct their icons of self-identification with codes specific to each historical context and relative to their historical context and relative to their political projects. (Castells, 2004, p. 53)

So the nation is not an intellectual narrative or the construction of the state, and the power of its identity is cultural and therefore autonomous from and not reducible to temporal politics, although this reality must be historically situated. From this, Castells (2004, pp. 35–6) provides four central points to navigate contemporary nationalism:

1 Nationalism, in contrast to the aspirations of its followers since the late eighteenth century, is now not necessarily oriented to the creation of a sovereign nation-state. This may be the aim but it is no longer a prerequisite for national liberation.
2 Nations and nationalism are not historically limited to the 200-year period following the French Revolution, which saw the creation of European and then Third World nation-states.
3 Nationalism is not necessarily an elite phenomenon and, in fact, contemporary nationalism is more often than not a reaction against global elites.
4 Because contemporary nationalism is more reactive than proactive, it tends to be more cultural than political and thus more oriented towards the defence of an already institutionalized culture than the construction or defence of a state.

This takes us to Castells' conceptualization of the relationship between globalization and nationalism. Based on the firm belief that nations are not artefacts that will wither once their social and political foundations are undermined, or at any rate their aspirations met, it is that the iniquities and inequalities of globalization will accentuate their struggles. In the following passage, Castells (2004, pp. 1–2) seems to suggest that globalization and identity are in opposition:

> Our world is being shaped by conflicting trends of globalization and identity. The information technology revolution, and the restructuring of capitalism, have induced a new society, a network society. It is characterized by the globalization of strategically decisive economic activities. By the networking form of organization. By the flexibility and instability of work, and the individualization of labor. By a culture of real virtuality constructed by a pervasive, interconnected and diversified media system. And by the transformation of the material foundations of life, space and time, through the constitution of a space of flows and of timeless time, as an expression of dominant activities and controlling elites. This new form of organization, in its pervasive globality, is diffusing throughout the world, as industrial capitalism did in the twentieth century, shaking institutions, transforming cultures, creating wealth, inducing poverty, spurring greed, innovation and hope, while simultaneously imposing hardship and instilling despair. It is indeed, brave or not, a new world. But this is not the whole story. Along with the technological revolution, the transformations of capitalism and demise of statism, we have experienced in the past twenty five years, the widespread surge of powerful expressions of collective identity that challenge globalization and cosmopolitanism on behalf of cultural insularity and people's control over their lives and environment.

This kind of analysis, the disruption of globalization versus the ethnic certainty of nationalism, was common to a number of commentators in the early 1990s. With Castells, it sets the scene for analysis across the pages of the third volume of *The Information Age* (2000) of various types of identity revolts, many of a national kind. Clearly, the second of his three types of identity – resistance – is considered key, as marginalized and displaced population groups cluster together in the face of networked global elites. In some cases, such as the Chiapas movement, Castells clearly regards the political movement that has arisen as progressive. Chiapas is a poor state in the southeast of Mexico. In 1994, a revolt (still ongoing) erupted between the Zapatista Army of National Liberation and the central Mexican authorities over the land rights of small, mainly indigenous, farmers. Other resistance identities, like right-wing political parties that oppose immigration in Western Europe, in a given defence of an existing culture, are semi-Fascist. In both cases, Castells seems to suggest that while the nation-state is undermined as its legitimacy is shaken, new identity-based national movements like those in Chiapas do not propose to capture the state and build an alternative institutional order.

This is made clear when referring in part to the political trajectory of contemporary Catalan nationalism. Castells (2004, pp. 53–4) refers to it as one of a number of 'postmodern nationalisms' that are currently 'deconstructing multinational states', while 'others [are] deconstructing pluri-national entities'. Neither movements are 'associated with the formation of classical, sovereign, modern states. Nationalism now exists as a major force behind the constitution of quasi-states.' This consists, he suggests, of devolved or even shared sovereignty, as in Canada with Quebec, and Spain – a 'nation of nationalities' – with Catalonia as well as the Basque Country, Valencia and so on.

As John MacInnes (2006) has pointed out, there are problems in Castells' understanding of both identity and nationalism. His conception of identity overlooks the dialectical construction of identity through the dual influences of an individual's sense of self and external influences that are socialized and imposed. His version of nationalism rests on an uncritical assumption of a common territorial basis and an overriding cultural proclivity. On the one hand, this fails to see that there are numerous, differentiated and even antagonistic, nations that claim the same territory. On the other, it imparts a mythical unity that, as suggested above, places the nation outside history in a fashion redolent of Herder. As examination of the historical record reveals, what is given as an ancient – so ancient as to be practically eternal – component of a cultural identity is often of more recent origin. For example, the Catalan language may be key to a sense of Catalan identity. However, in understanding its contemporary prominence in Catalonia, it is important to recognize the way in which it has been institutionalized in that society over the past 30 years by the local state. That Catalan is now the language of that society should be seen in this light, as much as it should be viewed as the romantic realization of a 1,000-year dream. We will return to the discussion of Catalan nationalism in Chapter 4. The central point for a general discussion of globalization and nationalism is that Castells argues that far from networked globalization leading to a decline in nationalism, it actually triggers revolts.

Conclusion

I suggested in Chapter 1 that it is too easy to dismiss accounts that suggest globalization is weakening nationalism by pointing to contemporary evidence to the contrary. This is because writers like Hobsbawm and Gellner are careful only to identify long-term trends. This is, in part, precisely what Castells does in a cursory dismissal of Hobsbawm's modernist account of nationalism on the grounds that it is clearly out of step with the present reality of its explosion. However, behind his mocking 'Never mind' is an intellectual and political tradition of explaining nations and nationalism that goes back to the eighteenth century. We saw that Herder's account of nations was a reaction to the globalization of his day. He categorically rejected the notion that a European, specifically French-led movement to a general improvement in humanity might erode cultural divisions between peoples. He thought that nations were in essence cultural entities whose language conveyed the essential soul of a people.

Such a view is not one that academic observers of nationalism, with the odd significant exception, share. But I would suggest that the approach of Smith and Hutchinson is closer to Herder than the modernist one. This is not simply because, as Nairn has recently remarked, it is possible to find passages in Smith's work that suggest, like a romantic nationalist might, that nations are permanent entities within history that were always waiting to be awoken (Nairn and James, 2005). Rather, it is because of the basic proposition of Smith and his followers that whatever role modernity may have played in the takeoff of modern nationalism, there was invariably an ethnic or ethnosymbolist precursor. This acted as a vital repository of culture and tradition that shaped the modern nation. If nations are not recent assemblages – the concoctions of various influences drawn together primarily by states for their political expediency in one phase of modernity – then it stands to reason that they are unlikely to unravel in another era. On the contrary, a project that may smooth cultural peculiarities is likely to trigger national resistance. And given the depth and legitimacy of the cause, this should assuredly not, *pace* Hobsbawm, be considered as a protracted series of last-ditch battles of nationalists while the productive forces march determinedly on towards global integration, leaving the former state platforms of nationalists behind them as they do.

Beyond this general position of the writers considered above, the chapter looked at the case made by Hutchinson. His contention is that whatever the homogenizing tendency of globalization, more important is the way in which nationalism has been propelled through waves of globalization. This is true in respect of the precedents and models of organization it imparts and through the backlash it provokes against an imperial power. When considered in this way over 1,000 years or more of world history, one has to conclude that the opposition between nationalism and globalization is more imagined than real. Hutchinson is not the first writer to suggest this. However, combined with the telling arguments that trade and war have historically served to highlight and strengthen ethnicity, the case is a powerful one. Nevertheless, familiar modernist criticisms of the ethnosymbolist position remain. They cannot, I submit, be constructively extended at a general level of debate. Rather, it is more productive to consider more applied, concrete areas of enquiry. I begin this process in Chapter 3, with consideration of economic nationalism and globalization.

Summary Points

- There is tradition going back to the eighteenth century of rejecting the suggestion that nations and nationalism are likely to fade.
- This tradition, found in the philosophical writings of Johann Herder, suggests that nations are cultural entities that are infused into the souls and languages of people.
- Contemporary commentators tend to reject this romantic conception of nations, as it is easy to show that national cultures are more recent constructions.
- Increasingly important in recent years has been the ethnosymbolist account of nationalism of Anthony D. Smith, which suggests that modern nations have crucial legacies of the memories and traditions of the ethnicities that preceded nations.
- This account has been supplemented by John Hutchinson, who suggests that rather than nationalism having been weakened by globalization over the past 1,000 years, it has actually carried it across the planet.
- As concerns the present, Tom Nairn suggests that the actions of the recent American government under George W. Bush have legitimated aggressive forms of nationalism.
- Manuel Castells suggests that far from globalization weakening nationalism, it is currently accentuating it, as people cling to their cultural identities, given the disruption and dislocation they experience.
- There are problems within the work of the writers discussed in this chapter – those of Smith and Hutchinson are highly abstract, while Castells misunderstands the modernist account of nationalism that he dismisses.
- Ultimately, only applied discussions of particular nations and forms of globalization can constructively add to the debate between modernists and ethnosymbolists on the future of nations and nationalism.

3
Globalization and Economic Nationalism

We saw in the previous chapter that assessments of the extent of economic globalization were not in themselves crucial to their authors' thoughts on the future of nationalism. Thus Hobsbawm and Castells come to quite different conclusions on this matter despite a shared assumption that globalization has led to profound change in the integration of world economic markets. It is not the extent of globalization that influences their opinions, but their understanding of nations and nationalism. If, as in the work of Castells, nations are viewed as historic cultural things, the building blocks of humanity, then it is unlikely that mere commodities and currencies that flow across them will weaken the power they exert over peoples. On the contrary, Castells – and he is not alone in this, the point having become a familiar academic counter to popular media assertions of global homogeneity – thinks that the inequalities inherent in globalization and the disruption of tradition it entails may trigger movements of archaic political and cultural compensation as peoples strive to reassert national identities. In the work of Anthony Smith, the theorist who has provided the most substantial contemporary account of the longevity of nations and nationalism, while there is no attempt to question the extent of globalization, it is suggested that it will barely scratch their surface.

The modernist school takes a quite different approach to nations and nationalism. Its fundamental assertion is that there is nothing natural or inevitable about them, but that they are the product of social transformation. In the most forthright account of this case, that of Hobsbawm, nationalism since the end of the eighteenth century has, in either popular or 'official' ruling class forms, been concerned with the building of nation-states. A central part of that endeavour was the acquisition and maintenance of national economies – clearly demarcated zones of economic activity corresponding to the political boundaries of the nation where domestic industry is nurtured and protected and foreign business through either sales or investment is of a fairly low order – through some form of economic nationalism. Initially, from the late nineteenth century, this consisted of the erection of tariff barriers on imported goods to guard and bolster distinctly national

industries, and then later, in the mid-twentieth century, the wholesale ownership and control of parts of domestic economies by the nation-state through
nationalization. If, as Hobsbawm thinks, global flows of goods and finance
now flood over national barriers and the prevailing opinion is that whatever
barriers that persist should fall further, then clearly the role and ultimately
the political salience of nationalism will fade. Possibly the single most influential modernist account of nationalism is that of Gellner. He thought that
nationalism was of central functional importance to industrialization as it
imparted a common but distinct culture to a technocratic and managerial
class within geographic units. If, as Gellner suggested towards the end of his
life, late industrialization is beginning to impart a shared culture throughout
the developed nations based on a high level of collective affluence, then the
points of distinction between peoples, and hence antagonistic national identities, will diminish. In sum, globalization will lead to the weakening of
nationalism.

So, on one level, argument about economic globalization does not impinge
on the key theoretical perspectives on the durability of nationalism. However,
that hardly makes the subject any less important. A discussion of the historic
and contemporary relationship of nationalism to the organization of
economic life and vice versa is fundamental to the broader subject matter of
this book. This will become clear in an initial section on the issues at stake.
Discussion will then move to the nature and role of economic nationalism
since its inception in the mid-nineteenth century. In the light of this discussion, the chapter will conclude by examining key questions on the continuing
relevance of economic nationalism.

The Issues at Stake

In coming to this subject, the relationship between globalization and
economic nationalism, there is no difficulty in defining the former.
Globalization involves such things as the integration of economic markets
through trade in commodities, the buying and selling of units of finance, the
purchase of manufacturing and service industries by external (that is, foreign)
buyers and direct investment by multinational companies. For some people,
especially those of a neoliberal economic persuasion, the very definition of
globalization is the opposite of impediments to the contrary. Neoliberalism
refers to those who advocate a contemporary return to the free-market
economics of the nineteenth century, associated above all with the eighteenth-
century economist Adam Smith. Martin Wolf (2004, p. 15), drawing on Brian
Lindsay from Washington's Cato Institute, defines globalization as a:

movement in the direction of greater integration, as both natural and man-made barriers to international economic exchange continue to fall. A necessary consequence of such a process of integration is the increased impact of economic changes in one part of the world on what happens in others.

Wolf believes that if globalization is allowed to proceed to its end point, 'the unilateral barriers of what remains of sovereign states' will become 'a structure of restricted national sovereignty similar to today's EU members, or a global federation'. There will be a continuing issue of the extent to which technology can render geographic distance obsolete. Wolf thinks that regardless of technological innovation, geography will continue to matter in human life. By contrast, the abolition of political division is conceivable but 'it is immensely far from where we are today. We are most unlikely to get there in this century, let alone the next decade' (Wolf, 2004, p. 15).

However, beyond the general implication that economic nationalism is concerned with barriers to globalization, this does not throw much light on what it actually is. In part, the problem with conceptualizing or even discussing this term is that it is nearly always used negatively. It is well known that the term 'patriotism' is normally used as a positive alternative to nationalism, but nationalism in everyday and media use can at least be neutral. By contrast, 'economic nationalism' has a pejorative implication. This point, made by Paul Burnell (1986, p. 22) before the contemporary dominance of neoliberalism had taken root, stands despite the current efforts of a group of scholars from the subject of international political economy, whose approach we will shortly consider, to rescue the term. The generally negative use of the term in part accounts for the small contemporary literature on economic nationalism.

There are broadly two reasons for this. First, it is associated with the knee-jerk protectionist reactions of national governments, themselves influenced by vested industrial and agricultural interests, to either the threat of economic recession and/or international trends that threaten their domestic economies. One can find predictions of a general rise in protectionism made over the past 30 years in both the quality business press and in semi-academic publications, often made by writers associated with free-market think tanks. Indeed, Harold James (2001, p. 204) says that: 'At regular intervals since the publication of David Ricardo's *Principles of Political Economy* in 1817, analysts have been predicting the imminent death of free-trade'. Speaking of the 1970s, Otto Hieronymi (1980, p. 11) stated that the period

witnessed an open revival of economic nationalism. This development has been in apparent contrast with the progress and the unexpected success of world-wide economic and financial integration of the last 30 years.

Similar sentiments, in a less sombre tone, were made in the mid-1980s by Robert Lawrence and Robert Litan (1986. p. ix), Washington Brookings Institute scholars, reacting against the then demand for 'tariffs, quotas and voluntary restraint agreements' to protect US industry. Gloomy pronouncements over globalization were made after the Asian financial crash of 1997 and have surfaced again more recently. Vendeline von Bredow, the European business correspondent for *The Economist* magazine, wrote in 2006 on the response to foreign economic takeovers:

> A spectre is haunting Europe – the spectre of protectionism. As economic national-ism is on the rise across the European Union alarm bells are ringing at the European Commission. The main offenders are France, Spain, Italy and Poland with threats – and measures – to raise new barriers to the free movement of capital across their borders. (www.axess.se/english/2006/03/outlook_bredow.php)

In America in the same year, Patrick Buchanan (www.realclearpolitics.com/articles/2006/11/return_of_economic_nationalism.html), admittedly a conservative critic of globalization, wrote of US fears over the further losses of US industrial jobs and the mounting trade deficit: 'But if the free-trade era is over, what will succeed it? A new era of economic nationalism. The new Congress will demand restoration of its traditional power in shaping trade policy.'

These sort of alarms usually indicate a wider, neoliberal objection to the state as an economic actor, and a belief that states' propensity to interfere with the natural workings of the market is, for the most part, counterproductive to prosperity. There may be some admission that the outcome of market forces is unpalatable from a national standpoint, but such a outlook is in itself thought to be out of date. For example, the takeover in 2006 by the Indian company Tata of Corus, the British owner of the privatized remains of the British steel industry, prompted the following editorial judgement of the *Financial Times* (21.10.2006): 'National pride may suffer a little but economic nationalism and imperialism have had their day and that can only be a good thing.' The likely writer, the *FT* editor Martin Wolf mentioned above, has provided an influential case that economic nationalism is not just obsolete but leads inexorably to international conflict and war.

In his book *Why Globalization Works,* Wolf (2004, p. 30) argues that individual freedom and democracy rest on free-market capitalism. He notes that one does not automatically give rise to the other, but is unequivocal that there is a general and longer term relationship: 'The market underpins democracy, just as democracy should normally strengthen the market.' In turn, market democracy gives rise to international peace as countries realize that it is folly to try to secure economic gain through military means rather than exploit comparative advantage, as the nineteenth-century classical economist David

Ricardo suggested, or, as it might now be put, to exploit their niche within an international division of labour. Again Wolf (2004, p. 33) is forthright:

> Liberal democracy is conducive to harmonious international relations because the prosperity of a nation derives not from the size of its territory or population under its direct control, but from the combination of international economic development and international exchange.

According to Wolf, this was the mutually beneficent direction – towards freedom, prosperity and peace – that humanity was headed in the nineteenth century before various forms of collectivism, chief among them nationalism, interfered. Although Wolf notes that nationalism played a functional part in the creation of states, *pace* Gellner, he sees it as a retrograde force that conservative elites used to corral emergent European working classes into integral and antagonistic forms, nations. The emphasis on the interests of the nation above the principles of individual liberty and market freedom led, on the one hand, to a rising tide of protectionism and the collaboration of industry and government – something known as 'corporatism' – in the latter part of the nineteenth century. On the other, it resulted in military expansionism and conflagration through imperialism and European war. The process went furthest in Germany where:

> collectivism and nationalism were brought together most completely . . . The glorification of war, the collective and the national contempt for peace, the individual and the cosmopolitan were to become the Leitmotifs of late nineteenth- and early twentieth-century thought. (Wolf, 2004, p. 125)

This was immensely destructive both in human and economic terms. Rather than being a positive product of modernity, nationalism, according to Wolf (2004, p. 37), coincided in the last three decades of the nineteenth century with the resurgence 'of pre-modern imperialist and protectionist ideas. The aim of these countries became to create a protected sphere of their own. From the point of view of promoting prosperity, these shifts were an error.'

There are a host of conceptual and historical problems with this account. Among historical ones is the fact that the champion of the story, British nineteenth-century laissez faire, was dependent on its integration of imperial markets, ultimately ruled by British bayonets, for raw materials and product sales. In some instances, this involved actively suppressing local manufacturers. For example, the East India Company was involved in the shutting down of Indian cotton-making workshops in the late eighteenth and early nineteenth century to guarantee export markets for British manufacturers, predominately based in Lancashire and Yorkshire. Concerning conceptual issues, the proposition that there is an integral relationship between the pursuit of free-market economics, liberty and human harmony is difficult to square with the foreign policy of the USA, the world's principal capitalist economy – unless perhaps one believes that the wars of George W. Bush's administration and now Barrack Obama's are genuinely designed to further democracy. But that aside, this assertion of a fundamental relationship between free-market capitalism, democracy and peace helps to explain why economic nationalism, as opposed to what may be seen as positive in cultural nationalism, is so discredited.

A popular version of this theory is on hand to make the case more simplistic still. In his bestselling book *The Lexus and the Olive Tree*, Thomas Friedman (2000, p. 251), suggests that no two countries with a McDonald's franchise had fought a war against each other since each got its own McDonald's – known as the 'golden arches' theory.[1] It would seem unkind to point out that a number of countries within the NATO alliance with MacDonald's restaurants attacked another with one, Yugoslavia, in 1999, the year the book first came out. Even where neighbouring economies have McDonald's and are highly integrated through trade and personnel, as in the case of Taiwan and mainland China, nationalist and subnationalist tensions hardly seem to have been reduced, if anything, the opposite is the case. Perhaps these kinds of issues are why Freidman (2005) has since come up with a new thesis entitled 'The Dell theory of conflict resolution'.

The second reason why economic nationalism is so negatively thought of is that after 1945 it was associated with the irrational actions of less developed countries. In an influential book on the subject, the Canadian economist Harry Johnson (1968, p. 14) argued that import substitutionism and other forms of protectionism were not a logical and successful route to industrialization. Rather, nationalism in Third World countries was motivated to 'direct economic policy toward the production of psychic income in the form of nationalistic satisfaction at the expense of material income'. This position seems close to the wider claim in postwar liberal political science, especially evident in industrial convergence theory as discussed in Chapter 2, that nationalism is a phenomenon that countries experience in the early stages of development that wanes with economic (and political and intellectual) maturity. Therefore, import substitutionism, nationalization, controls on foreign ownership and investment and so on made little strictly material sense, but upped the popular feel-good factor in the face of the former imperialist master. Such measures were political rather than economic in design.

This assertion made by Johnson and others overlooked, on the one hand, the argument of the emergent structuralist school of thought of various different political persuasions that, in the long term, the fortunes of economies reliant on the sales of raw materials decline because of a historic tendency of export prices to fall. On the other, it ignored the evidence of the emerging spectacular success of some, if not all, Third World countries – in particular

South Korea and Taiwan – in the postwar period that effectively prohibited foreign imports through exorbitant tariffs and in some cases formally did so. More generally, there was a certain conceit in Johnson's account, as 'irrationality' is in the eye of the beholder. Political intervention to control or prevent foreign business activity of some form after decades of economic subservience to an imperial ruler did not seem irrational in the view of the newly independent states in Asia and Africa.

Recent Accounts of Economic Nationalism

There is, however, a significant exception to the general identification of economic nationalism as being old, truculent and indicative of less developed countries. As mentioned, a group of scholars from the subject of international political economy, a subdiscipline of international relations, have attempted in recent years to revive the concept. This is not because of any shared political outlook nor commitment to economic nationalism as a practice. Nor do they share a common theoretical approach. Instead, their endeavour is motivated by the belief that the generally negative treatment of the term obscures the importance of nationalism in economic affairs. For the purposes of discussion, I will treat an article by Takeshi Nakano (2004) and *Economic Nationalism in a Globalizing World*, edited by Eric Helleiner and Andreas Pickel (2005), as representative of this case.

Nakano says that he wants to shift discussion of economic nationalism away from the brief but influential thinking of Robert Gilpin (1987) that nation and state are really one and the same thing.[2] Within Gilpin's work and realist international relations theory in general, however, the state is the key focus of analysis, with economic nationalism only figuring as one form of strategic mechanism employed to further its interests. Further, Nakano seeks to widen the scope of study by examining the nationalist motivation within economic affairs rather than seeing it simply as a set of narrow policy prescriptions – tariffs and so on. These starting points broaden into an attempt to formulate the role of economic policy within a Durkheimian construction of the national economic state.

Helleiner and Pickel (2005, pp. 7–8) endeavour to frame an appreciation of nationalism that is sufficiently broad to capture its various motivations rather than insist upon a set of normative concerns. As they state:

> Nationalism should be understood fundamentally as a generic discursive structure rather than any particular substantive doctrine . . . Nationalism is a combination of discourse, action and structure.

How nationalism and economics relate depends upon the particular conjuncture. As nations constantly reproduce themselves rather than disappear, so economic nationalism as an important part of their wider discursive remit will persist. Specifically addressing the question of whether globalization will make economic nationalism redundant, Helleiner and Pickel (2005, p. 228) state: 'From our perspective so long as nationalism and national identities endure, so too will various forms of economic nationalism'.

This approach to economic nationalism seems to have a number of advantages over the wider tendency among economic commentators to depict it as antiquated and dangerous:

1 The scholars recognize that although nationalisms generally rest on essentially timeless conceptions of territory, culture and character, the actual policy demands made in its name can change according to circumstances. There is, for example, no intrinsic relationship between tariffs and nationalism. As circumstances change, so will the sort of economic measures that nationalists of various stripes and persuasions favour.
2 Such a method is sensitive to the kinds of national choices that governments have and do make. For example, Rami Abdelal (2005) shows the role of nationalism in the economic orientation of the governments of Belarus, Ukraine and Lithuania after the break-up of the Soviet Union. He characterizes the directions as, respectively, cooperation, ambivalence and separation. With Russia itself, Andrei Tsygankov (2005) examines how different versions of Russian national identity – one of the insights of the study of nationalism over the past 15 years is the existence of nationalisms rather than a unitary nationalism – have corresponded to the shifts in Russian economic orientation. The embrace of the market in the 1990s under Yeltsin was in accord with the conception of Russia as a European nation; the path of Putin since 2000 to curtail market freedom fits more with Russia as an Eastern, 'Eurasian', power.
3 Most important with respect to globalization, this way of handling economic nationalism can recognize that policies associated with economic deregulation, above all privatization, can be pursued by governments that are by any criteria overtly nationalist. For example, in the 1990s, the governments of Croatia and India aggressively privatized swathes of their industry in line with their nationalist opposition to Communist Yugoslavia and Congress-controlled Indian states respectively.

However, the theoretical versatility of this recent approach to economic nationalism comes at a cost. The first point of criticism is that the definition of nationalism is incredibly loose. At times, the case seems to rest on the assumption that as national identity clearly exists, so everything governments do in respect to economics is 'nationalist'. From this standpoint, it is difficult to imagine what would not be included under the heading. Although the authors make no suggestion, the term might logically apply to the self-interest of a Third World government elite who openly embezzle state coffers while the mass of the population starve. Perhaps realizing that the definition given is rather vague, Helleiner and Pickel (2005, p. 225) address the matter directly in the Conclusion:

> If economic nationalism can be associated with very diverse economic policies, does this mean that economic nationalism is too vague a term to be useful? Is everything economic nationalism? No. Although its policy content can be everything, economic nationalism remains defined by its nationalism; that it is associated with core nationalist values such as commitment to sovereignty.

This is the first time in the book that the importance of sovereignty to nationalism – that it is not in itself coterminous with nationalism – is mentioned. We are left to wonder what the writer considers sovereignty to be and, given the title of the book, whether economic globalization is undermining sovereignty.

Second, there is very little coverage of the role of private capital within this new approach to economic nationalism. The assumption is that the state continues to be a key economic actor and states, nation-states, embody national identity in some form. Certainly one does not have to accept the sort of assertions made by the hyperglobalist Ohmae (discussed in Chapter 1) that the state is something of an irrelevance in a globalized economy. A cursory glance at the levels of state expenditure as a proportion of GDP within advanced economies is only one way of dispelling this notion. But one of the key points about globalization is that private capital, in the form of multinational companies, has increasing discretion in which country it will invest in. In doing so, in jumping and consequently wearing down the walls of national economies, private capital undermines the ability of the state to practise some form of 'economic nationalism'. A failure to consider the mobility of private capital indicates that the various writers seem reluctant to contemplate that globalization may have moved the economic earth on which nation-states rest. Therefore the standard criticism of realism within international relations of making the state the sole focus of inquiry still seems to apply to these writers.

Third, there is little consideration of how international economic institutions – principally the World Trade Organization (WTO), the World Bank and the International Monetary Fund (IMF) – are empowered to impose economic deregulation on nation-states, regardless of whether they consider the measures to be in their sovereign interest or not. For example, WTO rules now force all member countries, including Britain, to open up all public services, including the NHS, to foreign investors and foreign competition (Pollock and Price, 2000).

Fourth, there is no discussion in recent writings on economic nationalism of whether governments across the world conform to broadly similar neoliberal economic policies. It is now nearly 20 years since the term 'the Washington consensus' was first coined to capture the core measures – low tax regimes to stimulate foreign investment, privatization, financial deregulation and so on – that governments agree on or are coerced into accepting measures to which there are, in the words of the avowed market advocate Margaret Thatcher, 'no alternative' (the term was coined by the US-based British economist John Williamson). Across the world, regardless of whether a national government was formerly of the political Left or Right, the privatization of state-owned industry and services has been a basic feature of the past 25 years. This is true in Britain and France where successive governments, of whatever political hue, have relentlessly sought greater private sector involvement in the provision of state services. This move has only been reversed by the current recession that has seen governments – the British and the American leading from the front – move in the opposite direction to nationalize financial services such as banks and building societies, and bail out parts of manufacturing industry. However, although profound and involving massive sums of public money, it is doubtful that the move will herald a long-term ideological shift away from privatization, because the measures have only been taken as a necessity in the face of the possibility of a complete financial collapse. It is noteworthy that one current British Labour government minister (news.scotsman.com/latestnews/Mandelson-quizzed-by-MPs-over.4613015.jp), directly involved in intervention to prop up finance and industry, has simultaneously raised the prospect of the longer term privatization of the Royal Mail, a pubic service that even Margaret Thatcher vowed would remain in public hands.

In sum, the definitional looseness of the term 'nationalism' in recent academic discussion of economic nationalism from within international political economy robs the concept of any analytic purchase. It has the benefit of incorporating how nationalist governments might actively favour neoliberal policies and thereby shifts discussion away from a simplistic scorecard where state protectionism = economic nationalism, lack of state protection = globalization. However, at present, the writers seem unconsciously tethered to the assumption that states as the agencies of national identity are independent actors, when the whole point about globalization is that they must act in accordance with policies that favour the freedom of markets. Instead, I propose to make some historical assessment of the origination and rise of economic nationalism in order to assess whether or not globalization has led to a profound change in the conditions it operates in.

A Brief History of Economic Nationalism

The following is not intended as a short economic history of the world since 1800, but is an attempt to identify the emergence of economic nationalism and chart the contours of its role since the mid-nineteenth century. In doing so, it is useful to mention the names and principal ideas of several key economic thinkers who have contributed to this disparate body of thought.

From Mercantilism to List

The first point to make is that there is continuing disagreement among writers on whether the mercantilism of absolutist European states from the sixteenth to the eighteenth century can be seen as a form of nationalism or not. Mercantilism is the doctrine that the prosperity of government depends on its reserves of capital held as gold. To further their holdings, the state will encourage export sales and restrict imports. The economic historian Giovanni Arrighi (1994, pp. 49–50) thinks that the collaboration of the Dutch, English and Portuguese navies and chartered companies to dispel competition, both domestic and foreign, in the expansion of trade in Asia and the Americas equates to economic nationalism. Opposition to protectionism by economic liberals often makes comparisons between the mercantilist monopolies of absolutist monarchies and the protectionist policies of contemporary states. It is certainly true that in his most well-known book, *The Wealth of Nations* (1776), Adam Smith, the great advocate of free markets, counterposed free trade to mercantilism. In this we can see Smith's worldly Enlightenment outlook in distinguishing between the narrow and selfish stance of merchants and governments engaged in monopolies of trade and the wider benefit that humanity – and therefore whole nations within them – will enjoy by dint of free-market competition. By contrast, recent investigations of mercantilism by scholars primarily interested the history of nationalism question whether it makes much sense to apply the term. Liah Greenfeld (2001, pp. 113–14) is clear that there were seldom 'national' motivations, no matter how defined, in the actions of early European traders and royal navies so much as naked self-interest.

Leaving this matter aside, it is interesting to note that the British advocates of free markets in the nineteenth century, who drew inspiration from Adam Smith and other theoretical exponents, clearly thought within a national premise. As Lionel Robbins (1961. p. 9) pointed out many years ago:

It must be remembered that consumption which was regarded as the end of economic policy was the consumption of a limited community, the members of the nation-state. To the extent to which they repudiated former maxims of economic warfare and assumed mutual advantage in international exchange, it is true that the outlook of the Classical Economists seems, and indeed is, more spacious and pacific than that of their antagonists. But there is little evidence that they often went beyond the test of national advantage as a criterion of policy, still less that they were prepared to contemplate the dissolution on national bonds. If you examine the ground on which they recommend free-trade, you will find that it is always in terms of a more productive use of national resources ... We get our picture wrong if we suppose that the English Classical Economists would have recommended, because it was good for the world at large, a measure which they thought would be harmful to their own community. It was the consumption of the national economy which they regarded as the end of consumption.

This point can be widened to the appreciation that the advocacy by British capitalists and the government of free trade in the mid-nineteenth century was of direct economic benefit to Britain, given its manufacturing supremacy in world markets. Its short-lived intellectual leadership, in which the banner of free trade was raised up as a general principle, was a result of its economic dominance (Hobsbawn, 1988, pp. 53–4).

Most self-declared national spokesmen in the early to mid-nineteenth century supported free trade because of its general relation to liberation and advancement. Giuseppe Mazzini (1805–72) for example, often taken as the archetypal unificatory nationalist because of his tireless commitment to the unification of Italy and social justice, thought it one of a number of progressive forces of the age that patriots everywhere should favour (see Smith, 1994, p. 28). However, it was both the unacknowledged national bias among the followers of Adam Smith and the blithe, if somewhat deceitful, cosmopolitanism of British free-traders that drew intellectual and political reactions in this period that might more properly be termed as 'economic nationalist'. Among them, we can identify Alexander Hamilton (1755–1804), politician, lawyer and economist, in America and Friedrich List (1789–1846) in Europe as being of particular importance. The political influence of Hamilton, whose nationalism was somewhat more civic and secular in orientation, was no doubt greater as he was secretary to the US Treasury in the 1790s, while List provided the most substantial theoretical critique of free trade. Naturally, List's principal disagreement was with the free-market ideas of Adam Smith and his followers in Britain, while also making reference to Jean-Baptiste Say in France.

Like most intellectuals of the age, List acted as journalist, campaigner – in part as spokesman for the German Union of Merchants and Manufacturers – and administrator as well as a writer. Greenfeld (2001, pp. 208–14) suggests that his early advocacy of the abolition of internal tariffs within German states and the erection of some external ones to aid the development of infant

industries played a significant part in winning the uneducated German bourgeoisie to the economic benefits of nationalism – burghers who preferred the
bierkeller to reading Herder perhaps. But List's importance to actual policy
should not be exaggerated as he died a broken man, convinced that his ideas
were being ignored by the German governments of the day. Some 20 years
later they were realized through Bismarck's tariffs of the 1870s. List's most
important work, *The National System of Political Economy* (first published in
German in 1841 and in English in 1856) is of particular importance to the
history of nationalism. It combines pragmatic business arguments with the
cultural influences of German Romanticism, especially Fichte and Muller
(List, 1909).

List believed that physical and mental improvement depended on an
economy attaining a combination of manufacturing and agriculture. Success
in manufacturing could only be achieved by protection. Protection, he noted,
was condemned by British advocates of free trade, but this was driven by
their own self-interest:

> The system of protection, inasmuch as it forms the only means of placing those
> nations which are far behind in civilisation on equal terms with the one predomi-
> nating nation (which, however, never received at the hands of Nature a perpetual
> right to a monopoly of manufacture, but which merely gained an advance over
> others in point of time), regarded from this point of view appears to be the most effi-
> cient means of furthering the final union of nations, and hence also of promoting
> true freedom of trade. (List, 1909, p. 73)

This passage is notable for not rejecting free trade and calling for protection
per se, but suggests the latter is a temporary measure that should be used to
attain manufacturing parity by nations lagging behind the most advanced.
When they do catch up, free trade will have universal validity. In the interim,
Germany should take urgent measures to 'raise herself to an equal position
with the most advanced manufacturing nation' (List, 1909, p. 323).

Germany as a nation is defined in cultural terms. In this there is a clear
difference between List and Smith who, notwithstanding the assumptions
noted by Robbins, proceeded in his writings as if nations were merely aggre-
gates of people. List (1909, p. 99) characterizes this as 'cosmopolitanism'. He
notes that the more frank free-trade exponents of the day actually acknowledged that nations were theoretically irrelevant in the working of the market,
and looked forward to a time when collectives of any sort that hindered them
would dissolve altogether. List (1909, p. 140) thought such surmising fanciful
as it ignored the various intermediaries between economy and humanity,
above all the nation:

> The nation, with its special language and literature, peculiar origin and history, its

special manners and customs, laws and institutions, with the claims of all these for existence, independence, perfection and continuance for the future, and with a separate territory . . . [This organic society is] united by a thousand ties of mind and of interests, combines itself into one independent whole.

List argued that nations, as cultural hubs of humanity, are completely over-looked by 'the school' as this neat summation of its shortcomings reveals. Free-market economics is characterized by:

Firstly, a boundless *cosmopolitanism*, which neither recognises the principle of nationality, nor takes into consideration the satisfaction of its interests; secondly from a dead *materialism*, which everywhere regards chiefly the mere exchangeable value of things without taking into consideration the mental and political, the present and future interests, and the productive powers of the nation; thirdly, from a disorganising *particularism and individualism*, which ignoring the nature of powers in the higher consequences, considers private industry only as it would develop itself under a state of free exchange with society (that is, the whole human race) were not that race divided into separate national societies. (List, 1909, p. 140)

So within List one finds not just a pragmatic solution for the embryonic manufacturing industry, but also the assertion that free markets are not in themselves sacrosanct, rather, they should be subordinate to nations. Further, in certain circumstances, distinctly state-bounded national economies will emerge that are identical with 'the economy of the people'. Within them, peoples must pull together for the greater good:

The nation must sacrifice and give up a measure of material property in order to gain culture, skill and powers of united production; it must sacrifice some present advantages in order to insure to itself future ones. (List, 1909, p. 132)

Keynes and the End of Laissez Faire

It would be an interesting exercise in itself to try to assess the enduring importance of List's ideas. His ongoing relevance to political economy has been noted by several contemporary scholars trying to discredit the neolib-eral dogma that tariffs are always deleterious to the development of fledgling industries (see Levi-Faur, 1997; Schafaeddin, 2000). During the latter part of the nineteenth century, his ideas were of some direct influence on policy makers in the general drift towards tariffs and subsidies. His writings – notwithstanding how his remarks about national economies and state subordination might be read as anticipations of the twentieth-century shift towards autarchy – reflect the age before 1914 in which there was no general philosophical departure from laissez faire in the context of the actual and spectacular growth in world trade. Simultaneously, bourgeois governments in Europe, America and Japan made impatient attempts to force industrialization through piecemeal tariffs, amid periodic crises and a rising tide of popular nationalist sentiment.

Such sentiments acted as the backdrop to the sharp rise of government expenditure on the military before 1914, and in some instances, national tariffs were raised up very high. In Imperial Russia, they were 84% on manufactured imports by 1900, nearly double that of the nearest highest, the USA. But this was not accompanied by an attempt to keep out foreign investment. On the contrary, the tsarist regime actively welcomed it, with the result that by 1913 some 40% of industry was foreign owned (Frieden, 2005, pp. 65–6). Even in Germany, where there was a wholesale shift away from free trade towards tariffs between 1873 and 1879, Chancellor Otto von Bismarck seems to have harboured no long-term ambition to turn his nearly unified state into a self-contained industrial fortress. In Germany, as in Italy, the principal effect of protectionism in the form of tariff barriers and subsidy to domestic industry through state central banks seems to have been to bring about internal economic unification (see Kahan, 1968). Although the rise in tariffs was an important aspect of the latter part of the nineteenth century and differing models of national economic organization did emerge, it did not counter the rising importance of international trade. By 1913, trade composed between 35% and 50% of GDP of the advanced economies – higher in Britain, much lower in the USA (for statistics and an overview of this era, see Held et al., 1999, pp. 158–9).

If economic rivalry, as manifested in protectionism, was partly responsible for the outbreak of war in August 1914, the period after 1918 did not see an abandonment of a common commitment to international trade. The immediate aftermath of the war, a period in which the leading gentlemen of the victorious powers tried to turn the clock back to the pre-1914 era, witnessed chronic financial instability in Europe, giving way to economic boom among the industrialized and semi-industrialized countries in the second half of the 1920s. By 1929, world trade was 42% greater than it had been in 1913 and accounted for a significantly greater share of most national economies.

This made the subsequent economic collapse all the more dramatic. The world's economy contracted by a third between 1929 and 1934. Trade led the way in the fall, declining by a third within three years from the Wall Street stock market crash of 1929. Britain's withdrawal from the gold standard in September 1931 marked a symbolic and actual end of an era that, despite the ructions of war, imperialism and revolution, had stretched over the previous 100 years. As Frieden (2005, p. 194) says of the 1930s:

The classical world economy had failed. The halting recovery, the preliminary steps at reconstituting international economic order, the islands of growth in the midst of stagnation and the newly available products and techniques could not disguise this basic fact. The old order did not deliver economic growth, or stability or protection from chaos.

Hobsbawm (1992, p. 132) captures the retrenchment of the 1930s graphically: 'World capitalism retreated into the igloos of its nation-state economies and their associated empires.'

This is the context for the fundamental shift away, despite die-hard advocates in the world of high finance, government and academia, from the belief that economies should be self-regulating. The intellectual and political shift is discernible from the late nineteenth century, but it was not ordered and coherent. Instead, it was driven by immediate economic crisis and corresponded to medium-term financial fault lines. Crucial to whether or not a country moved directly towards economic autarchy (self-sufficiency) and political authoritarianism during the 1930s was whether or not it was an international debtor. Simultaneously, the shift was particularly pronounced within certain geographical and developmental sectors of the world's economy. Most political economies within Latin America and the advanced colonies of European empires that had relied on agricultural and raw material export markets moved towards the use of national resources to meet national ends. This involved the expansion of industry by the tried and tested means of making industrial costs exceptionally low and hence profits exceptionally high. At the same time, measures to restrict foreign involvement in domestic economies were introduced (Hobsbawm, 1992).

The shift was most explicit through the belt of Europe from Germany, through its centre and east, to the Mediterranean south, where Fascist and authoritarian regimes sought to make nationalist virtue from economic necessity. To the east of Europe stood the Soviet Union, which formally, although for ideologically different reasons, disavowed the world capitalist free market. Even in areas of the world where there was no official renunciation of free-market regulation, there were schemes to cope with its failure. The New Deal under Roosevelt in America (1933–36) defined the era. In Britain, was there no equivalent of this massive programme of government works. Instead, British industry increasingly relied on export sales to protected colonial markets to prop up its ailing industrial economy. It was not until around 1945 that the ideas of John Maynard Keynes, the British economist who was to become the most influential in the world for the next 40 years,[3] would find favour in government and Whitehall.

It is relevant to note the thoughts of Keynes on economic nationalism in this period. Although there is reference to the importance of the wellbeing of the British economy in his work in the 1920s, as a good classical liberal, his principal concern was the betterment of humanity a whole not a particular national sector. A contemporary noted his personal distaste for nationalism and other collectivisms, above all socialism (Skidelsky, 1992, p. 257). His approach to economics was to use it as a pragmatic guide to policy that should inform decision makers in governments on how to compensate for the inherent deficiencies and crises of free-market capitalism and, in particular, the greying financial ruling class of the city of London, by intervening to stimulate economic demand and hence production. This intellectual endeavour culminated in his well-known book, *A General Theory of Employment*, published in 1936. Three years earlier, in a speech in Dublin in April 1933, he had indicated a commitment to economic nationalism that should modify the assumption that Keynes was above all an economic cosmopolitan. The location for his remarks at University College, Dublin is significant, as Ireland had recently elected a Fianna Fail government under Eamon de Valera that was set on economic autarchy and Catholic austerity.[4]

Keynes had signalled an ethical commitment to the importance of the nation a few months earlier in a radio address, when he said that 'national self sufficiency' promised a 'well balanced' or 'complete' national life, allowing 'English people to display the full range of their national aptitudes in mechanical invention and in agriculture; as well as preserving traditional ways of living'. After linking various occupations to the breadth of English national character, he dismissed the notion that a balance sheet should alone determine the maintenance of industry. Speaking specifically of agriculture, Keynes stated (quoted in Skidelsky, 1992, p. 474):

> The country that cannot afford agriculture is deluded as to the meaning of the word 'afford'. A country that cannot afford agriculture, or invention, or tradition, is a country in which one cannot afford to live.

The Dublin lecture, however, was not national whimsy on the virtues of 'the homespun'. He argued first for greater economic self-sufficiency with characteristic lucidity on the grounds that he doubted the continuing economic viability of an international division of labour linked by trade. Instead, he wanted to 'bring producer and consumer within the ambit of the same national, economic and financial organisation'. Second, he suggested that free trade and the international mobility of capital were more likely to provoke war than keep peace. In times of stress, particularly, the ownership of national assets by foreigners was prone to 'set up strains and enmities', which had led to war in 1914. Third, in order to 'try to be working out our salvation. We do not wish to be at the mercy of the world forces working out, or trying to work out, some uniform equilibrium according to the ideal principles of laissez-faire capitalism.' Fourth, he stated that the perverse logic of capitalism condemns us to be poor because it does not 'pay' to be rich . . . Today, we suffer disillusion, not because we are poorer . . . but because our values seem to have been sacrificed . . . and sacrificed unnecessarily. For our economic system is not, in fact, enabling us to exploit to the utmost the possibilities for economic wealth afforded by the progress of our technique . . . leading us to feel we might well have used up the margin in more satisfying ways. But once we allow ourselves to be disobedient to the test of an accountant's profit, we have begun to change our civilization. (Keynes quoted in Skidelsky, 1992, pp. 476–8)

Robert Skidelsky, Keynes's authoritative biographer from whom this account is taken, comments that Keynes had seemed to swing full circle from Adam Smith to Friedrich List, German founder of economic nationalism, or, for the contemporary minded, to Dr Schacht, Nazi Germany's economic overlord (p. 476). However, the comparison with List is only half accurate because List, in part, only advocated economic protection as a temporal measure on the way to opening up all economies to market competition. But it is indicative of how profoundly the intellectual and political wheel had turned when an economic liberal of the twentieth century was more a 'nationalist' than the most prominent critic of laissez faire in the nineteenth.

From Managed Capitalism to Globalization

If Keynes chimed with the times in 1933, his wider thinking on managed capitalism, as set out in *A General Theory of Employment* and elsewhere, is indicative of attempts by the victorious, non-Communist allies to restore trade after the Second World War. The Second World War (1939–45) was an economic disaster for all the countries that had participated, with the spectacular exception of the USA, which had suffered no damage and had increased its GNP by nearly two-thirds (Hobsbawm, 1994, p. 258). The industrial and financial dominance of American capitalism after 1945 is one of the general features of the world's economy in the postwar era. The realization that the defeat of Nazi Germany would oblige the American federal government to become a international political and economic leader was grasped as early as 1939 within the Roosevelt administration, that is, before America actually entered the war. And it was something moderate presidencies were prepared to undertake after 1945 in the context of the Cold War with the Soviet Union, despite continuing isolationist strains in US politics and society that frequently surfaced in Congress. According to Frieden (2005), the general trajectory followed by the USA involved a rejection of both unfettered free-market capitalism and economic nationalism, a reflection of their disastrous impact over the previous 20 years. The rather grim prevailing mood was summed up by a supporter of Cordell Hull, secretary of state under

Roosevelt: 'If soldiers are not to cross international borders, goods must do so' (quoted in Frieden, 2005, p. 255). For goods to cross borders, the conscious administration of governments and large companies was required.

The actual arrangements for the postwar economic order were famously drawn up at Bretton Woods, New Hampshire in 1944, between British and American negotiators led by John Maynard Keynes and Harry White respectively. The single most important decision taken was that there was to be no return to the prewar gold standard. Instead, national governments and banks were to manage their currencies' exchange rates and their own capital accounts. To oversee development, financial crises and the gradual reduction of tariffs, plans were drawn up for the World Bank, the IMF and (what became in 1947) the General Agreement on Tariffs and Trade (GATT). The first two organizations were effectively bankrolled by the US Treasury.

The second major development in the postwar era relevant to the impetus of economic nationalism was the spread of nominally socialist countries under the leadership of the Soviet Union to encompass by 1950 central and southeast Europe and China. While trade and some travel existed between them, their economies relied on the planned investment and distribution of ruling Communist parties. If economic planning was most pronounced in socialist countries after 1945, it was found virtually everywhere.

The third development, the greatest nationalist wave in history, was that of colonial independence from the European empires. All such countries were committed to the development of national economies, regardless of whether they were formally part of the non-aligned movement of Third World states. As mentioned, less developed countries outside the industrial heartlands of the world economy had adopted protectionist policies as a response to international recession in the 1930s. Protectionism was formalized after 1945 and harnessed to the pursuit of forced industrialization through import substitution to boost domestic manufacturing, and given a theoretical underpinning through the work of the Argentinean economist Raúl Prebisch (1901–86) and the development of the so-called 'structuralist' school of economics. Prebisch had shifted his economic alignment from free-trade orthodoxy to Keynesianism while an adviser to the Argentinean Ministry of Agriculture in the 1930s and then as president of the nation's first central bank in 1943. After the war, he became director of the UN's Economic Commission for Latin America and in 1950 published his influential study, *The Economic Development of Latin America and its Principal Problems*. In it, he (together with Hans Singer) substantiated his nascent thinking on the long-term tendency of primary exports from the economic periphery of the world to fall in price, in comparison with the cost of manufactured goods made at the centre (known as the Prebisch-Singer hypothesis).

The technical argument for this need not concern us here. The obvious point for our purposes is that nation-states at the periphery must take steps individually and collectively to counteract this systemic and accentuating inequality in world trade. Later, while at the United Nations Conference on Trade and Development, Prebisch came to advocate greater regional economic cooperation between peripheral countries – sometimes referred to as 'collective nationalism', conceptually an oxymoron, as revealed in practice by internal tensions between participants – to counter deleterious trade relationships. The change in orientation of Latin American economies from being free-trade primary exporters to protectionist industrializers was profound during this period. By the early 1960s, for example, tariffs on manufactured imports averaged 74% for Mexico and 184% for Brazil. From 1954 to 1973, Mexico's industrial production quadrupled and Brazil's increased eightfold (Friedman, 2005, pp. 304–5).

The success of less developed countries echoes the fundamental feature of the postwar period as a whole up until the 1970s: it was the longest and most impressive boom in world economic history, one that ushered in the contemporary era of economic globalization. Like any sweeping claim made, some qualifications should be placed against it. This was not the most sustained period of growth of the British economy and, more importantly, growth in subsequent decades in Asia (which contains half the world's population) has been more impressive. Simultaneously, writers who are reluctant to concede to Keynesianism point to the exceptional circumstances of postwar reconstruction in economies like West Germany and Japan that benefited in part from the financial largesse of US Marshall Plan aid and unprecedented technological breakthroughs; the latter partly a reflection of massive US military spending (Wolf, 2004, p. 130). This obviously does not detract from the economic achievement. Despite the tariff prohibitions, total export sales as a percentage of world output grew by nearly 8% p.a. for the period 1950–73, considerably greater than the rise in output as a whole.

Hobsbawm suggests that the postwar period saw a shift away from national economies towards a transnational one, that is, one from where the boundaries of the nation-state are not the basic framework for economic activity but merely complicating factors. In his view, a world economy is one where territorial boundaries are largely irrelevant. The term 'transnational' is therefore a sort of 'halfway-house' between nationalism and globalization. In concrete terms, we can point to four developments that set the scene for the latter (Hobsbawm, 1994, p. 277):

1 The growth of transnational companies, often nineteenth-century European and American in origin, with investments and interlinked manufacturers as well as sales in multiple countries.
2 Emerging out of this, a new international division of labour that undermined, although it did not eliminate, the separation within the world's economy since the nineteenth century between essentially industrial and agricultural economies.

3   The rise of offshore finance involving 'multiplying floods of unattached capital that washed around the globe from currency to currency, looking for quick profits' (Hobsbawm, 1994, p. 278). These flows of liquidity made it increasingly hard for governments to control exchange rates. By 1971, they led to the fall of fixed exchange rates, the key feature of the Bretton Woods accords.

4   The spectacular gains in technology, in part a product of the colossal sums spent on military innovation.

The economic crisis of the 1970s, giving way to the turbulence of the 1980s, did not shift the momentum generated by the long postwar boom. Despite the devastation experienced by parts of the world's economy and population, internationalization as measured by key indices actually accentuated. Swathes of manufacturing industry disappeared in advanced capitalist countries. In the by now heavily indebted developing countries of the world's South, especially Latin America, there was severe overall economic contraction from the end of the 1970s. The 1980s were characterized by the austerity of World Bank and IMF-imposed structural adjustment packages, which tied further borrowing to radical reductions in state expenditure and market liberalization. Yet in every year, the growth in exports continued to outstrip the modest overall rise in world output. Between 1970 and 1990, exports as a proportion of total world output doubled. So in marked contrast to the slump of the 1930s, recession did not lead states to direct economies away from exports – the very opposite was the case.

Politically and intellectually, taken as whole, the era saw a definite shift away from the ideas associated with Keynes in the developed world, and Prebisch and others in less developed countries. Instead, a new breed of right-wing politicians, exemplified by Margaret Thatcher in Britain and Ronald Reagan in America, made reference to the economist Milton Freedman and the philosopher Frederick von Hayek, alongside Adam Smith, in attempts to curb the money supply ('monetarism') and reduce restrictions on the market. The turbulent decade of the 1980s ended with the apparent vindication of capitalism through the revolutions of Eastern Europe in 1989 and the unravelling of the Soviet Union. From 1992 through to 2005, the ratio of trade to GDP across OECD (Organisation for Economic Co-operation and Development)[5] countries increased by some 13% (OECD, 2007). The 1990s is the decade in which the very term 'globalization' became a universal catch-all for the outcome of the economic integration that had taken place over the previous 40 years.

As indicated above, it is not difficult to identify four contemporary predictions of a return of the hobgoblin of economic nationalism. Besides the somewhat alarmist fears of those who evoke this term together with socialism whenever they detect state intervention in market activity, around the millennium and after, there were more genuine concerns that the trajectory of globalization might be thrown into reverse:

1   There were the combined crises experienced by, first, Asian economies in 1997–8, and then Argentina in 1999, eagerly seized upon by the IMF and World Bank as a chance to subject their protected economies and overvalued currencies to world markets.
2   The popular protest against globalization across the world starting in Seattle in 1999.
3   On a quite different level, it was thought that the terrorist attacks of 9/11 2001 on New York might somehow lead to major disruption in the world economy. The event and its aftermath did cause a small but significant reversal in trade, capital flows and foreign investment, the former declining by 4% in 2002.
4   The Asian crisis convinced the Chinese Communist Party leadership to retain low exchange rates, making for a surge in export-led growth, something that has created employment and shored up domestic support. This has led to a massive trade deficit and a further decline of manufacturing industry for the USA, the principal recipient of Chinese exports.

It remains to be seen what degree of protectionism will emerge in the USA as a response to the onset of recession in the late 2000s. In Europe, leaving aside the alarmist fears expressed at the beginning of the chapter, there has been some shift in sentiment away from free markets as indicated by French success in reducing EU commitments to it, especially in respect to agriculture.

However, contemporaneous to all this, as Held and McGrew (2007) point out, economic globalization has proved far more resilient than many presumed. Trade in 2004 was the strongest in a decade, reaching historic levels of world GDP, foreign direct investment (FDI) flows rebounded to the level of the early 1990s, while financial flows increased and foreign exchange transactions reached historic levels. Thus the process of economic globalization continues apace. With this in mind, we turn to several key questions that emerge out of this overview of globalization and economic nationalism.

Whither Economic Nationalism?

Looked at in the long term, we can see that economic nationalism was something that arose in the nineteenth century as a response to the different takeoff points of industrialization and as a more directly politically motivated endeavour to create zones in which the cultural and the economic fuse. Although both factors played a part in the rise of tariffs in the nineteenth century, something which contributed to the rise of tensions culminating in war, the prevailing emphasis on trade continued until the late 1920s. Then, as a response to the economic slump that affected countries in Europe, Latin America and Asia, the 1930s saw an emphasis on a greater degree of economic self-reliance. This registered across the world but was especially acute within both Fascist and Communist states who embraced economic autarchy. It is testament to the strength of this intellectual trajectory that Maynard Keynes, a thinker who had hitherto been chiefly concerned with measures that might perpetuate free trade, spoke of the economic importance of industrial and agricultural national autonomy. The framing of the postwar economic order, under American domination, placed an emphasis on a renewed rise in world trade, but through the implementation of some of the methods of financial control that had developed in the previous era. The rapid period of growth that this initiated saw the development of a transnational trend in economic activity that gave rise to what became known as 'globalization' in the 1990s.

The first question we should ask is whether or not the move towards a national political economy, first depicted by List – at his most nationalist – in the mid-nineteenth century, is possible. It would be one in which economic activity returns to take place principally within the walls of nations as guarded by the high protective walls of the state. In such an economy, there would be a high degree of integration between the domestic state and business, either public or private, and a prevailing sense of national duty on the part of companies – as opposed to simply making money. Foreign economic activity, through either import sales, investment and ownership, or the buying and selling of national currencies, would be relatively unimportant and firmly controlled.

Opinions differ on this matter. Harold James (2001), a thinker from the discipline of economic history, suggests that such a return is possible, on the grounds that the wrench away from trade and overseas investment in the 1930s was as great as that which would be required now. To oversimplify, if it happened then, it could happen again.[6] Other writers, impressed by the scale of the unravelling of the nineteenth-century liberal order, take a similar view (see Beattie, 2006). For some, a return to national economies is all but impossible such is the extent of contemporary globalization. Nigel Harris, identified in Chapter 1 as a hyperglobalist, thinks that the growth of global markets over the past 60 years has decisively superseded national economies. Answers to questions of this type can only be provisional. Indeed, one could go further and say that futurology is rather a pointless exercise, if engaged in for the more distant future. Who knows what sort of world economy will eventuate in the longer term when the polar icecaps have been reduced to icebergs, large parts of the earth are uninhabitable and, as Keynes famously said, we, if not our great-grandchildren, are all dead?

What we can say is that a return to principally national economies – taken here to be economies that are largely self-sufficient save some reliance on external raw materials – seems in present circumstances highly unlikely for two reasons. The first is that the integration of markets through trade and investment would appear to make this practically impossible. Among OECD countries in 2005, some 45% of GDP was made up of foreign trade (over 50% for EU economies, the largest chunk of the world's economy), FDI accounted for nearly 20% of GDP and employment in foreign-owned companies was a little under 10% of the total OECD workforce (OECD, 2007). A large-scale reversal of this state of affairs, the scaling down of trade and so on to its level in, say, 1960 would not just involve a crisis of interwar proportions but an economic Armageddon. In fact, as mentioned, in recent times recession has accelerated global economic trends. Every indication, notwithstanding temporary blips, is that such figures are likely to rise.

The second is that models of national economic self-reliance – from the import substitution that originated in the 1930s, through the heavily state-managed and protected mixed economies of the long postwar boom, to the autarchy of Communist and Fascist regimes – have been discredited. Only the failing regime of North Korea continues to explicitly propound the latter notion. It is certainly true that national governments are extremely reluctant to remove key controls that either prevent or limit foreign economic activity within their national economies. Even within the global trend of the privatization of state-owned industries, there are often rules limiting foreign ownership. However, there are no contemporary examples of governments coming to power that are committed to actively reversing economic globalization.

There are plenty of radical, left-wing critiques of globalization, but they generally refrain from suggesting that the process should be reversed altogether. One such account is Waldon Bello's *Deglobalization* (2004), which does not in fact favour the curtailment of international trade, but maps a radical rethink of the institutions and priorities of the global economy. Opposition to globalization from the Fascist Right – who have historically associated it with Jewish financers – aims, vaguely, to regroup business within national economies. Some environmental campaigners suggest a reversion to local suppliers of goods and services, not out of love of country/loathing of foreigners, but to drastically reduce the emission of greenhouse gases.[7] There are radical Islamists who advocate the retention and use of oil resources within Arab countries as an aspect of jihad – one meaning of which is 'holy war' (bin Laden, 2005, pp. 163, 272). Even here, however, there seems to be no principled opposition to international trade per se. And despite the rhetoric, media profile and terrorist violence of al-Qaeda, these kinds of demands are fairly marginal even within the Middle East.

More mainstream critiques of globalization have been made over the past 10 years by political leaders, policy makers and even financiers. However, they have generally been of either the chronic instability of the present state of world finance and/or the dogmatic free-market prescriptions of the World Bank and the IMF. In the aftermath of the 1997 Asian crash, the Malaysian Prime Minister Mahathir Mohamad made a number of high-profile attacks on international financiers (especially George Soros), sacked his finance minister Anwar Ibrahim, who was responsible for economic integration, and charged him with criminal offences, and imposed capital and currency controls on Malaysia. However, as Frieden (2005, p. 394) comments:

> In another era the vitriolic Mahathir-Soros exchanges and the Malaysian prime minister's nationalistic rhetoric might have presaged long-lasting measures to turn the economy away from global markets. Yet within a couple of years the episode had largely been forgotten. After a severe recession the Malaysian economy began growing again. Despite the capital and currency controls, Malaysia continued to rely heavily on the international economy. Mahathir was indeed careful to avoid blanket condemnation of global capitalism. 'We want to embrace borderlessness', he said and 'We have always welcomed foreign investment and speculation'. It was just that 'we still need to protect ourselves from self-serving rogues and international brigandage' . . . Despite the great shock that international markets administered to the East Asian economies and the wave of crises that the shock caused, the advance of global economic integration was barely slowed.

The events in Asia in the late 1990s prompted Joseph Stiglitz, the chief World Bank economist, to resign from his position in protest at the bank's policies and set out a high-profile appraisal of his thinking in *Globalization and its Discontents* (2002). Stiglitz's account was acute but it was chiefly an attack on the World Bank's attempt to use the Asian economic crisis to open up the economies of the region by tying loans to deregulation. More widely, it offered a critique of economic liberalization in the developing world where domestic business is unable to compete with superior foreign competitors. This leads to consideration of issues such as global inequality and financial instability. However, he neither questioned the wider benefit of globalization nor suggested a radical alternative to the present system. Instead, he called for greater accountability and transparency among international institutions. Some influential academic figures, such as Ann Florini and Dani Rodrik, have taken the idea of reform of the international financial system further, to what Bello (2004, pp. 98–9) refers to as 'global Keynesianism' and 'back-to-the-Bretton-Woods'.

Interestingly, some of the proposals for reform of international institutions have been taken up by Soros himself, an archetypal, billionaire financier. His *On Globalization* (2002) provides an exacting assessment of what he terms 'free-market fundamentalism' as it emerged in the 1990s and was visited upon Eastern European and Asian economies. This is followed by a comprehensive set of proposals for the reform of global governance. They are designed to improve the sorry record of the World Bank and the IMF in respect of less developing countries, and to create and augment other international institutions like the International Labour Organization, strengthening what he calls 'global public goods'. These include labour rights, the environment, consumer safety and public health. Whatever the worth of these proposals, they are in no way, shape or form concerned with anything that might possibly be termed 'economic nationalism'. In sum, the momentum towards market integration through the reach of multinational companies and finance, combined with the prevailing political and intellectual orthodoxy, means that economic globalization is likely to intensify. This is the context against which the continuing relevance of economic nationalism should be measured. Simply to say, as some contemporary scholars do, that nationalism and national identity exist and count for something in the world economy is undoubtedly true, but not particularly useful in understanding globalization. However, a number of important qualifications should be made:

1   Capitalism has not brought about anything like the complete integration of national economies. The general rule of thumb is that small, rich and medium income economies are highly globalized. Thus the ratio of trade to GDP in Ireland, Austria, Mexico, Hungary and Korea is above 50%, while the figure is less than 15% for Japan and the USA.

2   The indices of globalization are in themselves highly uneven. Trade is the most highly globalized indicator of globalization, the best to make the case, but other indices, arguably better gauges of globalization such as the stocks of foreign investment and the employment share by foreign companies, are significantly lower. Ireland stands at the head of OECD countries in respect of foreign investment, but the proportion of workers in foreign-controlled manufacturing enterprises is less than half the total workforce, while the figure is 22% for services. In the USA, the figures are 11% and 3% respectively for foreign employers; in Japan the numbers are negligible. The level of inward and outward flows of FDI was approximately 20% of GDP for OECD countries in 2004. Even with trade, for obvious geographic reasons, it is significantly higher for manufactured goods than for services.

3   Trade is principally conducted between the richer countries of the world located in North America, parts of Latin America, Europe and parts of Asia. In 2005, 70% of the trade of OECD countries was with other members of this 'rich man's club', a figure that had fallen some 10% in the previous period solely due to the rise of China as an economic superpower. Only 3% of OECD trade was with Africa (OECD, 2007). This is the context for the enormous and widening inequalities of world capitalism.

4   National protective measures still exist through tariffs, subsidies and regulations on foreign business activity. A glance through the databases of the WTO at the most important hindrance to international trade, tariffs levied on imported goods, reveals that they are approximately 15% for agricultural products for the EU and the USA, twice as high in Japan and over 100% for India.[8] Obviously GATT and subsequently the WTO have reduced tariffs substantially for non-agricultural goods since their high watermark in the postwar era. In the short to medium term, however, WTO talks on further trade liberalization seem mired in intractable disputes on universal reform. Recent deadlock has been at least as much over the refusal of the EU and the USA to bring down their agricultural tariff walls, as the unwillingness of developing countries to allow non-agricultural products to freely enter their consumer markets. The historic importance of national farming constituencies has been central to this deadlock.

Taken together, these things suggest that economic globalization is extremely uneven, limited by the extent of penetration into national economies, its international reach and continuing state imposed national barriers. As Wolf (2004, p. 134), not a sceptic given to playing down the process, puts it: 'Globalization is not rampant. It remains remarkably modest.'

A fifth qualification that should be set beside the achievement of globalization is of a rather different type: the contemporary economic nationalism of the world's superpower, the USA. This might be better termed a global corporate US nationalism or simply imperialism. It reached its peak (or nadir) with the unashamed unilateralism since 2000 of George W. Bush's administration, but there is a clear continuity of the policies of American governments favouring US business interests on the international stage since 1945. There are presently a number of aspects of this to which we might point:

1   The control and use of organizations that are nominally international to break into national economies that were previously protected. For example, according to Bello (2004, p. 48), the Asian financial crisis of the late 1990s (when Bill Clinton was in power) shows that:

> the stabilization programmes imposed by the IMF on the key countries of Malaysia, Indonesia and Thailand reveal that the rollback of protectionism and activist state intervention were strategically incorporated into them. These programmes went beyond mere stabilization and short-term adjustment, leading credence to the claims that in the critical years of 1998 and 1999, the USA was interested not in the economic recovery of the Asian tigers but their resubordination.

Bello quotes several US and IMF negotiators who were quite explicit that the ability of foreign firms to enter previously restricted markets through sales and ownership was in the interests of the USA.

2   The use of international agencies like the WTO to promote and enforce agreements that favour US and European multinationals. One of the most important moves of the WTO since 1995 has been TRIPS (the Trade Related Intellectual Property Rights Agreement) that consolidated the hold over high-tech innovation by US corporations such as Intel, Microsoft and Monsanto.

3   The holding up and ultimately the wrecking of negotiations of the WTO Doha Round talks over, among other things, the attempt by developing countries to tie health issues to trade agreements through the weakening of patent rights.

4   The pursuit not of multilateral, that is, global, trade agreements to reduce tariffs and so on, but of preferential, bilateral agreements in contravention of WTO rules (Krushna, 2005, pp. 10–11).

5   America's so-called 'war on terror' has had an economic dimension that has added to the US trend towards protectionism. In 2006, the US Congress blocked the attempted takeover of US ports by a consortium from the United Arab Emirates (UAE) on the grounds that it did not want foreigners, especially Muslims, acquiring a key US strategic asset. Although the then Bush administration opposed this move, probably as much on the grounds that the UAE is an ally in the Gulf region as a commitment to free trade, the bar attracted cross-party Congressional support. As Representative Jerry Lewis, a California Republican, put it before the vote: 'We want to make sure that the security of our ports is in America's hands' (http://news.bbc.co.uk/1/hi/world/americas/4784842.stm). The issue was followed by calls for tougher and more systematic control of Arab investment in the USA.

6   Most dramatically, the extension of the US military across the world with the clear intent of securing markets and natural resources. This process is at its most stark and lethal in the Middle East, where the Bush administration (2001–09) attempted to take over Iraq, install an acquiescent government and, whatever the final outcome, leave a substantial political and army presence in order to secure access to oil supplies.[9] The vast sums spent by the Bush administration with the consistent support of Congress have been of massive benefit to some American multinationals and domestic markets, often connecting business and government in what can only be described as 'crony capitalism'. The example of Republican ex-Vice-president Dick Cheney's connections to Halliburton, a recipient of massive contracts for the US military in Iraq, is well known.

This most brutal – if contested and deeply troubled – manifestation of American imperialism should be set beside the fanciful scenarios that globalization is making state and national interests obsolescent, or that 'actually existing economic liberalism' is somehow a neutral and natural process – an extension of man's propensity to 'brook, barter and trade', as Adam Smith put it. However, there is still the question of whether or not American actions are likely to set back the advance of market integration. Certainly American protectionism has triggered occasional trade spats with the EU – an organization that uses its own economic muscle vis-à-vis developing countries – that have damaged certain industries for a short period of time. More widely, it is likely that the brazen pursuit of American corporate interests by US negotiators at WTO talks from 2000 to 2008, together with a wider hostility to the Bush administration's foreign policies, have significantly delayed further trade liberalization. It remains to be seen to what extent President Obama's administration will further the cause of economic internationalism.

Arguably too, US foreign policy has fanned the flames of a resurgent Russian nationalism under Vladimir Putin, who heads a government that is quite prepared to use energy supplies as well as its military to try to reassert its position of influence across Eastern Europe and in the Caucasus region in particular and the world in general. The latter may involve the development of an Eastern zone of authoritarian governments, including China, that could act as an alternative zone for business. There is some evidence that some Eastern European countries, notably Serbia, tired of being rebuffed in their attempts to enter the EU and incensed over the EU and US push for Kosovan independence, are gravitating towards it. China itself has cultivated markets and raw material supplies from parts of the world that American and European business has only limited interest in, notably sub-Saharan Africa. All this suggests that future economic development is likely to be further skewed by national and regional interests and alignments.

Conclusion

This chapter first noted that the conception of the degree of economic globalization is not in itself crucial to theoretical conceptions of whether nationalism is set to weaken. This depends on how nations are conceived. In the estimation of those writers who think they are relatively recent, the product of the transformations of modernity, there will be a decline in their long-term power as the nationalist project, the nation-state, becomes progressively less viable in the global age. For those who think that nations have deeper historical roots and therefore greater, even immutable cultural durability, globalization will have little, if any impact on the hold of nationalism over peoples. Notwithstanding this intractable theoretical disagreement, the subject of economics is integral to understandings of globalization and nationalism. At stake is whether or not nations, through their given organizational structure of the state, have the ability to direct economic affairs in their own interests.

The fundamental issue is the role and salience of economic nationalism in relation to globalization.

I noted that there is an initial difficulty in discussing economic nationalism as it generally has a poor academic profile. While this has been the case for some time, the term has undoubtedly suffered further through the dominance of neoliberalism, an integral part of globalization. For neoliberals, or 'economic liberals' as some prefer, economic nationalism is not quite a term of abuse but is something that is taken to be all that globalization is not. They are given to raise the spectre of economic nationalism at regular intervals. According to this school of thought, economic nationalism is about the artificial protection – through tariffs and other measures – of national economies from external, foreign businesses. National economies are geographic areas where economic activity largely occurs. For more idealistic neoliberals, that is, those who are not just concerned about capitalists making profits, the openness of markets to trade and other forms of external economic activity is equated with individual freedom and political democracy.

In contrast to this general neoliberal denigration of economic nationalism, there has been a recent attempt to rescue the term by several scholars within international political economy. In part, they are motivated by the desire to dispel the simplistic assertion that economic nationalism is really 'about protectionism'. Also, they are concerned to give an adequate independent role to nations and nationalism within international political economy and international relations where historically it has been subsumed within considerations of the state. I argued that although the flexibility of this approach has some benefits, such as the appreciation that privatization was carried out by aggressive nationalist governments in the 1990s, its loose definition of nationalism robs it of analytic purchase.

With this in mind, I suggested that a better approach is to try to trace the modern rise of economic nationalism since the mid-nineteenth century. Here we saw that its first theoretical exposition was set out by List in an account that combined, not altogether coherently, support of tariffs for infant industries, based on differing levels of the industrialization of Germany and Britain, a longer term commitment to free trade and a cultural nationalism that seemed at points to advocate the creation of national economies as an end in itself. List prefigured the rise in economic nationalism, as realized in an increase in tariffs, in the late nineteenth and early twentieth centuries as part of a wider ascent in the phenomenon that contributed to war in 1914. However, it was not until the late 1920s that the importance of trade to world economic output was thrown into reverse. The 1930s saw both a substantial decrease in actual trade and an accompanying ideological movement that rejected on nationalist grounds its pursuit in favour of 'homespun' production. This trend was both institutionalized and ameliorated after the horrors of the Second World War through an international acceptance, under the leadership of the USA, of the role of nation-states in organizing their national economies, together with an emphasis on reviving world trade. This gave rise in the half-century following 1945 to a globalizing trend in economic activity that has surpassed in depth and range the phase before 1914. The trajectory has hardly been a smooth, even and politically neutral one. On the contrary, it has been marked as much by crises as by pacific development. However, it is a fact that at every conjuncture where the pundits predicted a reversal of the process of economic integration, the period after 2001 being the most recent, levels of world trade and investment have outperformed domestic growth. In other words, economic globalization has consistently become more important and pronounced, not less. It is difficult to see a wholesale reversal in this state of affairs, particularly as there is no prominent political and intellectual case distilled into economic nationalisms intent on so doing.

However, this is not the whole story. There are a number of important qualifications that should be set beside the claim that there is no turning back to distinctly national economies. Among them are that economic globalization is limited by its extent within all economies, its only partial integration of the different geographic regions of the world and the continuing protection of national markets by governments. These things apply to the world's biggest economy, that of the USA. I suggested that in an imperial form, the USA pursues a form of contemporary economic nationalism through imperialism that in several respects reached its zenith under ex-President George W. Bush. This has set back the cause of globalization through the undermining of WTO free-trade negotiations in various ways. However, regardless of how unilateral US foreign policy is in pursuit of American corporate self-interest, there is little or no prospect that a presidency and Congress will be elected in the near to medium-term future committed in some way to reversing America's economic integration into the world economy. But American imperialism, combined with a number of sub-imperialisms elsewhere in the world, Chinese and Russian the most important among them, indicates that globalization is not a benign process of mutual enrichment imagined by economic liberals. Rather it is something shot through with antagonistic national interests that both impede and propel it forward.

Summary Points

- Economic nationalism concerns the attempt by governments to largely confine economic activity to the geographic area of the nation using a number of policy instruments. It is generally seen as a negative phenomenon.

- Although there are intimations of economic nationalism in mercantilism from the sixteenth century onwards, it arises in a modern form in the mid-nineteenth century through, in particular, the writings of Friedrich List.
- List advocated government policies to protect infant industries, especially those of his native Germany, given the contemporary dominance of British manufacturers.
- Such policies were increasingly adopted in the subsequent period in an era that was still characterized by a commitment to free trade. However, as recession struck in the late 1920s, there was a marked shift away from the principle of free trade towards a emphasis on national economic self-reliance.
- The disasters of Fascism and war gave rise to a US-led attempt – in the context of a developing Cold War with the Soviet Union – to manage capitalism in the period after 1945.
- Taken as a whole, this period has seen a spectacular internationalization in the world's economy. In the process, the 'managed' aspect of global capitalism has broken down – although recession governments are now frantically attempting to restore some degree of regulation and control.
- However, given the extent and dependence on trade, it is unlikely that there will be a wholesale political attempt by governments to restrict business activity to national economies. Furthermore, there is little apparent ideological enthusiasm for such a move. This does not mean that globalization has now 'won' and is complete, as it is partial and uneven.

4

Small Nations in a Globalized World

Introduction

From the subject of globalization and economic nationalism, we now turn to that of small nations in a globalized world. I use the term 'small nations' to indicate the wider subject matter; most of the discussion is actually about stateless nations or minority nations – peoples within larger geographical and numerical nation-states who desire greater autonomy or seek actual independence from the central state. Specifically, it is about Catalonia within Spain, Scotland within Great Britain and Quebec within Canada. The principal issue, its importance to the wider subject of this book, is whether or not globalization is energizing and enables their desire for a greater degree of independence. To this end, the chapter looks at the leading writers on these advanced minority nations set within wider states, who argue that globalization, far from weakening the power of nationalism, is actually increasing its power. It is a matter that has already been touched on. In Chapter 2, we saw that some writers think that globalization stimulates the viability of small nationalisms. With reference to Catalonia, Castells (2003) argues that, on the one hand, the loosening of the bonds of the central Spanish state since the death of General Franco in 1975 has enabled the renaissance of Catalan cultural identity. He suggests that it is not a singular identity, but one Catalans share with wider Spanish and European identities. On the other hand, he says that Barcelona and its environs are tied into international networks that are not primarily determined by the broader economic orientation of Spain. In this way, according the Castells, Catalans – historically a people of merchants, traders, financiers, seafarers and so on – have been able to reaffirm these occupational traditions alongside their historic culture, above all the Catalan language.

Against this, we saw in Chapter 3 that the neoliberal advocates of globalization equate nationalism – specifically economic nationalism – with state protectionism of one type or another. Protectionism is contrary to the unfettered workings of free markets, the holy grail of neoliberals prior to the current recession. According to their argument, free markets are not just fundamental to prosperity, but also to individual liberty and freedom. So neoliberals are likely to treat small nationalisms as backward forces that will act as impediments to trade through the erection of additional barriers. Instead, the governments of existing nation-states through international organizations like the WTO should be concerned with removing the plethora of tariffs and so on that still remain. There is a logic to this argument, inasmuch as we saw that between roughly the mid-nineteenth century and mid-twentieth century, national movements were concerned with using the state first to nurture infant industries and then, in changed circumstances, to build national economies through degrees of economic self-sufficiency and isolation. We also saw that the extent of contemporary economic globalization, a product of postwar economic development, would now prevent a small national newcomer from using protectionist measures to try to bolster its economy.

This is the context for the point made by Hellenier and Pickel (2005) in Chapter 3 that contemporary nationalism is quite compatible with globalization in general and neoliberalism in particular. They refer, as does Michael Keating, one of the writers dealt with in this chapter, to 'free trade nationalisms' as distinct from the traditional conception of nationalism as being concerned with protection. I briefly mentioned Croatia as an example of a small nation (some 5 million people) that, having achieved independence through the leadership of the Hrvatska Demokratska Zajednica (HDZ) in 1991, set about privatizing major parts of the old Yugoslav national economy, while fighting initially defensive wars against the Serbs in 1991–2 and then offensive campaigns against the Bosnian Muslims in 1993 and the Serbs in 1995 in pursuit of a Greater Croatia. While Croatian privatization in the 1990s was characterized by corruption and nepotism, arguably a feature of the wider 'gangsterization' of Balkan politics and society in this period, the point is that far from seeking to take the economy under state control, as the Communist Party had under Tito after the reformation of Yugoslavia (1943–6), the HDZ government of the late Franjo Tuđman sold it off into private hands, domestic and foreign.[1] The example of Croatia is not one that the academic writers on the minority nations – principally Scotland, Quebec and Catalonia – examined in this chapter refer to. On the contrary, as we will see, contrasts are generally made between aggressive nationalisms like those in the Balkans and more tolerant, democratic strains that Scotland et al. represent.

Scottish nationalists often point to the economic success of small nations like Ireland and Norway. The former is positively identified as a country of only 4 million people who have benefited from global-led growth, the latter as a Scandinavian nation that has effectively used (through international sales) its primary natural resource, oil, for its own purposes rather than having it taken by an overarching state. Ireland is sometimes branded the 'Celtic tiger', a name derived from the success of four relatively small Asian tiger economies over the past 50 years: South Korea, Taiwan, Singapore and Hong Kong. Comparisons to these economies are not generally made in academic writings on Catalonia, Scotland and Quebec. In fact, the writers on these minority nationalisms generally refrain from wider assessments, tending to treat their 'advanced' cases as distinct. There is understandable academic caution in this, but such an approach does appear to sit beside a degree of methodological parochialism in some of the accounts discussed below.

The argument that small nations are viable economic entities is also at odds with older conceptions of the nation-state that originated in the mid-nineteenth century. If the assumption is that the states should bound and protect a national economy, as List (1909) thought, it makes obvious sense to enlarge its boundaries, political and economic, as far as is naturally, or 'nationally', possible to maximize consumer market size and access to raw materials. Such thinking is discernible in unificatory nationalism in the nineteenth century and was particularly important to Communist-led approaches to the nation in the twentieth century. The idea that a central state should stimulate demand within a substantial territory also figured as a tenet of Keynesian economics of the mid-twentieth century. Therefore the proposal that it is legitimate to parcel the world up further into lesser economic units is contrary to traditional approaches of economic liberals and nationalists alike.

Within the recent study of nationalism, the promotion of specifically small nationalisms runs counter to a wider academic scepticism, sometimes hostility. There were various reasons for this; probably the most important immediate cause was their obvious destructive potential in the former Yugoslavia. In this period, the early 1990s, Tom Nairn (1993, p. 3), a stalwart of the positive potential of nationalism, referred sardonically to the language of 'nuclear abyss' of the 1980s being replaced by a discourse of 'ethnic abyss'. It should be said that academic accounts came to the fore in this period, above all the ethnosymbolist thesis of Smith, which rejected the claim that nationalism, small or large, inevitably entails violence. However, the idea that nationalism, especially small nationalisms, can be 'good' did seem to run against the grain of academic and media commentary after the notion that the fall of the Berlin Wall signalled the end of history had perished in the Balkans.

In fact, a certain contempt for small nations within scholarly and more general discussion of nationalism is apparent from the nineteenth century on. Hegel (1994, p. 279) famously drew a distinction in his *Philosophy of Mind* between those peoples that could, thanks to inherent 'natural and spiritual abilities', establish a state and act as bearers of historical progress, and those that lacked such qualities, had no state and in fact have, 'strictly speaking, no history – like the nations which existed before the rise of states and others which still exist in a condition of savagery'. Besides more immediate political considerations, such a division influenced Fredrick Engels in his dismissive attitude towards the very existence of small, non-historic peoples. Much has been made by postcolonial critics of the writings of Marx and Engels on early Indian and Algerian independence struggles. What such accounts omit, however, is that Engels had equally derogatory things to say about some small European nations. Here he targets the various Slav nationalities – especially the Czechs and Slovaks, but also the Croats, Slovenes and Serbs – of the Austro-Hungarian Empire for their failure to support the 1848 revolutions:

> But at the first victorious uprising of the French proletariat ... the Austrian Germans and the Magyars will gain their freedom and take a bloody revenge on the Slav barbarians. The general war which will then break out will scatter the Slav Sonderbund [alliance], and annihilate all these small pigheaded nations even to their very names. The next world war will not only cause reactionary classes and dynasties to disappear from the face of the earth, but also entire reactionary peoples. And that too is an advance. (Engels, 1975, p. 227)

This cannot be attributed to anti-Slav racism because Engels and Marx supported the liberation of the Poles from the Russian Empire. The scornful language is not dissimilar to that of the great liberal of the day John Stuart Mill. He similarly favoured the forced incorporation of small peoples within larger entities led by historic nations on the grounds that 'absorption is greatly to their advantage'. The alternative, speaking of the Breton and the Basque in France and the Welshman and Scottish Highlander in Britain, was 'to sulk on his own rocks, the half-savage relics of past times, revolving in his own mental orbit without participation or interest in the general movement of the world', rather than being 'brought into the current of the ideas and feelings of highly civilized and cultivated peoples' and 'sharing the advantages' of the 'dignity and prestige of a great power' (Mill, 1882, p. 122).

In one of the first extended academic considerations of nationalism, Lord Acton (1909) condemned the modern theory of nationality as a 'retrograde step' that had arisen after the French Revolution – 'more absurd and more criminal than the theory of socialism' – on the grounds that it negated liberty through the extension of the right to form a state to all. Using the term 'race' in discussion of the mixture of nationality, he contended that smaller entities 'can be converted into efficient members of a free community only by the contact of a superior race in whose power will lie the future prospects of the State'. Britain counted among those states that were 'substantially the most perfect' in the 'establishment of liberty for the realization of moral duties within civil society' through their inclusion of 'various nationalities without oppressing them'. By setting itself against the contact of nations, the modern theory of nationality was, according to Acton, 'the greatest adversary of the right of nationality' (Acton, 1909, pp. 297–8). Among noted contemporary commentators, only Max Weber (1948, pp. 171–9), while disdainful of the Poles of West Prussia for expressly political reasons, seems to have looked favourably on small Slavic nations for the strength of their common sentiment.

Of course it was not only critics in this era who were contemptuous of the claims of small nations. At major international gatherings, like the Congress of Berlin in 1878, called by the great powers of the day to settle the Eastern Question – principally to affix borders – delegates from the emerging Balkan nations had difficulty in gaining entry even to the social events of the conference let alone the actual diplomatic negotiations (Glenny, 1999, p. 141). Such derision was a staple feature of great power diplomacy in the nineteenth century. At the Versailles negotiations and treaty following the First World War, this changed somewhat through the insistence of the American delegation led by Woodrow Wilson on the principle of self-determination for all European nations. The alleged 'balkanization' of Eastern Europe this created from the Austro-Hungarian Empire is one of the aspects of the Treaty of Versailles that Carr took issue with in an influential book, *The Future of Nations*, written in 1941, while a propagandist at the Ministry of Information and a deputy editor at *The Times*. The thrust of Carr's case, an extension in key respects of *The Twenty Years' Crisis, 1919–1939* (1939), was that the political right to self-determination 'must be conditioned and restricted not only by the military necessity, but by the exigencies of economic interdependence'. In other words, he thought history between the wars had conclusively demonstrated that small nations simply are not economically or militarily viable. Furthermore, he thought that the independence claims of minority nations must be placed against the 'needs of the wider community', that is, the wider state. However, while his argument was against the unchecked principle of self-determination for reasons of realpolitik rather than the inadequacies of small peoples, he simultaneously spoke of the 'helplessness and hopelessness of the small national unit'. Speaking of a supposed nostalgia of small Slavic nations for the grandeur of imperial rule, he warned that 'the crabbing and confining effects of small national markets, small political systems and even small national cultures come to be felt as restrictions' (Carr, 1941, p. 424).

Such a disavowal of the right of all nations to self-determination characterized the postwar era, in which the interests of the powerful, mainly but not exclusively the USSR and the USA, trumped political rights, regardless of what the United Nations constitution may have declared. Simultaneously, the period did see a wave of national movements in Africa, Asia and the Caribbean attaining independence from European empires. As for the study of nationalism, Hegel's distinction between historic and non-historic nations occasionally surfaced, expressly so in Hugh Seton-Watson's *Nations and States*, published in 1977. In everyday life it is, of course, not uncommon to hear references to a particular people referred to as a 'great nation' and/or a patronizing tone adopted towards small nations. Such a description refers not just to population and geographic size, but also a conception of culture, history, military capability and sporting achievements.

Unsurprisingly, the writers we are about to consider – principally Michael Keating (2001), Montserrat Guibernau (1999), David McCrone (2001) and Nairn and James (2005) – reject any division of the world into historic and non-historic nations. It is obviously the case that the nations they are concerned with – Scotland, Catalonia and Quebec – are smaller than the larger states in which they exist: Great Britain, Spain and Canada. But as we will see, part of their argument is that the case for larger states in the previous era no longer exists in a global world. Before going any further, it will be useful to briefly outline the position of Scotland within Great Britain, Catalonia within Spain and Quebec within Canada in order to give context to the discussion that follows of their contemporary nationalisms.

Scotland

Scotland has been a part of Great Britain since 1707 when the Treaty of Union was passed by the Scottish Parliament. In the 300 years since then, the cause of Scottish independence has taken a variety of political and military forms in different periods, while Scotland has simultaneously been fully integrated into the wider British economy and state. It is significant that, in line with most considered academic accounts of the place of Scotland within the UK, McCrone (2001) does not claim that the English as a people have historically oppressed the Scots.

Modern Scottish nationalism in the form of the Scottish National Party (SNP), a product of the merger of recently formed smaller parties, emerged in 1934. However, it was not until the 1960s, in the context of the latter period of the break-up of the British Empire and the discovery of large reserves of North Sea oil, that the issue of independence and the less all-embracing option of home rule – some form of devolved government short of outright secession from the Union – entered mainstream Scottish politics through the election of Scottish Nationalist MPs. The SNP subsequently increased its number of Westminster seats in the 1974 British general election won by the Labour Party. That government, committed to devolution and with a parliamentary majority dependent on the support of minority nationalist parties, put forward plans for a Scottish Assembly through the Scotland Act 1978. However, a stipulation of the parliamentary bill was that 40% of the Scottish electorate had to subsequently endorse such an assembly in a referendum. Although a majority of Scots did approve the legislation, the proportion was well short of the 40% required, so plans for the assembly were repealed in March 1979.

The Conservative Party, under the leadership of Margaret Thatcher between 1979 and 1990 and then John Major until 1997, was implacably opposed to any form of devolved government for Scotland on the grounds that it would injure the Union. As a result, there was no possibility of a Scottish Assembly until the Conservatives were defeated and replaced by the New Labour government of Tony Blair in 1997. Shortly after taking power, Labour, under Scottish Secretary Donald Dewar, drew up plans for an elected Scottish Parliament with legislative responsibilities for domestic affairs in Scotland. The Parliament was overwhelmingly approved by a referendum and elections were held in May 1999. The Scottish Parliament was convened and sat for the first time since 1707 in July 1999. Labour held power in the Parliament until May 2007, when the SNP narrowly won an overall majority under the leadership of Alex Salmond.

Quebec

Quebec is a majority French-speaking province in eastern Canada. It was founded by French Catholic settlers in the early seventeenth century under the rule of Louis XIII. After war with the British, the province was ceded to the British in 1763. Certain cultural and Catholic religious rights were granted to the population in 1774 by the British government and subsequently insti-tutionalized. An armed attempt to acquire independence by insurgents in 1838 was crushed by the British Army. The area became a province within the Federation of Canada as it emerged through varying degrees of independ-ence from Britain from 1867 onwards.

Modern Quebec nationalism stems from a complex set of factors in the 1945 era. In certain respects, it drew on conservative clerical nationalism, typified by the long period in office of Maurice Duplessis, leader of Union Nationale, who dominated the provincial government between 1944 and 1960. Conversely, it was influenced by the progressive era of the 1960s, dubbed the 'quiet revolution', under the leadership of the Liberal Party. The decade saw the emergence of the terrorist Front de libération du Québec and, of lasting importance, the formation in 1968 of Parti Québécois, which was committed to work for Quebec independence through constitutional means. Parti Québécois was elected in 1977 under the leadership of René Lévesque. By that time it had softened its demand for outright secession from Canada to one of sovereignty association within a much looser Canadian federation. Quebec sovereignty was put to the people of the province in a referendum in 1980, but only 40% of the population voted for it. The 1980s saw much consti-tutional wrangling in Canada as a whole, giving way to a second referendum on Quebec sovereignty in 1995. Parti Québécois had been returned to government in 1994 following years of Liberal Party administration. This time the vote was far closer, with sovereignty being rejected by just 50.4%, 49.6% voting in favour. As in the previous referendum, the vote was cast along ethnic/linguistic lines, with a high majority of French speakers voting yes, and a majority of English speakers, immigrants and indigenous peoples voting no to Quebec sovereignty. Jacques Parizeau, Quebec premier and leader of the sovereigntist cause, controversially claimed that the vote was lost due to 'money and some ethnic votes', reflecting a divisive campaign involving claims of corruption and a lack of loyalty. Parizeau resigned shortly afterwards. Parti Québécois subsequently won the elections of 1998 under Lucien Bouchard, but lost them to the Liberals in 2003 and again in 2007. It is committed to another referendum on sovereignty should it take power again.

Catalonia

Catalonia is a nation within Spain. Its territorial beginnings took place in the ninth and tenth centuries through the fusion of several monarchies under the control of the kings of France. This culminated in the declaration of independence of the Barcelona court in 989 from the French King Hugh Capet. The subsequent period saw the amalgamation of the region into the wider Kingdom of Aragon and its rise as a maritime power. The term 'Catalan' seems to have entered popular usage in the late eleventh century. The marriage of Ferdinand II of Aragon and Queen Isabella of Castile in 1469 marked the starting point of Catalonia's incorporation into Spain, as the state was centralized under the authority of Madrid in the context of imperial expansion. Especially important in this was the abolition of its special status as the former Kingdom of Aragon in 1714 by the Bourbon monarchy.

Various forms of nationalism influenced by Romanticism can be found in nineteenth-century Catalonia. However, it was not until the turn of the twentieth century that it found an organized form through the formation of Lliga Regionalista in 1901. In the subsequent period, Lliga Regionalista acted as a key force in Catalan society through promoting a regional cultural identity and calling for a Spanish federation to replace a unitary state, without unsettling the powerful industrial bourgeoisie who were wary that independence might risk the loss of Spanish markets. By this time, Catalonia was the most industrialized area of Spain, and to this day, it is the richest. Lliga Regionalista's aim was partially achieved through the grouping of the four Catalan provinces into a regional administration. The move was abolished, however, by the dictator Primo de Rivera after he took power in 1923. Autonomy was briefly achieved during the democracy of the Second Spanish Republic, 1931–36. The ensuing civil war culminated in the final victory of the Fascist forces under General Francisco Franco in 1939. On taking power, Franco revoked autonomy and outlawed and repressed any public manifestation of Catalan separatism. It should, of course, be pointed out that dissent of any kind against the regime's authoritarian rule was brutally crushed. Although there was an easing in the suppression of the use of the Catalan language in public life towards the end of Franco's rule, it was not until his death in 1975 and the restoration of democracy that autonomy became a possibility.

The new Spanish Constitution of 1978 included a Statute of Autonomy recognizing Catalonia, along with the Basque Country, Galicia and Andalusia as autonomous nationalities. In 1979, the constitutional change was approved by a referendum and in the elections of 1980, the Convergència Democràtica de Catalunya under Jordi Pujol was elected as the Catalan regional government. Convergència and Pujol remained in office for the next 23 years. In 2006, autonomy was taken a step forward through a further constitutional change, endorsed by a referendum, the Statute of Autonomy of Catalonia, which states that 'the Spanish Constitution recognizes Catalonia's national reality as a nationality' (see www.guardian.co.uk/commentisfree/2006/jun/19/smallearthquakeincatalonia).

National Allegiance and Detachment

This, then, is the predicament of the minority nationalisms under consideration in this chapter. All are contained within wider democratic nation-states but have some degree of self-governance. It is obvious from reading the texts of the writers on these minority nations considered in this chapter that they favour devolution or outright independence for Scotland, Quebec and Catalonia. None of them, however, make clear their own national identities, although it should be said that Keating (a Scot) provides a genuine comparative analysis of the three cases, rather than first and foremost a case study of his nation. This is despite the fact that at points in the writings, there is a suggestive, even programmatic quality to the discussion, that is, what form the nationalism should take to realize its aspirations. Towards the end of Guibernau's most recent book on Catalonia, for example, she claims:

> Democratic nationalism is legitimate. It defends the right of nations to exist and develop while recognizing and respecting internal diversity. It rejects the territorial expansion of nations and shows a commitment to increasing the morality of the nations' citizens. Only by being committed to these principles can democratic nationalism become cosmopolitan. (Guibernau, 2004, p. 164)

Elsewhere I have noted that in the work of McCrone, there is a tendency to assume the 'good' in Scottish nationalism as a given (Pryke, 2002). Now perhaps it would be too much to say, as Hobsbawm (1992. p. 12) does, that 'no serious historian of nations and nationalism can be a committed political nationalist'. But obviously the judgement of an observer can be influenced by their allegiance, in this instance their national loyalties. A recent critique of

Castells for his casual cultural conception of nation and a failure to fully acknowledge massive immigration into Catalonia suggests that his national- ism colours his sociological judgement (McInnes, 2006; see also McInnes, 2004). However, nationalists can actually be the most harsh and discerning critics of their country and people. No doubt they themselves alternate between positive and negative feelings, hope and frustration. And perhaps such ambivalence is particularly found in small nations' spokespeople, who love their country but tire of their people's seeming sense of complacency, even inferiority, vis-à-vis a larger neighbour.[2] So the point is not that some- body who in the broader sense might be termed 'a nationalist' cannot under- stand nationalism. Within the accounts discussed below, Asifa Hussain and William Miller (2006) present an analysis of Scottish nationalism as a multi- cultural force in respect to its incorporation of Asian Muslims that is free of any illusions about the Scots as a particularly inclusive people. Rather it is that the background and political sentiments of the writer should be made clear at some point within their account in order to, as it were, square it with their analysis. Thus it would be revealing to know what degree of national separa- tion Guibernau and McCrone favour for Catalonia and Scotland respectively.

The final point to mention before examining the various arguments put forward is that the approaches of the writers to small nations will be taken as a whole. This is not to suggest that there is agreement between them on all points. There is not and, on occasions, this will be noted. However, all share the conviction that globalization, far from constricting the room for manoeu- vre of small nations and blunting their impetus, actually serves to heighten their viability and vitality. The rest of the chapter is approached as follows:

1 I discuss some points the authors make about the changed nature of nationalism.
2 I look at their treatment of globalization.
3 I note the perceived decline of the larger nation-states in which the minor- ity nationalisms in question, Quebec, Scotland and Catalonia, are found.
4 I map the given characteristics of the minority nationalisms.
5 I look at recent political developments in Scotland, Catalonia and Quebec.
6 I assess whether or not the case made for these small nations applies more widely.
7 I conclude with some possible criticisms of the accounts.

A Changed Nationalism?

In Chapter 2, we discussed Nairn and James's contention in their recent book *Global Matrix* (2005) that any pretence that we live in a postnational age has been blown apart by the strident nationalism of the USA post 9/11. We will return to Nairn later in this chapter. The relevant point here is not that Nairn and James 'favour' American nationalism, certainly not in an aggressive impe- rial form, but that it gives the lie to the great power conceit that the phenome- non is the property of quarrelsome little peoples. Similar sentiments to Nairn and James are found within the writings of Keating, Guibernau and McCrone. For example, McCrone (2001, p. 176) stated that 'The tide is turning in the direc- tion of nationalism'. The reason for this is a new-found 'agency' on the part of nationalist political parties in the context of favourable wider 'structures'.

None of the writers appear to disagree with the convention that national- ism as a political movement places the interests of the nation above all others.[3] Such an understanding has been used to try to identify at which point historically it gained centre stage as a political ideology as opposed to the preoccupation of a few intellectuals. At the same time, they all stress that it has become a commonplace to say that national identity coexists with a number of other identities such as those of religion, class and so on. For example, an individual living in Glasgow may feel himself simultaneously a Scot, a Muslim of Pakistani origin, a small businessman, a supporter of Celtic Football Club, a parent, British and so. Given the nature of identity, in normal circumstances it is unlikely that such identities will collide and vie with one another, that is, be felt to exist in contradiction to one another. It is generally the case that identities buttress and support one another. However, different identities come to the fore and are felt most keenly according to the particu- lar context and conjuncture. Of key importance for discussion of minority nations is that writers on them argue that the political programme of nation- alisms, the substantive demands that nationalists make, change considerably over time. As Keating (2001. p. 18) puts it:

> Nationalism in the age of the nation-state differed substantively from the proto-
> nationalisms of earlier periods; it is equally true that nationalism is changing its
> meaning in the contemporary era, in which the classic nation-state is being trans-
> formed.

Central to this is the contention that contemporary nationalisms in Scotland, Quebec and Catalonia, as well as other small nations like Wales, have to some degree edged away from the insistence that they should secede and create an independent state to organize their interests. The very title of Keating's book is *Nations against the State* (2001). This refers not just to the desire of the Scots, for example, to extricate themselves from the union with England, Ireland and Wales, but that this may be achieved through some- thing other than the creation of a traditional nation-state. Guiberneau's book is entitled *Nations without States* (1999), while McCrone refers to nationalism as the 'gravedigger' of the nation-state. McCrone (2001, p. 186) claims:

What is indubitably clear is the historic creation of classical nationalism, the nation-state, is losing its *raison d'être*. The nation-state is a historical product, not a fact of nature, and emerged as the dominant political formation between the mid-nineteenth and mid-twentieth centuries.

This is of course contrary to most analyses of nationalism. Whatever the profound disagreements between ethnosymbolist and modernist schools, none of the writers would depart from the view that the state has played a central role in unifying a people through the provision of a national education system, broadcasting service, defence forces, immigration control and so on; the difference of opinion between them is in the extent to which the endeavour was one of social construction or rested on genuine cultural sentiment. However, for reasons we will examine, the proponents of small nations think that the age of state-led nation-building has now passed. In my view, nationalism is certainly a political chameleon, something that is open to updates and revisions as much as to opportunistic manipulation by political adventurers. In part, its very flexibility accounts for its enormous and enduring power. However, if it is to progress beyond a sentiment into an organizational form, if it is to properly exist at all, it can only operate in relation to the state and seeks progressively greater state power. This may not involve the creation of a new state, although it generally still does, even in the somewhat exceptional circumstances under examination here. What it inevitably involves is greater devolved or autonomous state power.

We will return to this issue later. The point is that the writers on minority nationalism argue that the historic link between nation and state has been loosened in contemporary times. So too apparently has the link, usually made at the beginning of the chain, with ethnicity. This is true at any rate of the writers on Scotland. At times, Guibernau's writings, influenced by Anthony Smith, seem to allude to an ethnic conception of nationhood. Guibernau (1999, p. 17, emphases added) tells us that: 'A nation without a state is based upon the existence of a nation, that is, community endowed with *a stable but dynamic core* containing a set of factors which have generated the emergence of a specific national identity.' By contrast, a clearer division is drawn by Keating (2001, p. 3):

> Ethnicities, states and nations are analytically quite distinct categories, which empirically may or may not coincide. Nations are not necessarily either ethnic groups or states, and conditions in the contemporary world may be pushing these categories further apart, to produce societies whose organising principles are quite distinct.

The implication in the second part of this quote is slightly different from the commonplace that the nation-state is an inherently imprecise term we are stuck with, something of a misnomer, which obscures the fact that almost all nations are composites of peoples, cultures and religions. For this reason, some writers prefer the term 'national state'. Keating's suggestion is that the linkage there once was between an ethnicity, a nation and a state is now being eroded. This is topped with the familiar claim of all the writers that we now live in an age of multiple identities, one in which an individual can feel themselves to belong to different if often overlapping groups.

As with the suggestion that the relationship between nation and state is no longer symbiotic, this claim, that ethnicity and nation have become decoupled, is at odds with established understandings of nationalism. Obviously, it is contrary to the influential ethnosymbolist account of Smith, Hutchinson and their followers; indeed Smith's best-known work is entitled *The Ethnic Origins of Nations* (1996). Their case is that there is an intrinsic relationship between the two things: nations have ethnic origins that impart vital stability to subsequent state formation. Other writers, especially Hobsbawm and Gellner, are generally sceptical of the veracity of this thesis, but would accept that a political link is generally made between ethnicity and nationalism. Hobsbawm (1992) documents how in the late nineteenth century, nationalism became ethnic (or racial) at the same time as it shifted sharply to the political Right and became a political option open to all takers, large and small. As such, it ceased to be an ideology of unification concerning forming larger units out of multiple strands of ethnicity, but a claim for independence any group might raise, no matter how small. The divisiveness this involved, given the scattering of nationalities, meant, as Porter (2000) puts it in relation to a case study, nationalism began to hate in this period. From then on, ethnicity has been used by nationalists as a qualification of membership, a means to identify who belongs inside the given boundary. This tendency continues in the twenty-first century. As Perry Anderson (2001, p. 13), somebody whose writings on nationalism would broadly be described as modernist, puts it in an essay on the Palestinian–Israeli conflict: 'All ethnic nationalisms – and all nationalisms are in some measure ethnic – contain seeds of potential violence against other nationalities.'

So the accounts examined here run counter to established understandings of nationalism in that they take a generally positive stance towards small nations and question the historic link between ethnicities, nations and states. Crucial to this contention is an understanding of contemporary globalization.

Small Nations in a Globalized World

It would be too much to say that the case made for small nations rests solely on the claims made about globalization. All the writers would agree, indeed it is an obvious fact, that Scottish, Catalan and Quebec nationalisms and modern political movements predate contemporary globalization. It is certainly the case, however, that writers on small nations think that globalization is of key importance. Guibernau (1999, p. 20) states:

> The re-emergence of nationalism in nations without states is directly related to the intensification of globalization processes which have proven capable of altering the political, economic and cultural structures of current societies.

Similar kinds of sentiments can be found in the writings of Keating and McCrone. There are of course a number of aspects of what globalization is taken to be.

In Guibernau's *Nations without States* (1999, p. 21), there is simply the assertion, without qualification or support, that globalization has 'broken up the classic nation-state's monopoly of the economy'. This kind of claim may capture the general shift of Spanish capitalism away from the autarchy of the Franco years towards world markets since the mid-1970s, but clearly takes no account of earlier periods of globalization. By contrast, Keating has provided in various writings of his own and edited collections a more substantial analysis of the decline of the postwar Keynesian state (Keating, 2001; Keating and Loughlin, 1997; Keating and McGarry, 2001). He argues that after 1945 both social democratic and conservative governments were able to integrate and manage regional economies within broader structures of state control. However, with the greater mobility of capital and fundamental shifts in the location of production, regional economies, especially those formally reliant on heavy industry such as Scotland and Quebec, have been vulnerable to prolonged recession. This has been compounded, a central point of McCrone, by a tendency of central governments to direct economic policy in the interests of its primary electoral constituency within the majority nation at the expense of the periphery. This was typified by the orientation of the British Conservative governments of Margaret Thatcher and John Major between 1979 and 1997 towards their political base in southeast England.

As this claim about Thatcherism perversely demonstrates, Keating is clear that economic globalization does not mean that geographic territory is somehow redundant. On the contrary, drawing on Kennichi Ohmae, he argues that specifically regional economic interconnections, as distinct from the wider relationships of trade and finance between nation-states, have reinvigorated the importance of place and territory. This has not made the state per se outmoded, but accentuates how responsive governance should be located within smaller regions to stimulate and coordinate, among other things, investment and training. The case for greater autonomy or even independence for minority nations within wider nation-states is thus strengthened. According to Keating (2001, p. 53), globalization has resulted in a 'decreased capacity of national states to deliver the goods. In an international order they are no longer able to manage their own spatial economies.'

Added to this, the writers make a number of other points under the heading of globalization. Guibernau refers to the internationalization of human rights norms and the ubiquity of calls for democracy from which no state is immune. Such claims are part of what Archibugi and Held (1995) refer to as 'cosmopolitan democracy'. The essential argument, one that Guibernau uncritically draws on, is that globalization has seen the proliferation of international organizations and conventions, to which governments are signatories, that oblige states to observe treaties in respect of, among other things, crime and justice, trade, broadcasting and communication, biological and chemical weapons, land mines, the conduct of war and environmental emissions. This has had the effect of limiting the ability of governments to do as they like. To oversimplify somewhat in relation to our subject, nation-states, especially those with formally democratic systems, can no longer ignore the rights of minority peoples with impunity; the mesh of international democratic standards, combined with the constant scrutiny of the media, prevents them from doing so.

All the writers refer to how small nations are better equipped than the cumbersome wider states in which they reside to protect and promote identity in the face of global cultural homogeneity. Some reference is made to how the place of minority nations within the wider structures of the European Union (EU) allows the expression of national identity. Such a belief contrasts with the wider distrust of the EU – 'Euroscepticism' – in larger nations, especially evident in England. The fear is that, far from the organization nurturing national identity, it threatens to swamp national cultures through the imposition of federal symbols, flags and so on to create a soulless euro culture.[4] In the work of Guibernau, Keating and McCrone, the way in which the EU can apparently protect small national identities forms part of a wider case of how the organization – and to a lesser extent the North American Free Trade Association (NAFTA), an organization comprising the USA, Canada and Mexico that was formed in 1993 – are beneficial to small nations.

The key to regional organizations relates to the above. The claim is that regional organizations provide minority nations with wider economic markets. The case is not unique to Scotland and Quebec. An early slogan of the separatist Northern League in Italy was 'Away from Rome closer to Europe'. During the break-up of Yugoslavia, Slovene and Croat politicians argued that part of their motivation for secession was to facilitate integration into Europe. The advantages of access to a national market within a larger nation-state clearly do not exist if there is wider free trade within a regional single market. Therefore a firm in Glasgow or Barcelona that does most of its business in England and Castile respectively will not face repercussions through tariff barriers if they detach themselves from the British or Spanish states through Scottish or Catalan independence. The economic impact will be reduced further if EU economic and monetary union exists as it does in the case of Spain. The SNP supports British inclusion within the Eurozone precisely because 'Euro membership hastens and facilitates the process of Scottish Independence by rendering Westminster redundant'.[5] Moreover, both the EU and NAFTA accentuate the argument made above for change in the organization of governance in respect to small nations. McCrone (2001, p. 190) argues that:

> Global economic transformation has crucially taken place within a new geometry of power. Instead of the territory relating only and directly with the state of which it is part – classical centre-periphery relations – a further dimension of supra-state power has been added. In the case of Scotland (and Catalonia), this is the European Union such that there emerges a complex and variable speed geometry in which the nation in question is engaged in relationships with both the state and supra-state body.

McCrone is presumably referring to Scotland's inclusion in Europe through the Committee of the Regions. Whether or not this body does actually represent a level of genuine governance is open to question, but certainly the authors think the possibilities the EU offers small nations are propitious. A Scottish or Catalan government would exist both independently and in concert with other European countries through the medium of the EU, an organization whose powers extend to justice, criminal investigation, security from terrorism, immigration and workplace conditions. The EU is therefore far more than just a single economic zone or a temporary crutch to overcome the problems of further distancing itself from the existing state centre. Rather, it affords a crucial set of durable structures in which small nations can operate. Apparently, as European integration deepens – regardless of whether independence, greater autonomy or the status quo pertain to stateless nations – so it is likely to become more accommodating to them. Guibernau (1999, pp. 27–8) claims: 'There are strong chances that further European integration will favour a greater presence of nations without states such as Catalonia, Scotland, the Basque Country and Flanders in the international political arena.'

These, then, are the features of globalization for writers on small nations: transnational capitalism, a changed spatial economic role for governance, cosmopolitan democracy and regional organizations, above all the EU, that provide access to wider markets and facilitate economic convergence through monetary union. Globalization has deepened the problems afflicting large nation-states that group several smaller nations under an overarching political structure. But it is not the whole story of their demise in the accounts under consideration here. Some further coverage is required of the decline of the wider states – Britain, Spain and Canada – in question.

The Decline in the Legitimacy of Nation-states

The understandings of this differ according to the country in question. In the cases of Catalonia's place within Spain and Quebec within Canada, the suggestion is that it is no longer possible to attempt to forcibly assimilate minority nations as they have in the past. Speaking generally but clearly with particular reference to Catalonia, Guibernau (1999, p. 17) claims:

> The nation-state has traditionally based its legitimacy upon the idea that it represents the nation, in spite of the fact that the state once created had to engage in nation-building processes aiming at the forced assimilation of its citizens. It now becomes apparent that, in many instances, these processes have largely failed; the re-emergence of nationalist movements in nations without states proves it. At present, the state becomes increasingly unable to fulfill its citizens' needs, and as a result of this they turn away from it and search for alternative institutions.

Although claims of 'forced assimilation' are no doubt made by Scottish nationalists on occasions, any academic analysis would refrain from such assertions, given the voluntary nature of the Union of 1707 (at least among Scottish elites), the continuing institutional autonomy of Scotland after that date, the weak attempts to foist a northern British identity on Scotland and the prominent role of Scots and Scottishness within the distinctively British Empire. Even in relation to Spain, unqualified talk of forced assimilation, which is tantamount to oppression in this context, overlooks the role of the collaboration of sections of the Catalan ruling class with the Francoist regime in Madrid during this most violent phase of attempted Spanish absorption.

Keating makes a rather different argument about the loss of legitimacy of the central British state. In line with his general remarks about the predicament of the post-Keynesian state and a sometimes critical attitude towards globalization, Keating (2001, p. 47) says:

> The resulting fiscal and monetary austerity [of neoliberalism globalization] and the subordination of social issues to a particular definition of economic necessity serve to delegitimize the whole political process and citizenship is itself emptied of its meaning.

As indicated above, this opens the possibility for the reconstitution of state, territory and nationhood on a smaller scale. Recent remarks made by Nairn (2007, p. 125), specifically on the faltering of democratic reform under New Labour, are in line with such an argument:

> 'Modernization' of this kind has generated a UK climate recognizable enough in many other parts of the neoliberal world: generalized scorn and despair of politics and

politicians, and mounting anguish about what the country now *means*, in a shrinking world-web that somehow renders identity more, rather than less, important.

As we will see, this is part of the case that Nairn makes for the resumption of Scottish independence.

Besides these general claims, there are, of course, more detailed histories that chart the waning of states that incorporate small nations. The case of Britain with Scotland, effectively made by McCrone (2001; see also McCrone et al., 1989), serves as a particular instance that has some parallels to Catalonia and Quebec. Among other things in his account, we can mention:

1   The fading of the memory of empire as an integrative British force that, under the figurehead of monarchy, served to meld the union of not just the English and Scottish but also the Welsh and Irish through military conquest, economic enrichment and large-scale emigration.
2   The decline from the late 1970s onwards of a Keynesian managed economy with governments committed to full employment and a welfare state designed to impart collective standards of health and social security.
3   The growing political division within the UK from the 1980s through the 1990s as a succession of right-wing Conservative governments pursued fiscal objectives of principal economic benefit to parts of England through increasing reliance on the electoral support of the English alone.

This trend of political disaffection of the Scots with the trajectory of UK central government policies in London has, according to Nairn, continued through revulsion north of the border at New Labour's foreign policy subservience to the Bush administration and the decision to locate a new Trident nuclear missile system in Scotland.

The Characteristics of the New Nationalisms

The characteristics of the new nationalisms flow from the reasons provided by Keating, McCrone, Guibernau and Nairn for their revival. In line with the argument that nationalism is now dissociated from the state, they contend that national movements in advanced democracies are no longer besotted with achieving their own independent statehood. Keating (2001, p. xiv) says of Scotland, Catalonia and Quebec:

> [There is] convergence of opinion around a 'post-national', or at least a post-statist, agenda as nationalist parties are abandoning traditional notions of independence while the non-nationalist parties are taking more national colours.

Quite what the replacements are to 'traditional notions of independence' is slightly opaque in his account, a matter we will return to in the next section. That aside, the point is supplemented by McCrone's claim that the politics of small nations are, like politics more generally, shifting beyond Left and Right as ideologies are compressed, in part by the limitations of globalization.

All writers agree, although as mentioned there is ambiguity in the work of Guibernau, that small nationalisms, certainly those at the forefront like Catalonia, are not ethnic or cultural in orientation. Because of the traditional view that small nationalisms are particularly intolerant – small and narrow-minded – writers on minority nationalism are forceful in their attempts to rebut this perception. As Will Kymlicka (2001, p. 74), who has written widely on the subject especially in relation to Quebec, puts it:

> The inherited view that minority nationalisms represent an illiberal, exclusive and defensive reaction to modernity is multiply mistaken, at least in the context of Western democracies. Some minority nationalisms represent a liberal, inclusive and forward looking embrace of modernity and globalization, and are potentially just as 'civic'-post-ethnic and cosmopolitan as majority nationalisms.

McCrone (2001, p. 177) claims that Scotland 'belongs at the "civic" rather than the "ethnic" end of the spectrum'.

In relation to Scotland, this claim is backed by an impressive marshalling of statistics and new qualitative data by Hussain and Miller in *Multicultural Nationalism* (2006). They note in their Introduction that this term, 'multicultural nationalism', would seem a conceptual oxymoron as nationalisms are about *a* culture – the culture of a people singular. Although they arrive at the conclusion that multicultural nationalism does apply to Scotland, their argument is measured. They find that the support for independence entails higher than average negative feelings towards the 'auld enemy', the English, but less negative feelings towards Asians, Muslims and others than is the norm in either England or Scotland. This tendency has accentuated since 2000 as Muslims in Scotland have become the group with the highest levels of support for an independent Scotland and the SNP. Hussain and Miller (2006, p. 199) feel justified in claiming in their conclusion: 'So, for the moment, and against the theoretical odds, multiculturalism and sub-state nationalism have not merely coexisted but actually interacted positively within Scotland.'

This civic, or even multicultural, direction to minority nationalisms is apparently in accord with a generally positive, certainly open stance to economic globalization. In line with the wider contention that 'free-trade nationalism' is perfectly possible in our global times, Keating in particular claims that 'minority nationalisms are committed to global and continental free trade'. Given that he thinks that national movements within Spain, Canada and Britain are likely to remain stateless, logically this would have to be the case. As Keating (2001, p. 63) puts it, 'protectionism is by definition is ruled out'. This contrasts with a sometimes more critical tone in relation to neoliberalism, where he talks of small nations as social movements 'challenging the dominant logic of state and market' (p. 48). Others, while not calling for Scotland to introduce some form of protectionism, clearly think that an unchecked embrace of economic globalization is dangerous. Jim Harvie, a SNP minister in the Scottish Parliament, thinks, for example, that Scotland is a 'high-maintenance society which has taken a battering from globalized capital and its indifference to human outcomes'. Harvie calls for a 'rational allocation of latent or misapplied wealth to bridge the social divisions this gives rise to'.[6]

Clearly, at such points, there is a danger that discussion can cease to be about small nations per se in democratic countries – Scotland, Catalonia and Quebec anyway – and simply develops into a debate about a particular instance. Notwithstanding this, it is interesting to note that Nairn, who is attentive to wider trends in the history of nationalism, also thinks that Scotland's 'outward-bound mentality', a product of its long history of emigration, is in keeping with the times. Nairn (2007, p. 128) refrains from claiming Scottish nationalism as a laissez-faire movement, but says that: 'Just as free trade was impossible without assorted forms of protection and barriers [in its classical nineteenth-century phase], so globalization will only work via renewed forms of nationalism and identity conservation.' Added to this, as might be expected given their generally positive opinion of regional organizations, in the work of Keating, McCrone and Guibernau is the claim that minority nationalisms are more pro-EU and NAFTA than their majority big brothers.

Despite the optimistic case made for small nationalisms as vital forces in the contemporary world, the authors acknowledge that nationalism is simultaneously a somewhat more measured, even ordinary, political movement, given the strictures imposed by globalization. If, as Keating (2001, p. 74) puts it, 'sovereignty is itself now greatly attenuated', clearly the promise that independence holds for a 250-year dream (Quebec) or a 300-year (Scotland and Catalonia) dream is, if not tarnished, then somewhat reduced. Nairn (2007, p. 125) thinks that the way in which the issues are now stacked makes it increasingly appear to Scots that there is '"no alternative" to resuming independence'. As noted elsewhere, nationalism is a political chameleon that marries pragmatism and principle. However, there is perhaps a danger that it will devalue its ultimate goals in an effort to appear respectable. We will reflect on this and other issues in the final section of this chapter.

A Rather Dull but Irresistible Force?

The thesis that the case for small nations is strengthened rather than weak-ened by globalization cannot simply be confirmed or denied by a snapshot of current political trends in Scotland, Catalonia and Quebec. The political and economic developments that the accounts identify go deeper than that. Nevertheless, it is interesting and relevant to point to some recent political developments to place beside the analyses of Keating, Guibernau, McCrone and Nairn.

First, the momentum towards greater autonomy is mixed:

- Catalonia has certainly acquired it. A referendum held in June 2006 granted the Catalan regional parliament constitutional control of taxation, immigration and employment legislation, an independent judiciary and a greater share of central Spanish revenue. This was followed in November by the re-election of Convergència i Unió, the moderate separatist party, which had held power in Catalonia since the introduction of devolved government in 1979.
- In Scotland, the narrow election victory of the SNP without an overall majority in the Assembly elections of May 2007 has presaged a possible referendum in 2010/11 following an extended national debate.
- In Quebec, the so-called 'sovereigntist' cause received a set-back in elec-tions in March 2007 when the Parti Québécois (PQ) came third in the polls behind the Liberals and Action démocratique du Québec (ADQ), a populist right-wing party that favours autonomy for Quebec.

Second, there appears to be some evidence of greater political convergence around moderate nationalism:

- In Catalonia, the 2006 referendum was a product not of a Convergència i Unió administration, but a Catalan socialist one (the Partit dels Socialistes de Catalunya), admittedly in coalition with the smaller pro-independence parties. The only electoral group to oppose greater Catalan autonomy was the conservative Partit Popular de Catalunya, a party that only receives around 10% of the vote in elections. Simultaneously, there appears little immediate or even medium-term prospect that a majority of Catalans would vote for outright independence from Spain in the unlikely event of being offered it in a referendum.
- In Scotland, all four major political parties – Labour, the SNP, the Liberal Democrats and the Conservatives – now back the devolved Scottish Assembly established in 1998. The issue of independence remains highly divisive in party political terms as witnessed by the present inability of

the SNP to find a stable coalition partner from among the opposition parties, despite its obvious strategy to take the sting out of the issue of independence. Meanwhile, among Scots, Britishness remains an important source of identity beside Scottishness and support for outright independence is, according to one recent survey (polls on this appear to fluctuate widely, no doubt a reflection as much on the methodology used in their collection as in dramatic shifts in opinion), at a 10-year low of 23% – lower than English support for such a move.[7]

- In Quebec, continuing political division among political parties on sovereignty is more salient than consensus, although it is worth pointing out that a majority of voters support the parties – the ADQ and the PQ – that broadly favour greater self-determination for the region. Opinion polls show a steady advance in support for sovereignty, especially among younger age groups (www.cbc.ca/canada/story/2005/04/27/sovereignty-poll050427.html).

Third, it is possible to discern a certain normalcy of nationalism in the three nations:

- In Quebec, there is little sign that nationalism will take Canada to the edge of break-up as it did in 1995, although it remains a latent political force.
- In Catalonia, almost three-quarters of those who took part in the 2006 referendum backed greater autonomy, but less than half of those eligible bothered to vote at all. The run-up to the poll was marked by a warning from General José Mena Aguado, head of Spain's 50,000-strong land forces, that the army might have to intervene to protect the country's territorial integrity as Article eight of the national Constitution entitles it to do. A month later, this was followed by an angry letter to a local newspaper in Meilla, a Spanish enclave in North Africa with strong connections to the Franco era, from Antonio Tejero, leader of the 1981 attempted military coup in Madrid. 'Who do these people think they are to play with the [physical] integrity of Spain?' he fumed in his letter to the *Melilla Hoy* newspaper. 'We would be real cowards if we let this happen.' Tejero himself only proposed a national petition of protest, but another old Francoist threatened to take a company of the Spanish Legion to Madrid to complain about the proposed Catalan autonomy bill. The most notable thing about the episode was not that the referendum infuriated a few old Fascists and some serving army chiefs, but the limited media attention and public interest it generated across Spain as a whole. One journalist commented: 'The fact that Spain's national press paid little attention to Tejero shows how far the country – where no one really believes the army would ever take to the streets again – has moved on since the fraught days of 1981.' The reaction of the socialist government, far from being alarmed by the warnings, was

one of 'barely-concealed gloating', as they sought to tie the general's rumblings to the rightward direction of Spain's main opposition party Partido Popular (*Guardian*, 2006). As mentioned, in Catalonia itself, such incidents failed to galvanize more than half the electorate to vote at all.

• In Scotland, there is evidence that independence is becoming an unremarkable future; certainly this strategy is being pursued by the SNP. Nationalism, as Nairn (2007) suggests, is beginning to appear at once an irresistible historic force and a more mundane matter of day-to-day politicking that lacks the fire to, as it were, set the heather blaze.[8] In this way, the momentum towards independence in the medium to longer term is strengthened, because Scottish nationalism no longer takes the terrain on which its opponents can attack it with dire forebodings of the grave dangers of breaking up the Union. Certainly there were attempts to demonize it prior to the last Assembly elections in May 2007 – elections in which the SNP became the largest party. The Labour Party focused on the destruction that would be wrought by independence. The *Financial Times*, which opposes nationalism precisely because it thinks that it runs counter to globalization, warned that:

The goal of independence has not changed. But the SNP leader has exchanged the fiery belligerence of Braveheart nationalism for a dark suit and a soothing tone. Instead of wrenching separation, Mr Salmond now proposes what, on the other side of the channel, France's Nicolas Sarkozy calls 'une rupture tranquille'. (Stephens, 2007)

Since then, however, Alex Salmond has succeeded in initiating a debate on the possibility of further autonomy/independence, something that the other main political parties had previously refused to countenance. In line with this, a prominent Labour Party spokesman has been forced to concede that an independent Scotland would not 'wither and die' as it had previously claimed.[9] As regards business, the SNP now has an eminent socioeconomic advisory group, chaired by Sir George Mathewson, former chairman of the Royal Bank of Scotland and recent convert to the independence cause. Announcing his support for the SNP in early 2007, Mathewson said of independence:

Comments that have been made on [the potential lack of] access to the English market are patently absurd. Currently, a huge proportion of the English financial services market is supplied by companies in the US, in Holland, Germany, Ireland, etc. Globalisation is here and Scottish companies have embraced it and indeed have benefited from it. (quoted in Larsen, 2007)

Because of these kinds of developments, the *Financial Times* has subsequently spoken of a new 'serenity' pervading Scottish politics and society (Reid, 2007).

Does the Case Made for Scotland, Catalonia and Quebec Apply More Widely?

Besides these developments, which appear to confirm aspects of the case for small nations, there are several criticisms of the authors that can be made. First, although the authors are generally careful about the application of their thesis, it is worth underlining how limited their case is. Their claim that the wider democratic framework in which Catalan, Scottish and Quebec national movements exist has allowed them to transcend a fixation with secession and outright state independence is obviously not a luxury for Chechens, Kurds or Palestinians. In such minority nations, whatever the 'rights and wrongs' of their nationalism, achieving a viable independence from Russia, Turkey and Israel is, quite literally, a matter of life or death. Even among the three movements considered, it is not as if all the principal political parties have renounced the aim of independent statehood. The SNP is committed to national independence for Scotland – albeit in a somewhat gentler form, given its commitment to remain within the British Commonwealth with the monarch as head of state and so on. In fact, this position is close to that of the sovereigntist Parti Québécois in Canada.

Similarly, it bears emphasis that the claim that small nations are no longer reliant on ethnicity or culture to define membership certainly does not apply outside the three cases discussed. Such a contention would appear absurd in the case of Kosovo, the latest European 'nation' – whatever one thinks of Stalin's attempt to define the objective traits of a nation, the term does have to be used advisedly sometimes – to have achieved independence, where hostility to Serbs and Serbia is the defining feature of Kosovan nationalism, whatever constitutional and rhetorical claims are made to the contrary. Kosovo might appear an extreme instance, as its Albanian national consciousness was hardened through several decades of bloody ethnic conflict with the Serbs, but the general point stands. And again further qualifications need to be emphasized in relation to Catalonia and Quebec where writers, including in part Guibernau, habitually refer to their basis as cultural entities through the historic retention and use of the Catalan and French languages respectively.

In a certain sense, there is nothing 'wrong' with this, as ethnicity is, after all, a typical way in which nations are conceived. But without qualification it poses problems for the civic incorporation of the substantial numbers of immigrants (from the wider nation-states and beyond) within those nations. In Scotland, data from the late 1990s shows that 72% of Scots reveal that being born in Scotland is important or very important to being Scottish (Bechhofer et al., 2001). Now place of birth is not quite the same thing as ethnicity, as for someone who thinks that parental lineage is key, being born in a particular country does not necessarily confer nationality. One only has to think of the racist rhetorical question: 'If a pig is born in a stable, does that make it a horse?' However, if a majority of Scots – and the claim would no doubt be as high or higher everywhere else – think that someone has to be born in their territory to be a Scot, then clearly there are limits to how permeable this nationalism is. Even with Hussain and Miller's (2006) measured thesis of Scotland's nationalism, there is evidence that general levels of what may be termed 'ethnic sentiment' are high. Thus while they show that there may be no correlation between Scottish nationalism and anti-Asian racism, general unhappiness among Scots over such things as marriage of a family member or relative to an Asian is more than six times higher than marriage to an English partner (Hussain and Miller, 2006, p. 75). This is certainly not to suggest that minority nationalisms – or nationalism per se – are incapable of degrees of inclusiveness. But it is to caution against trite references to them as post-ethnic as if this were an established fact. Ethnicity is and will continue to be one way in which nationalisms define who is a genuine member of their nation and who is not.

Second, it is fanciful to suggest that any of these nationalisms have moved beyond a central relationship to the state. This line of reasoning rests on the kinds of hyperglobalist claims examined in Chapter 1 that the state is a spent force. They became all too frequent in the social sciences in the 1990s, but have since rather died out. In this period, McCrone (2001, p. 186) claimed that the nation-state is 'going out of fashion'. The implication of Guibernau's work is that the state is losing its economic role. Since then, the military power of the world's largest state, the USA, has been dramatically demonstrated across the world through the invasions of Iraq and Afghanistan. As of spring 2009, governments across the world are playing a crucial role in propping up large sections of financial and industrial capitalism facing bankruptcy through unprecedented loans and part-nationalization, that is, state ownership.

In Chapter 3, I argued that a return to economic autarchy is practicably impossible, given the extent of economic globalization. Although this is of profound importance – the world has moved on by dint of globalization – this should be set beside a wider appreciation of the continuing economic role of the state with respect to its expenditure as a proportion of economic activity, its role in promoting exports, in training, subsidizing small business, intervening in financial markets and regulating labour markets. The fact that states seldom get all, or even most, of these functions 'right' does not mean that they are now irrelevant to contemporary capitalism, far from it. More widely, states continue to impart law and order, provide social security systems, school and university education, attempt to control immigration and so on. Far from their reach and control over citizens diminishing, it is more plausible to argue that the use by state police and security services of new technology is extending surveillance over their citizens to levels unimagined even by George Orwell.

As regards the claim that these minority nationalisms have superseded the historic demand of liberation through independence, we have noted that the most important political expression of Scottish nationalism, the SNP, continues to favour secession from the UK. Meanwhile, it remains to be seen if the enhanced powers Catalonia has as a result of the 2006 referendum will weaken demands for secession or, as Spanish nationalists often predict, augur a rising demand for outright independence. Even if a national party does not have the ambition of independence, it will attempt to take a greater share of state power – autonomous or devolved if not separated power – from the wider structure. The point is not a semantic one. There is a necessary relationship between the state and nationalism when nationalism becomes a political force. This is because the state provides systematic organization to the basic things that nations are about in the estimation of their advocates: the national language, wider culture, history, defence, employment, laws and so on. It does this through state bodies like schools and universities, institutes of language, broadcasting organizations, remembrance days, armed forces, civil services, courts and judiciaries.

A third criticism is that in the work of McCrone, Guibernau and Keating there appears a consistent exaggeration, arguably a misunderstanding, of the nature of the EU vis-à-vis small European nations. Such a misunderstanding is less true of Quebec with NAFTA, as Keating (2001, p. 59) is clear that it offers small nations even less opportunity than the EU: 'NAFTA is a strictly intergovernmental affair' that is 'concerned almost exclusively with trade issues'. In consequence, it does not increase the powers of subnational governments but 'may erode them since it permits national governments to invade their spheres of competence in order to secure their international commitments'. There is no mention at all in the various accounts of how the Asian intergovernmental organization, the Association of South East Nations, might provide a nurturing framework for the various stateless nations of the region.

As regards the EU, it should be said that commentators on small nations are not unique in portraying the organization as an essentially progressive force that somehow represents all that is positive in Europe in marked contrast to its bloody past. The EU website showing the gates of Auschwitz surely tries to project this imprecise but powerful line of thought. We as a unitary organization of different nations, it seems to say, embody a common rejection of our continent's terrible history. But references to the past are rare in how the EU depicts and justifies itself. Instead, the representatives of the EU set out, in the introduction to specialist conferences or in the preamble to technical documents, a resolutely positive vision of the future. It is this that several recent books on the subject emphasize. For example, Mark Leonard, the New Labour foreign policy adviser, writes in his book *Why Europe Will Run the 21st Century* (2005, p. 7): 'Europe represents a synthesis of the energy and freedom that come from liberalism with the stability and welfare that come from social democracy.' Jeremy Rifkin, former adviser to Romano Prodi while he was president of the European Commission, is more effusive still. Seeking 'harmony, not hegemony', Rifkin (2004, pp. 256, 382) tells us, the EU:

> has all the right markings to claim the moral high ground on the journey towards a third stage of human consciousness. Europeans have laid out a visionary road map to a new promised land, one dedicated to reaffirming the life instinct and the Earth's indivisibility.

Within the study of nationalism, there are those who laud the development of the EU as innately democratic in comparison to the states that it comprises. Without reservation, Josep Llobera (2005, p. 175) writes:

> One of the most distinctive features of the EU, which contrasts with the way in which the national state developed, is precisely that the former is the result of a voluntary pact entered into by democratic states, while the latter was constructed on the basis of coercion and carried out by non-representative elites.

The fact that the EU, as even supporters would concede, was essentially an elite construct, while nation-states involved genuine popular participation and stake (unless one is to believe that they were purely the imposition of the ruling classes), seems absent from Llobera's picture. More measured case studies of nationalism have attempted to argue that the EU is a positive force as it provides an external forum through which national antagonisms may be reduced. Simultaneously such inquiries suggest that a common European identity may emerge to sit beside local national identities (see, for example, McCall, 1999). The notion that a common European identity will actually supplant national identity has been subject to much criticism by Smith and Hutchinson, writers who, as we have seen, reject the idea that globalization will weaken nationalism. They do this without actually referencing an author(s) who has made this case. Now perhaps it would be too much to say that the idea of a common European identity is a fiction created by Smith and Hutchinson for the sake of argument, but it is worth pointing out that no serious scholar has suggested that this is likely to happen.[10] Hutchinson does refer to William Wallace's work on the EU in his critique. However, Wallace (1997) is careful only to suggest that the EU is taking over some functions of the traditional nation-state, not that it is building a supranational identity.

I should also point out that among the writers considered in this chapter, there is actually some caution about the EU in relation to minority nations. We saw above how the general case of Keating, Guibernau and McCrone is that the EU is a particular manifestation of globalization. They argue that it provides a framework in which small nations can access markets and find international representation outside their historic nation-states. But besides such a claim, there are other passages that are more sceptical of the EU. Keating (2001, p. xv) states:

> There is still not, however, a clearly defined place for stateless nations within the EU ... The Europe of the Regions movement did not make much progress in the last revision, the Treaty of Amsterdam, and the Commission has retreated from its more ambitious regional policy strategies. The Europe of the Peoples favoured by the Esquerra Republicana de Catalunya in which the big states would fade away to allow the regions and peoples to fill the space, is still a utopian dream.

In light of this, he forecasts a bifurcated Europe in which some minority nations are able to attain substantial autonomy, while others remain dependent on their nation-states. Guibernau (1999, p. 174), while not questioning the long-term movement of Europe towards the incorporation and representation of autonomous nations, is highly critical of the Committee of the Regions (CoR), which represents national areas like Catalonia and Scotland as well as individual cities. Even Llobera (2005, pp. 174–5) recognizes that a federal Europe that genuinely represents 'ethnonations and regions' is dependent on a wholesale democratic overhaul of its institutions. Despite such reservations, the general belief is that the EU will 'favour a greater presence of nations without states', as Guibernau puts it. It is in the light of this mostly positive assessment that the following observations are made.

First, the precedent of the enlargement of the EU, its principal recent achievement, is not an optimistic portent for small nations. The key organizational change that preceded enlargement, a new constitution, was drawn up under the direction of former French President Giscard d'Estaing prior to the entry of the newcomers in the east and south of the Continent. When the constitution was put to a referendum in the existing 15 states in 2004, it was generally rejected, causing some temporary problems for the EU. The hiatus did not affect the lack of involvement of the accession states. Anderson (2007a, p. 16) comments that countries to the east were relegated to mere 'onlookers': 'The logic of a constituent will was inverted: instead of enlargement becoming the common basis of a new framework, the framework was erected before enlargement.' The procedure of constitutional imposition – which has now been completed through some minor alterations and signed off by prime ministers and presidents, this time without risking referenda – is mirrored by its actual effects. According to Anderson (2007a, p. 16), its 500 pages, 446 protocols and 36 procedural protocols will

> increase the power of the four largest states in the Union, Germany, France, Britain and Italy; top the inter-governmental complex in which they would have greater sway with a five-year presidency, unelected by the European Parliament, let alone

the citizens of the Union; and inscribe the imperatives of a 'highly competitive' market, 'free of distortions', as a foundational principle of political law, beyond the reach of popular choice.

If this is the context for the entry of states as numerically large as Poland into the EU, it is difficult to imagine that far smaller nations like Scotland and Catalonia (although of course in per capita terms generally much richer, except for newcomer Slovenia) would be able to gainfully represent themselves as equal partners.

The case of the constitution mirrors a wider absence of democracy within the EU. The Parliament in Brussels lacks initiative and contains no pan-European parties. More important in the passing of laws than the European Parliament is the permanent Council of Ministers and the European Council of heads of state that meets every three months. Yet only the unelected European Commission can propose legislation upon which the Council and Parliament can deliberate. Between the Commission and the Council, there are a number of COREPER committees where proposals are thrashed out before being given the stamp of parliamentary approval. In addition, the CoR exists as a consultative body that 'the Commission and Council are obliged to consult whenever new proposals are made in areas that have repercussions at regional or local level'. Established in 1994, the rationale of the CoR is that as most EU legislation is implemented locally, it 'makes sense for local and regional representatives to have a say in the development of new EU laws'. Additionally, there 'were concerns that the public was being left behind as the EU steamed ahead. Involving the elected level of government closest to the citizens was one way of closing the gap.'[11] The CoR comprises 344 members drawn from local and regional government drawn from 27 national delegations (subnational ones are not actually named). In this way, it includes representatives from regional parliaments, Scottish and Catalan among them. However, it has no particular brief to represent minority nationalities; indeed, they have no special role within it. Delegates from Britain include representatives from the southeast and northwest as well as the various areas of Scotland, and Spanish delegates are from Sevilla and Valencia as well as Barcelona. Given the CoR's brief, this is entirely logical, as it is not even a body tacked onto the existing order of institutions in recognition of stateless nations. There is no such facility within the EU and, given its wider 'democratic deficit' and its domination by its most powerful member states, it is inconceivable that one will be formed.

The remote and opaque nature of the EU no doubt accounts for the general lack of interest in the EU among European citizens. It might be true that there are somewhat more positive attitudes towards Europe in Catalonia and Scotland, but apathy characterizes peoples and electorates as a whole in respect to the EU.[12] This is of course true of politics per se, regional, national and subnational. As mentioned, less than half of Catalans bothered to vote on greater autonomy in 2006. However, it is worth pointing out that that voter turnout for EU parliamentary elections, when not combined with domestic polls, is generally only around 10% in all parts of the Continent. When European citizens do get the chance to have a say about the direction of Europe, as some of them briefly did with referenda on the latest constitution, they generally reject the move – not, I would suggest, as a result of xenophobia but through alienation from its bureaucracy and business imperatives.

Finally, it is not the case that all political parties in small nations across Europe set store by the EU. An essay by Janet Laible (2001) finds that both separatist Flemish political parties in Belgium – Belgium is currently a state in a considerably more unstable situation than Spain or Britain – are suspicious of the EU. Interviews that Laible conducted with senior party figures in Volksunie and Vlaams Blok reveal that they think that Europe has infringed upon their hard-fought attempts to promote and protect Flemish culture and language, and consequently they regard the EU 'not as an ally in the nationalist struggle, but as a problematic partner and even as a threat'. In addition:

> both parties suggest that the disrespect for their national culture within European institutions reveals deeper problems of democracy in the EU . . . small or weak polities are endangered by centralization of the EU but at the same time there is insufficient institutional means to articulate their concerns. (Laible, 2001, p. 225)

Conclusion

This chapter has discussed the case for small nations, specifically minority nations – namely Scotland, Quebec and Catalonia – within established, democratic Western nation-states through the writings of Keating, Guibernau and McCrone. I also discussed some of Nairn's recent thinking on the subject. The arguments made were rehearsed in earlier chapters when we saw how those who posit the power of identity within a globalized, networked world think that their claims to self-determination will rise in the twenty-first century. By contrast, economic liberals suggest that such nationalisms run counter to the globalized trend in world history as they are apt to impose restrictions on the movement of capital. The argument that minority nations should either further detach themselves or even leave wider states is also at odds with older ideas of strong, centrally managed states that control integrated national economies that extend over a significant territory. It is partly through scepticism of the economic viability of small nations that a historic condescension exists towards them.

Against this background, Keating, McCrone and Guibernau contend that the context for nations and nationalism has altered in recent history. They argue, primarily in relation to the cases they are concerned with but with a seeming wider application, that nationalism is not so tied to the state as it was in previous eras, nor is it so ethnic in orientation. There are several reasons for this that the writers group under the heading of 'globalization'. They suggest that the transnational movement of capital has undermined the form of state organization, the Keynesian welfare state (in Social Democratic, Conservative or Fascist form) committed to full employment, which existed after 1945. National economies have been replaced by regional economies that pay less heed to the borders of states. This has not superseded the importance of geography to economic governance but strengthens the case for a closer, more localized relationship to cope with the challenges of globalization. Simultaneously, a higher tier of government exists for the three nations that challenge their nation-states through regional organization. Some reference is made to NAFTA by the writers dealt with in this chapter, but really the reference is the EU. Their claim is that the EU provides an open market within which the economies of minority nations are already integrated and is an organization committed to the democratic inclusion and therefore representation of small nations. In addition, there is mention of how globalization has furthered international standards of democracy – 'cosmopolitan democracy' – and human rights that aid the attempts of minority nations to win greater devolution or even outright independence.

If globalization is central to the case made by Keating, McCrone and Guibernau for minority nations, it is not the whole story. Important to the thesis is the decline in the legitimacy of the old nation-states of which they are part. The arguments are, in part, particular ones. In the case of Britain, for example, the passing of the integrative force of empire is thought to be of central importance to the waning of the Union of England, Ireland, Scotland and Wales. A more general argument, but clearly one with particular application to Spain and Catalonia, is that the period in which states could, without impunity, attempt to forcibly assimilate minority nations has now passed. Nairn's distinctive contribution to the debate is that neoliberal policies of modernization, combined in the case of Britain with slavish adherence to American foreign policy, have disaffected electorates, especially minority nations, from remote central governments.

In the estimation of Nairn, this augers well for the resumption of Scottish independence. The other writers are similarly optimistic about the prospects for the nationalisms with which they are concerned. Keating, McCrone and Guibernau think – with differing degrees of emphasis – that the Scottish, Quebec and Catalan movements are civic rather than ethnic in orientation. They are thus inclusive to both immigrants and minority ethnic/religious groups, rather than being concerned with a population majority defined by historic culture or ethnic features. Relatedly, they are not introverted but inclined to free trade within regional and global markets. Nairn's variant on this argument is that the Scots are an outward-looking people, given the experience of centuries of emigration and return.

Recent political developments in Spain, Canada and Britain perhaps inevitably both confirm and question aspects of the thesis made by the writers on minority nationalisms. Of importance in this chapter was the finding that nationalism has become 'normal' in Catalonia, Quebec and Scotland. As a result, it takes on a certain respectability as it heads towards, in the estimation of its leaders, medium-term national self-realization. I suggested that a drive towards a certain political decorum, combined with commitments to retain strong links to the structures of the existing nation-state, risks making such nationalisms somewhat boring in their everyday sensibleness. The low voter turnout in the recent Catalan referendum is perhaps indicative of this trend.

Besides this observation, certain criticisms can be levelled at the case. It can, perhaps, be argued, as McCrone attempts, that Scotland, Quebec and Catalonia are indicative of an emerging international trend with respect to a shift away from the demand for independent statehood. However, the quest of minority nationalist movements across the world for state independence is actually fairly unequivocal: they demand independence. Related to this is that national movements necessarily have a central relationship to the state. Even if they wish to stop short of the creation of a new nation-state – and the principal nationalist party in Scotland, the SNP, has not abandoned this goal – as political movements, they will seek greater state power. Part of the rationale for a shift in orientation away from the accomplishment of state-hood is that it is superfluous, given the opportunities presented for small nations in the EU. I suggested that this interpretation of European develop-ment and trajectory is mistaken. The EU is not predisposed to minority inter-ests and is essentially undemocratic.

A final observation is that the principal case of McCrone, Keating and Guibernau – if not Nairn, whose recent use of globalization is one in a long line of sticks with which to beat Britain and Britishness – appears redolent of trends of the 1990s. Despite the fact that their enthusiasm for nationalism ran counter to wider intellectual trends in the decade, their arguments combine hyperglobalist claims about the demise of nation-states with the belief that they are inherently unstable political structures. While the point is not made explicitly by any of the writers, one feels that this stems from the influence of watching the collapse of Stalinist state structures across Eastern Europe between 1989 and 1991. This remarkable period of history was, in part, testi-mony to the enormous power of nationalism in all its guises. But it was a collapse of states that were bankrupt and lacking in any popular legitimacy. Whatever the historic strains within nation-states such as Britain, Spain and

Canada, they are in relatively good health and have been sufficiently flexible to introduce a level of devolved government that may keep them together at the seams. The more mundane, if not hushed, nature of national politics in Scotland, Catalonia and Quebec is indicative of this.

Summary Points

- The issue considered in this chapter is that globalization will motivate the quest of small nations – Scotland, Catalonia and Quebec – within wider nation-states – Britain, Spain and Canada respectively – to achieve greater autonomy or outright independence. The argument that it will is contrary to the claim of economic liberals that globalization is making nations and nationalism less relevant.
- The academic writers who make this case actually accept the contention of hyperglobalists and economic neoliberals that globalization is making the nation-state less relevant. But they suggest that more localized levels of government and administration, such as that provided by small nations, are better fitted to the twenty-first century.
- The risks of greater autonomy or independence from the bigger nation-states of which they are currently part are apparently reduced by the support they receive through regional organizations, especially the EU for Scotland and Catalonia.
- The external orientation of small nationalisms in respect to governance and trade mean that they are not culturally introverted and prone to ethnic exclusiveness, but are tolerant and democratic in orientation.
- Recent political history seems to confirm and contradict aspects of the case made by the writers examined.
- In both Scotland and Catalonia, there has been movement to greater autonomy, but there is little evidence that the demand for full independence attracts much enthusiasm.
- Meanwhile, claims that the nation-state is a redundant political entity and the EU represents a federal institution that can nourish regionally autonomy are, at best, naive.
- More fundamentally, there are questions over whether the cases of these 'advanced nations' are really representative of the character and predicament of small nations across the world.
- Within these cases, it is questionable to what extent the bases of national inclusion – culture and ethnicity – have been replaced by a civic understanding.

5

Culture and Nation in a Global World

Introduction

Culture, whatever it is exactly, is often evoked directly or indirectly in every-day conceptions of globalization when the pervasiveness of consumer forms and media images is under discussion. Ask what globalization refers to and one might well hear references to McDonald's, Nike, Vodafone and Facebook as 'being everywhere', possibly with mention of how such things are readily available on holiday abroad as well as at home. Such an awareness of trends in cuisine, clothing, communication and viewing habits indicates the fusion of economy and culture the world over. Within the study of globalization, Marshall McLuhan's (1962) conception of the 'global village', which now sounds a little quaint, brings to mind images of an all-embracing closeness as technology makes the world into a parish. More recently, writers who have had an influence across academic disciplines and among general reading publics have emphasized how the integration of economic markets produces sameness. This is true, for example, of George Ritzer's bestselling 1993 book *The McDonaldization of Society*, now in its fifth edition (2008). In it, Ritzer draws on Max Weber's emphasis on rationality as the steamroller of moder-nity to analyse how the internal organization of contemporary capitalism, exemplified by the famous burger chain, is characterized by control, predictability, quantification and efficiency. According to Ritzer (2008), the result is a set of consumer products that are as bland and uniform as McDonald's food. Such a methodology has subsequently been used by soci-ologists to examine, among other things, higher education, theme parks and pornography. In Weber's (1930) words, 'the victorious capitalism that rests on mechanical foundations' is one side of another popular account of globaliza-tion, Benjamin Barber's *Jihad vs. McWorld* (1995). First published in 1995 and attracting a rise in sales and influence after 11 September 2001, Barber sets the levelling effect of contemporary business against the archaic compensations of ideological movements that are at once complementary to 'McWorld' and opposed to it. With less emphasis on outright opposition, the binary of the global and the local is a central way in which culture has been discussed over recent years.

Within earlier chapters of this book, culture has been of greater or lesser importance. This book began with a glimpse of how even in the context of warring states, communication – a constituent of culture and the means of its transition – between peoples, at least individuals, is still possible. In Chapter 1, I noted the influential understanding of Gellner (1964) that the boundary of polity and culture is the same. Gellner and the so-called modernist school suggested that this was a new notion of the industrial age, that is, of modernity. According to this account, the belief inspired movements and states in nation-building from the late eighteenth century on, something that involved, in the words of the titles of two of the best-known books on nationalism, 'imagined communities' (Anderson, 1983) and 'the invention of tradition' (Hobsbawn and Ranger, 1983). Further to this, the extended definition of a nation that I took from Hroch (1993) was explicitly cultural in respect of the way in which a degree of cross-class, horizontal unity is assumed for all citizens through their ability to communicate and interact more readily within it than with those outside. The definition of globalization that I took from Held et al. (1999) emphasized how it should be understood as a set of processes, cultural among others. According to this approach, culture is one means by which national societies are increasingly enmeshed in a global world.

In the discussion of industrial convergence theory in Chapter 1, we saw how Gellner (1964) suggested that once the cultural expression of the early industrial takeoff had been rounded off with the full onset of industrialization, so antagonism between nations would recede. Against this position, writers on globalization like Castells (1997) suggest that the inequalities of globalization trigger cultural revivals at a local level as an aspect of political reaction to economic inequality. More fundamentally, we saw in Chapter 2 that for Smith (1995), culture – or ethnosymbolism – is a key expression of the historic accumulation of a people's experience. As such, it should *not* be considered the arbitrary assemblage of nationalists within modernity that is now susceptible to being washed away by globalization. There was less mention of culture in Chapter 3 on economic nationalism, although the reader may have noted the particular sensitivities that are involved in cultural ownership, given its direct line to nations. In Chapter 4 on small nations, we noted that their academic advocates argue that globalization facilitates their cultural revival in the face of cultural homogenization.

This chapter begins with an attempt to formulate a working definition of culture and makes some broad and provisional points about the context for discussion of cultural globalization and nationalism. It then examines issues of homogenization. Academic writers have actually been rather cautious in suggesting uniformity so the account is inevitably a little fragmented; it is a case of piecing together aspects of this understanding. It goes on to look at cultural hybridity, in some respects the converse of homogenization. Here I base the discussion on an account of the influential work of Arjun Appadurai. Finally, I look at three forms of academic cosmopolitanism put forward over the past 15 years.

Culture and National Culture

The term 'culture' is subject to such varied and differing meanings that it seems that in academic discussion, as much as in everyday life, users of the term are happy enough to assume definitions are unnecessary as 'everyone knows' what it denotes. Matthew Arnold (1978) famously thought it consisted of intellectual and artistic worth that could bring 'sweetness and light' to counter the philistines of the Victorian age. This projected thread of 'high culture' differs from less elevated levels of individual and collective expression conveyed by the term 'popular culture', and culture as in the code of everyday life in the anthropological conception of the term. In relation to the attempt to establish a scale of cultural merit, Arnold stands poles apart from contemporary postmodern rejections of judgements of taste and discernment.

In debates on the study of nationalism, there is an implicit disagreement over the conception of culture. For modernists, culture, as in a national culture, is something that can be assembled in a relatively short space of time.[1] By contrast, ethnosymbolists suggest that cultures – as the historic embodiment of the experience of peoples – are altogether more durable entities that can only be supplemented through invention if the addition conforms to the mores of the existing culture. Within the academic study of globalization, considerations of its cultural aspect were to the fore as the concept moved from business studies to the broader social sciences in the late 1980s and early 1990s. Of particular note was a special issue of *Theory, Culture and Society*, published in 1990 and subsequently released as *Global Culture: Nationalism, Globalization and Modernity* (Featherstone, 1992), which brought together a number of distinguished scholars to discuss the theoretical and applied implications of a global cultural trajectory.

Mike Featherstone stated that the term 'global culture' is a misnomer if it is conceived as akin to a national culture writ large, that is, one of homogeneity and integration. This would require a global state, 'a highly unlikely prospect', he asserted. However, he set the tone for the subsequent contributions by suggesting that the definition of the term 'culture' should be broadened from such a narrow remit to include a range of transnational processes – 'flows of goods, people, information, knowledge, and images' – which are not replacing the national culture so much as serving to create 'communication processes which gain some autonomy on the global level'. Featherstone (1992, pp. 1–2) referred to this as the emergence of 'third cultures', something he claimed that methodologically postmodernism is able to conceptualize through its emphasis on diversity rather than uniformity. Although not actually mentioned, such postmodern influences are notable in many of the discussions of global culture over the past 20 or so years.

Probably the most influential contributions to the collection edited by Featherstone were those of Roland Robertson and Appadurai, whose work we will shortly consider. In a subsequent book, Robertson (1992, p. 177) defined globalization as: 'The twofold process of the particularization of the universal and the universalization of the particular'. This emphasis on the interrelation of the global and local in relation to culture and society more generally was put in a more straightforward fashion by Anthony Giddens (1990, p. 64) in his summation of globalization as: 'The intensification of worldwide social relations which link distant localities in such a way that local happenings are shaped by events occurring many miles away and vice versa.' Such a distinction between the global and the local became influential in sociological accounts of globalization over the subsequent period. More recently, for reasons we will touch on later, theoretical and empirical accounts have questioned such divisions. Tomlinson (2007, p. 154) suggests, for example, that any global–local assessment of culture overlooks the way the latter is shot through with influences of the former.

However, before going any further, it is important to try to affix a definition of culture. In doing so, I use the broad remit provided by Held et al. (1999, pp. 328–9):

> Culture refers to the social construction, articulation and reception of meaning. Culture ... [is] a lived and creative experience for individuals as well as the specialised discourses of the arts, the commodified output of the culture industries, the spontaneous and unorganised cultural expressions of everyday life and, of course, the complex interactions between all of these.

In the subsequent discussion, I will have less to say about expressions of everyday life than about the arts and cultural industries, but as the definition recognizes, there is no neat separation between the two. For example, the worldwide success of television shows like *The Dragon's Den* and *The Apprentice* may be encouraging universal rude and abrupt management styles – not least in British universities. No doubt talent shows like *Pop Idol* and *The X Factor* lead directly to youth video expression on YouTube and Facebook the world over. At an interpersonal level, it may well be that pornography, unquestionably one of the great commercial successes of globalization, is shaping common, predictable and ritualized expressions of sexual desire.

Perhaps the 'high five' greeting, originally of US sports, is replacing indigenous forms of greeting. But such observations possibly overlook forms of
reflexivity that global medias enable and, as such, imply that globalization
consists of cultural homogenization. As already indicated, this is something
over which observers disagree. More pertinent to the discussion here is to try
to set out in a little more detail what a national culture might comprise.

In doing so, it is necessary to avoid somewhat overdrawn assessments that
imply that the national cultures of yesteryear were essentially endogenous
and stable in comparison to the jumbled and fluctuating nature of culture
today. This sort of impression is given by, among others, John Urry (2003) in
his book *Global Complexity*. Urry (2003, p. 107) suggests:

> There are various networks and fluids roaming the globe that, unlike societies,
> possess the power of rapid movement across, over and under many societies as
> 'regions'. Societies are transformed by 'becoming elements within the system of
> global complexity . . . For the past couple of centuries apparently separate societies
> (especially those within the north Atlantic rim) have been characterized by a 'banal
> nationalism' that separated one from the other.

He proceeds to enunciate the various aspects of banal nationalism – flag
waving and so on – and suggests that in many instances they date from the
late nineteenth century.

The identification, in particular, of this historical period in European
history as formative to national cultures is not at issue. However, Urry overlooks that, whatever the political pretence, national cultures in this age were
frequently of diverse origins, the products of the global influences of that age:
free trade, rapid developments in communication systems, empire and
migration. For example, to choose one example among many, when football
was first played in Germany in the 1890s, it was labelled an 'English game'
by nationalists who saw gymnastics as the appropriate Teutonic pastime.
Within a few years, it was not only accepted but widely considered a national
pursuit to which Germans were exceptionally well suited (Noam, 1991, p. 23).
A similar, if now too familiar, point could be made about how quickly Indian
food – albeit Anglicized – became a staple feature of an English night out in
Britain in the latter half of the twentieth century. The general point is that
although the degree of internal and external influence differs, culture is
always protean in composition.

Putting aside the endless business of qualification, a national culture can be
considered, at the risk of tautology, the culture that belongs to and therefore
predominates within a nation. According to a civic approach, this consists of
the collective values and pastimes of a group sharing the same geographic
space. Less politically acceptable now is the assertion that a national culture is
the reserve of an ethnic group – culture in the blood, in the final analysis –

although no doubt such a view is for many a simple matter of common sense, and all the more powerful for that. It is not necessarily, however, a more contentious view than the former. One has only to think of the controversy generated by the insistence of the French that Islamic headscarves (the hijab) and other religious paraphernalia should not be worn in state schools as the country is formally secular. National cultures, whatever the imprints of the past, emerged as recognizable assemblages in the age of nationalism from the nineteenth century on. In doing so, they drew on and replaced aspects of older national culture and pre-existing global cultures. One of the weaknesses of the recent accounts of globalization is a failure to recognize the extent of cultural diffusion prior to the twentieth century. As a result, contributions generally lack balance through a tendency to exaggerate or underestimate the salience of contemporary forms. A further methodological point worth mentioning here is that writers usually fail to distinguish between impact qua cultural globalization on values and identity and impact qua the transformation of the context and processes of cultural transformation (Held et al., 1999, p. 328).

Historic global cultures were created through the domains of ancient and modern empires and world religions. To this we could add the cultural impact of large-scale migrations (often as the result of wars and famines) and networks of trade. Such influences were not just historic and therefore only of academic note. For example, the contemporary cultural, linguistic and religious similarity of most of central and Eastern Europe is attributable to the common legacies of Slavic invasion and Christianity. Equally, the Hispanic and Catholic culture of Latin America was a product of Spanish and Portuguese invasion starting at the end of the fifteenth century. The degree to which local, regional traditions remained intact was due to the strength of resilience to the external cultural influence and the degree of effort invested in its imposition (Held et al., 1999, pp. 330–6). This issue is important, as scholars have made the point that, for example, with the spread of Islam between the seventh and eleventh centuries, internal diversity was as great as the overall similarity (Gilesman, 1990). Whatever the level of local resistance, it was, in general terms, likely to be less pronounced than that which succeeded within modernity. This is because within modernity, external influences were subject to the barriers erected by nation-states. Therefore it follows that peoples were more susceptible, and global cultures were potentially more profound in their impact, prior to the age of nationalism. The place of culture within more modern empires is more complex still. While modern European empires acted as incubators of national liberation struggles in Asia, Africa and the Caribbean by generating much resentment towards the foreign master, they did not generally involve a wholesale rejection of, in particular, French and British cultures per se. A bizarre indication of this would be Robert Mugabe's identification of cricket as the greatest bequest of the British to a newly independent Zimbabwe in 1980.

Whatever the influences wrought by historic forms of globalization, the amalgams of vernacular languages and local cultures were shaped into distinctly national cultures by national movements (in the first instance, as Hobsbawm (1992) notes, more cultural than political), the organizations of civil society and, most importantly, the state. An appreciation of the social construction involved in this process of nation-building does not have to rest on contemporary modernist accounts of nationalism. Quotes ultimately cannot prove a case or substitute for historical detail, but the following statements are revealing. Massimo d'Azeglio, the first prime minister of Piedmont, is supposed to have remarked of the continuing north/south squabbling after the unification of Italy in 1861: 'Now we have created Italy, we will have to create the Italians' (Alter, 1985, p. 23). That national unification was only to be the starting point of nation-building is indicated by the fact that, in the case of Italy, only a little over 2% of the population spoke Italian at the point of unification and the rest knew only various mutually incomprehensible regional idioms. Nation-building in Italy also included the promotion of common cuisine. Pizza, originating in Naples, was promoted in the late nineteenth and early twentieth century as an Italian-wide 'typical' form of food. Issues of language divisions and a wider lack of national self-consciousness were voiced by the first leader of Poland, General Pilsudski, after the mass of peasants had shown themselves to be indifferent or even hostile to the attempts of the nascent bourgeoisie to rid the country of the Russian tsarist yoke in the nineteenth century: 'It was the state that created the nation, not the nation the state' (Hobsbawm, 1992, pp. 44–5).

In a cultural sense, nation-building consisted of the writing of often mythologized national histories, the framing of symbols, the designation of national holidays and commemorations, the standardization and enforcement of national languages through schools, universities and academies, the setting up of postal and transportation networks, the establishment of broadcasting authorities and the formation of national sporting sides. Concerning the arts, we can cite the establishment, with varying degrees of state involvement and funding, of national galleries, libraries, museums, orchestras and operas. As with the military, political and economic aspects of nation-building, such as the enlargement of standing state armies, attempts to regulate immigration and various levels of involvement in the economy, cultural developments depended on an enlarged state personnel and income. The course of development thus involved the extension of the state and the binding together of common sentiments.

Since the above definition of culture emphasized that it exists at two broad levels, purposive creation and everyday life, it is worth emphasizing that nation-building drew in artists, intellectuals, teachers and bureaucrats in the depiction and standardization of nations, and socialized cultural norms and expectations that left some imprint on routine behaviour. Therefore we can give some credence to the emergence of national character, as distinct from more self-conscious national identities, in this period (for a discussion of the distinctions between national character and national identity, see Anderson, P., 1992). The idea of national character is an older one – a product of climate and geography, according to prominent eighteenth-century Enlightenment thinkers. The point here is that in some instances, notions of the particular national character underpinned educational reform in the period before 1914.[2] Even where the concept was more implicit, as in British public schools and youth organizations like the Boy Scouts, there was an obvious endeavour to produce a certain personality type (see Mangan, 1986; Rosenthal, 1986). Although eminent sociologists have taken national character seriously, Max Weber and Norbert Elias among them, it is a difficult concept to sustain intellectually because of the internal differences of class and region besides the crudity of stereotypes. But who would now, or then, seriously wish to argue that the attitudes, disposition and patterns of consumption of, say, the people of Switzerland, Japan and the USA are indistinguishable?

Nation-building is not, of course, something that was undertaken, achieved and put to one side as finished products over the nineteenth and twentieth centuries. National reproduction is an ongoing process with its various banal, that is, commonplace, activities (Billig, 1995). More pointedly, governments, or at least political figures, make periodic attempts to update the process, in part expressly due to phenomena associated with globalization. Proposals for educating immigrants who wish to naturalize as British citizens – possibly to be extended to young people of all backgrounds, indigenous and foreign – would be one example of this (Travis, 2008). The contemporary challenge of mass migration to nationalisms is not new of course. What is different, as we will discuss, is the media technology that enables migrants to retain contact with their culture of origin.

The particularity of nineteenth-century nation-building, the attempt to impart distinctiveness, vied with universal ideologies that stemmed from the universal scientific rationalism of the Enlightenment. Of particular importance in this respect were liberalism and socialism. Liberalism always had an inherent ambivalence as nationalists – or patriots as they preferred to be known – of the early to mid-nineteenth century saw their national independence and unification struggles as part of humanitarian progress per se. Socialism presented a more overt challenge to nationalism in principle as it proclaimed the common goals of, broadly, equality and emancipation, and posed an international solidarity in the face of nations – one encapsulated in Marx's clarion call in *The Communist Manifesto* that 'workers of all countries unite'. As socialism developed through the Communist internationals, so it acquired its own culture through symbols, figureheads and vocabularies, especially after the Russian Revolution of 1917. Thus Communist workers the world over marched under red banners with the heads of Marx, Engels, Lenin and Stalin on them, the hammer and sickle in the corner, while singing the 'Internationale'. However, in practice, socialist movements were generally only successful during the twentieth century insofar as they were able to adapt their movements to nationalist imperatives. In a world riven by impe-rialism, Fascism and war, Communist parties often proved the most politi-cally adept and militarily effective organizations in the struggle for national liberation, their partisan programmes fusing demands for self-determination and social justice with an internationalist rhetoric taken from 'Marxist-Leninism'. Simultaneously, the foreign policy interests of the socialist 'great brother', Soviet Russia, trumped internationalist principles in the policies dictated to Communist parties by Moscow after Stalin had taken effective dictatorial power of the USSR by the end of the 1920s. So it is somewhat misleading to pose nationalism as contrary to the internationalism of liberal-ism and socialism because they themselves were influenced by it.

Be that as it may, Held et al.'s (1999) assessment of the success of nation-alisms in relation to international ideologies is accurate: 'On balance, it was nationalism that became the more powerful cultural force, at least in part because it was systematically backed, funded and deployed by modern states.' In line with the above points on the historical impact of global culture, Held et al. (1999, p. 341) continue: 'On this reading, the high point of cultural globalization lies in the past, while the most powerful and significant cultural flows and cultural relationships have the boundaries of modern nation-states.' The question remains whether this is still the case in, as Held puts it, the era 'of CNN and the internet'. Before considering writers who have in general terms addressed this question, I next consider some of the relevant trends in respect to culture to add some context to discussion.

Trends in Global Culture

Obviously no comprehensive overview can be given of the trends in global culture, it being such a massive and often transitory subject, let alone one inevitably restricted by the limitations of space. I hope simply to raise some key issues as they affect national culture. For the sake of clarity, these are discussed under three headings, but this should not be taken to mean that I think this is somehow a summation.

Economics and Commercialism

The first point relates to the definitional issues discussed above. It is that culture cannot be separated out from economics to produce causal conceptions that Tomlinson (2007, p. 150) objects to, such as 'the impact of globalisation on culture'. It appears that he rejects this line of causation as it implicitly denies culture its own efficacy, that is, it assumes that culture is a passive medium that market forces shape. A more basic point is that culture in respect to commodities *is* economics, that is, it is a massive industry that involves millions of people producing cultural products that are sold to make profit. The point is a familiar one. For example, George Yudice (2003, p. 17) remarks on 'the ad nauseam repetition that the audiovisual industry is second only to the aerospace industry in the United States'. Yet it is one offset by the lingering of the ideology of the aesthetic, something that insists that artistic expression takes place outside market relations. Leaving this chimera aside, it is important to note that some regional economies are largely dependent on employment generated by films, TV, video games and the internet. The production and display of 'cultural commodities' within contemporary capitalism are naturally subject to the same trends as other sectors of the economy with respect to mergers and acquisitions, outsourcing and so on. What is particularly marked is the dominance of key US multinationals like Times Warner and Disney, which has implications for issues of homogenization we will shortly consider.

Commercialism is not simply apparent in respect of the marketing of a cultural product like a film and its associated merchandise – video games of children's movies often gross more than cinema box office receipts. The staging of an art exhibition will typically draw in several sponsors – a merchant bank and a car maker, say – besides some state backing and then charge visitors good money to see the paintings and buy reproductions on posters, mouse mats and so on. Integral to the cultural aspect of globalization considered in this way has been the extension of intellectual property rights through WTO negotiations. Within the various rounds of talks, there has been discord over whether or not culture should be subject to the same market rules as other economic sectors. French and American delegations have disagreed over whether or not French film companies should receive government subsidies. Commentators see this as indicative of a wider transatlantic difference on the national importance attached to culture (Yudice, 2003, p. 18).[3] In general terms, the French argument is that as its cinema embodies themes and traditions within its national culture, efforts should be made to protect its share of available viewing in its cinemas. The American case is that excessive government subsidies distort the workings of the market. It follows that if French films are commercially unpopular with cinema goers in France and elsewhere compared to Hollywood blockbusters so that their makers are forced out of business, then so be it. Perhaps the single most economically open cultural industry is found not in film but sport. The English football Premier League is now largely composed of non-English players, managers and owners – several of whom have acquired their fortunes in less than scrupulous ways – with the biggest share of its income coming from foreign TV rights to show matches. References to globalization are often made to justify the almost total lack of regulation by its administrators. It is fitting that a recent suggestion of the Premier League chief executive to stage matches overseas from 2010/11, notably in China, between its top four global clubs – Manchester United, Liverpool, Arsenal and Chelsea – were kicked into touch by European and international authorities, not by anyone within the domestic game.

Technology and Migration

Technology and migration have produced a partial separation of geography and culture, something that is captured by the term 'deterritorialization' (Tomlinson, 2007, pp. 152–3). Put directly, this refers to the fact that the culture of a human group(s) is not determined and limited by the geography in which it is found. Caution is needed when discussing this point, lest the impression is given that this is a historically recent development or is free of restraint. Instantaneous transnational communication is not new, but has existed through the telegram since the 1860s. Although straight comparisons are no doubt problematic, it is worth considering whether the telephone – an ongoing technology – or the internet has had the greatest impact on human communication. As concerns agencies of control, it is not the case that states are now obsolete in their control and regulation of media flows. The success of the Chinese government in preventing the free flow of information on the internet, admittedly in the case of Google through craven commercial acquiescence, is indicative of this. As regards migration, it is true that ethnic and religious groups have historically migrated and managed to retain their original culture. Migration is now more extensive and intensive than at any previous point in history, but the case is not clear-cut, given the scale of movement during the 'age of migration' before 1914 (Castells and Miller, 2003), something we return later in the chapter.

Yet with these important qualifications aside, it is the case that for much of human history, culture was circumscribed by time and space – for the most part inevitably, given the technological limitations of communication, and, since the rise of nationalism, intentionally – in ways in which it clearly now is not. Referring to this process, Tomlinson (2007, p. 152) refers to a global connectivity 'reaching into the localities in which everyday life is conducted and experienced'. In basic terms then, it is generally no longer the case that interaction and cultural absorption are determined by the constraints of geography. A corporate instance of this that relates to the above point about economic dependence is that media industries can now be located outside the national markets for which they cater. The biggest centres for Latin American

TV, film and web production are, for example, Los Angeles and Miami (Yudice, 2003).

High Art

The distinctions of high art, with an attendant defence through national academic establishments, have been much reduced. One result is that the avant-garde of early twentieth-century artistic modernism lack clear conservative targets against which to pit their radicalism (Anderson, 1998). In a certain sense, the loss of distinctions is not of direct detriment to national culture, as high art always had a universal aura of bourgeois civilization. However, an appreciation of great European authors, artists, poets and novelists, of culture as civilization, simultaneously involved distinctions of different national schools and traditions in a way that, for example, the contemporary preoccupation with the celebrities of film, sport and pop music clearly does not. Thus someone versed in high culture might draw distinctions between the prose of Dostoevsky and Balzac that relate to themes and antecedents within their wider French and Russian national literatures. Would anyone seek to make such distinctions between the pop music of the American Beyoncé and the British Girls Aloud? The result is that a notion of a national canon as an acquired taste is undermined. Coupled with this is what has been described as a 'culture of immediacy' in relation to the acquisition of information (the phrase is from Tomlinson, 2007, p. 156, although he does not use it in quite this sort of context). The point could be extended to the ownership of consumer durables, beauty, success and physical and sexual gratification. Of course, in a world beset by congestion, bureaucracy, human inefficiency and security fears, besides the limitations of income, it is obviously not the case that all wants are immediately met. Furthermore, as always, we should be careful about how recent such developments are. Nineteenth-century sociologists like Georg Simmel and Emile Durkheim warned of psychic exhaustion and social 'anomie' through a maelstrom of wants and information in *fin-de-siècle* Europe. Nevertheless, it is the case that human expectations of and therefore toleration for a period of waiting have been much diminished in our global world. This no doubt affects the salience of cultural forms such as books that take an extended period of time to absorb in comparison to media signs, symbols and sounds. So possibly a culture of immediacy, with its technology-obsessed emphasis on novelty, implicitly undermines an appreciation of history, something intrinsic to understandings of individual and collective national identity.

Once again, in making these points, the inference is that we are witnessing cultural homogenization through globalization, something that is disputed. It is to that subject that we now turn.

Cultural Homogenization

As indicated in the Introduction, the idea of the homogenization of culture – the process of making the cultural all of the same kind – fits with everyday understandings of globalization, in part derived from perceptions of American and, more generally, Western dominance. It is one that is likely to register in any overview of the contemporary world, particularly one concerned with political and economic outcomes. For example, in a typically perceptive consideration of current affairs, Anderson (2007b, p. 18) comments on India: 'There is now a middle class that has internalized Western consumer and celebrity culture even more avidly than its Chinese counterpart.' By contrast, in talking of the relative failure of American hegemony in the Middle East, he says of Muslim culture: 'At a social and cultural level, it has remained the strongest of all barriers to ideological victory of the American way' (p. 18).

As mentioned, American writers of mainstream influence have put forward this view. Ritzer's McDonaldization thesis need not concern us further as he has little directly to say about nations and nationalism. Barber's (1995) book is more directly concerned with the issues pursued in this chapter. The paradoxes that fill the book are undoubtedly telling. For example, Barber (1995, p. 3) conjures this ironic image of jihadists: 'Iranian zealots keep one eye to the mullahs urging holy war and the other cocked to Rupert Murdoch's Star TV beaming in *Dynasty* and *The Simpsons* from hovering satellites.' Written in 1995, one could imagine how the line could be updated to take in the internet. Barber does not think that 'McWorld' and 'Jihad' are equal and opposite forces. The driving force is that of McWorld bringing in the longer term 'the slow certain thrust of Western civilization', an 'unstoppable' force (p. 7). Fundamentalisms – clearly, in Barber's scenario, Islamic ones are foremost – are forces that 'not only revolt against but abet McWorld'. The dual forces at work create a momentum that is 'tearing the world apart and forcing it reluctantly together at the same time' (p. 3). This may make for lurches backwards in history's 'twisting maze', creating a 'shifting amalgam' that suspends the world in chaos. More dramatically still, Barber warns that the world risks 'falling apart'. As suggested, the ultimate trajectory is likely to be towards greater cultural homogenization. In part, this is due to the subtle if temporary concessions that business may make in establishing itself:

> McWorld does take on the cultures it swallows up – for a while: thus the pop music accented with Reggae and Latino rhythms in the Los Angeles barrio, Big Macs served with French wine in Paris made from Bulgarian beef in Eastern Europe, Mickey speaking French in Euro-Disney. But, in the end, MTV and McDonald's and

Disneyland are American cultural icons, seemingly innocent Trojan-American horses nosing their way into other nations' cultures. (Barber, 1995, p. 29)

Whatever force ultimately triumphs, Benjamin is clear that the dual forces of the conjuncture, with their mutual contempt for the freedoms and rights guaranteed by nation-states, are crushing democracy. Barber thus opens the way to a call for a revitalized civic nationalism on American lines.

As this book has pointed out, we are inevitably stuck with dualisms. Dichotomies help us to think straight. However, the titular terms of 'Jihad' and 'McWorld' are too overdrawn, too polemical in this account. While there is no denying that Barber's contradictory depictions are thought-provoking, too much of the book seems to be spent in evoking their paradoxes. Despite the counter of jihad, there are some similarities between the given scope of McWorld and the hyperglobalist exaggerations of the extent of globalization made in the 1990s. Like such projections, there is little in the way of empirical evidence produced. A further problem, conceptual and actual, is that far from being a powerless actor, the American government in particular and states in general are actively involved in the furtherance of corporate culture (Cheah and Robbins, 1998, p. 18, n. 51).

Elsewhere in the globalization literature, one can find writings that seem to echo the older critique of cultural imperialism derived from Third World variants of Marxism in the social sciences. For example, in an essay entitled 'Dollarization, fragmentation and God', Egyptian commentator Sherif Hetata (1998, p. 285) comments:

> The globalization forces are homogenizing other cultures everywhere. In villages that continue to be deprived of the basic necessities of life it is possible to see Star TV, MTV, Zee TV, cable TV and blue movies. The cultural invasion by consumerism is becoming pervasive, creating severe conflict between what is desirable and what is available. The invasion by images is critical. For the first time in history countries like ours are watching the homogenizing of Western or Northern culture into a consolidated, alluring image of the other, of a liberal, capitalist, materially and sexually enticing market, of a world where comparison with our life can only force us to look up to it in reverence.

Seen in this way, globalization imparts cultural imposition through historic patterns of First–Third World patterns of dominance and subordination.

There are various criticisms that can be made of this approach. In fact, critics seem generally wary of the idea of globalization as homogenization. A first response is that it conforms to a standard model of development that has been superseded by global technological diffusion. Anna Greenspan (2004), an independent scholar of digital culture and globalization in China and India, argues that such a model derives from the historical sociology of Marx and Weber. More appropriate than Marx and Weber would be the identification of the postwar modernization theories of incremental growth of Rostow (1960) and others that explicitly took Western Europe and North America as exemplars of development. Some of Greenspan's case is actually quite compatible with what Marxists used to call 'uneven and combined development'. But that aside, the important point is that Greenspan (2004, p. 14) seeks to cast doubt on the validity of clichéd conceptions of Western dominance:

> Today it is common for people to label all signs and expressions of modernity – from the skyscrapers of Shanghai to the futuristic neon-laden streets of Japan and Hong Kong, to the techno parks of India – as 'Western', despite the fact that there is really nothing in the West that compares with the science-fiction landscapes of Asia.

Much of her account is concerned with what she terms 'anachronistic rupture', a process whereby technologies appear spontaneously rather than following the 'route of "normal" progress'. Greenspan finds that this has occurred with IT when, for example, an individual who previously has never had any kind of telephone suddenly gains access to the most advanced communication devices like a wireless mobile phone. Thus 'cultures cease to play "catch up" and begin to "leapfrog" past the developed world' (p. 6).

The degree of adaptation and reflexivity this involves is apparent in other fields. Greenspan uses the fate of English in India as an example. At one level, the rise of English as a world language might, of course, be considered a striking instance of the Western face of globalization, as its use reflects British imperial rule in the nineteenth century and American dominance in the twentieth and twenty-first. Greenspan argues that actually the inventive way in which English has been transformed into 'Hinglish', through its incorporation into indigenous languages, demonstrates how malleable culture is. Greenspan (2004, p. 6) comments:

> Hinglish (in comparison to Indian English) is more obviously hybrid, striking and inventive. It is used to describe the process in which a speaker switches back and forth between an Indian language and English. This process of punctuating sentences with English words and phrases is technically called code-mixing and beginning to be studied as a language of its own. While Indian English is only being spoken by a fairly small elite, Hinglish is more widespread and can be found in publicity blurbs, class room interactions, public addresses, TV and radio interviews … The fact that a Hinglish ad slogan can spread through a local culture embodying everything from the most fervent nationalism, to Bollywood hype, to IT success, illustrates the extent of India's participation in the language of global culture.

In the final sections of her book, Greenspan almost seems to want to completely redraw traditional notions of Westernization by suggesting an

Eastern basis to computation through the Indian invention of zero. This aside, the challenge to conceptions of Westernized development and resulting homogenization is clear.

A second criticism of cultural homogenization is one that takes the commercialism of the case head on, but argues that far from capitalism producing uniformity, its global expansion brings greater cultural diversity. A lively form of this argument is provided by Tylor Cowen. Cowen, an academic economist, something that in itself seems to irritate some of his critics, takes an avowedly market approach to global culture in his book *Creative Destruction* (2004). Cowen is highly sceptical of the view that cultures have in any sense ever been pure – as in uncontaminated by external influences. He notes that alarms over cultural levelling are not new. In late medieval Europe, eminent authorities predicted that the rise of printed Latin would displace local alternatives. In fact, the direct opposite was the case, as printing in a universally understood language allowed the dissemination of the books of writers of various periods and backgrounds to a vastly expanded audience. Printing was of course crucial to the linguistic diversity institutionalized by nationalism, as Anderson (1983) – a source Cowen does not draw on – has shown. In discussing the hybrid nature of a given language, something that is generally inimical to the strictures of cultural nationalism, he cites the now forgotten work of Rudolf Rocker, *Nationalism and Culture* (1937). Much of this book is a polemic of the age levelled against Nazi Germany whence Rocker had fled, but it contains interesting passages that broadly prefigure the case that Cowen makes. On language, Rocker (1937, p. 281) writes:

> Every new intellectual development, every new social movement which transcends the narrow frontiers of a country, every new device borrowed from other people, every advance in science and the immediate effects in the field of technology, every change in the general means of intercourse, every change in world economics with its political consequences, every development in art, causes the intrusion of newly borrowed words into the language.

Now, as historically, Cowen suggests that cultural diversity should not be understood in zero-sum terms. Diversity can increase within societies while decreasing between them. For example, he points out that the international spread of the Borders chain of shops is obviously an instance of homogenization as the consumer can find the same store selling much the same products in a number of countries worldwide. Simultaneously, it retails a vast and heterogeneous range of books, films, and music. Further to this – and this is a more controversial point – Cowen argues that the penetration of one culture by another and the subsequent market opportunities that arise are creative. He gives various examples of how European and North American technology enabled the enhanced production of traditional cultural forms. One instance is how electrical instrumentation taken to Africa by Europeans was the basis of the commercial explosion in so-called 'world music' in Britain in particular in the 1980s. Cowen (2004, p. 18) puts his general case in the following somewhat provocative terms:

> The creative destruction of the market is, in surprising ways, artistic in the most literal sense. It creates a plethora of innovative and high quality creations in many different genres, styles and media. Furthermore, the evidence strongly suggests that cross cultural exchange expands the menu of choice, at least provided that trade and markets are allowed to.

This thesis is taken to a slightly bizarre extreme when he argues that the very popularity of Hollywood movies – whose financial and artistic make-up is far more cosmopolitan than critics suggest, but whose themes, he concedes, are predictable – allows European film makers to produce innovative cinema precisely because they do not try to compete in the same commercial market. They can thus specialize in superior, more artistic films that cater for niche audiences.

A quality of Cowen's account is that he is attentive to the limited period of time that creative destruction occurs vis-à-vis poorer countries. In the longer term, he all but concedes that greater homogeneity is the likely outcome through a threefold process of saturation by the dominant culture, the ameliorating effects of market exchange and the softening result of greater wealth. The case of Hawaii provides an example:

> This fertile period for Hawaiian culture in the twentieth century, however, did not last forever. American dominance of the island – in cultural, economic and political terms – was only a matter of time. This vital indigenous Hawaiian culture has since dwindled precipitously, having been swamped by the greater numbers and wealth of mainland Americans and Asians. Contemporary Hawaii is hardly a cultural desert, but it is more like America than in past times. The region is not producing a stream of distinctive creative achievements comparable to its peak years earlier in the century. (Cowen, 2004, p. 57)

Cowen's reaction to this is a familiar one offered to critics who bemoan the loss of indigenous cultures. He suggests that those who would seek to freeze development to preserve the context for cultural creativity are actually seeking 'diversity slaves', that is, those whose poverty is the economic backdrop to the particular milieu of artistic expression.

A third criticism of cultural homogenization, already noted in Featherstone's postmodernist rejection of grand narratives and present in Cowen's account, is that it conceives culture as an inert substance, not something that can be accepted, rejected or reinterpreted by its recipients. Further, envisaging globalization as a smothering blanket of bland consumption often involves a degree of anti-American moralizing, something that is not uncommon on the academic Left. Interestingly, these points and aspects of the kind of case made by Cowen are acknowledged by Frederic Jameson, somebody whose work over the past 25 years has attempted to situate postmodernity within a Marxist account of late capitalist development. In direct consideration of cultures and globalization, Jameson (1998) held out at least the possibility that market forces may be enabling greater creative endeavour as they loosen the hold of state bureaucracies in less developed countries and elsewhere. Furthermore, he acknowledges that condemnations of American culture as 'materialistic' and 'corrosively individualistic' are too simplistic. This is not to say that Jameson is uncritical of America, specifically the ideology of neoliberalism that American government and business further, because he is. The economic dominance of America results in a 'cultural dissymmetry' between the US and the rest of the world in Jameson's view, and he is quite prepared to use the term 'cultural imperialism' to describe the promotion of consumerism as being at the core of 'the American way of life'. Such promotion is carried out by 'our culture and entertainment industries' that 'train us ceaselessly day after day, in an image media barrage quite unparalleled in history'. He identifies Hollywood films as being of particular importance in this process of 'changing traditional practices' to create 'something allegedly resembling the American way of life':

> Alongside the free market as an ideology, the consumption of the Hollywood film form is the apprenticeship to a specific culture, to an everyday life as a cultural practice: a practice of which commodified narratives are the aesthetic expression, so that populations in question learn both at the same time. Hollywood is not merely a name for a business that makes money but also for a fundamental late-capitalist cultural revolution, in which the old ways of life are broken up and new ones set in place. (Jameson, 1998, p. 63)

Jameson suggests, not altogether convincingly, that ethnic warfare in African and other less developed countries is primarily a form of nationalist resistance against imperialism rather than an atavistic expression of culture. But this aside, the identification of the wash of consumerism within American cultural forms seems a powerful one. His case is not limited to America and Americanism as encapsulated in the way of life represented by Hollywood, but he suggests that it plays a leading role in this ideological expression of capitalism.

The difficulty with Jameson's thesis is that it is not clear what effect consumerism will have on national identities. Speaking generally of global culture, Held et al. (1999, p. 328) comment that it is a 'exceedingly difficult

task to interpret accurately, the impact of this new form of [cultural] globalisation on political identities, national solidarity, cultural values etc'. In fact,
there is some empirical evidence that young people are quite capable of
consuming global, particularly American, cultural forms while retaining
commitments to local cultures (see Day and Thompson, 2004, pp. 184–7). One
writer, Yuanxiang Yan (2002), discussed in greater detail below, finds that
some Chinese youths quite literally 'buy into' American sports while being
strongly opposed to the actions of the US government. Jameson's account
lacks not simply empirical evidence but even examples of specific Hollywood
films.

One account that does attempt to research the question of global culture in
a structured, case by case manner is *Many Globalizations*, a collection edited by
Peter Berger and Samuel Huntington (2002). The international contributors to
the book were commissioned by the editors to examine Berger's (1997, pp.
23–9) typology of global cultures, something they do with varying degrees of
direct application. Berger's typology posited four possible kinds of global
culture that might be emerging:

1 'McWorld', which takes its name from and broadly corresponds to that set
   out by Benjamin Barber.
2 A 'Davos culture', consisting of not simply the business and political elites
   who attend the annual symposium in Switzerland, but those who aspire
   to do so. According to Berger (2002, pp. 3–4), they form:

   a global network of ambitious young people who popped up in every country
   studied in our project, a sort of yuppie internationale, whose members speak
   fluent English and dress alike and act alike, at work and at play, and up to a point
   think alike – and hope that they might one day reach the elite summits.

3 Also at an elite level, there is a 'Faculty club culture'. This group is a
   product of 'the globalization of the Western intelligentsia'. It sometimes
   merges with the business world of the Davos culture, and it is in tension
   with it. It comprises academic networks, foundations, NGOs and some
   governmental and intergovernmental agencies. It seeks to promote not
   the interests of multinational companies but the 'ideas and behaviours
   invented by Western (mostly American) intellectuals' such as 'the ideology of human rights, feminism, environmentalism and multiculturalism
   as well as the politics and behaviours that go with these ideologies' (p. 4).

   Of these two cultures, Berger thinks that the latter is the more 'cultural
   imperialist' of the two, as it largely emanates from universities and foundations in America, while the Davos culture is emerging within Asian
   cities.

4   Without a handy name tag, Berger identifies 'popular movements of one type or another' (p. 7). These sometimes promote the agendas of the faculty club with respect to health, feminism and environmentalism. On occasions they find a toehold in countries outside the West, and some-times they act essentially as missionary organizations. Interestingly, Berger (2002) does not mention the so-called 'anti-globalization move-ment' or Islamic movements under this subheading, but says that 'evan-gelical Protestantism, especially in its Pentecostal version, is the most important popular movement serving (mostly inadvertently) as a vehicle of globalization' (p. 8). This form of globalization seems the least covered in the book.

According to Berger (2002), the emergence of these cultures may result in one or a combination of four things:

1   replacement of local cultures by a global culture
2   coexistence
3   synthesis
4   rejection.

Berger does not attempt to specify which form of global culture is likely in itself to have the single greatest impact. But with the analytic basis of cause and effect, global cultures are examined on a case by case basis.

Space does not allow a full consideration of the generally high-quality contributions by sociologists and political scientists to *Many Globalizations* (Berger and Huntingdon, 2002). There seems to be evidence of Davos and faculty club cultures worldwide. The strongest single affirmation of this is, as one might expect, from the senior American executives of what appear to be top US companies interviewed by Davidson and Yates. The researchers find that they see no tension whatsoever in seeking to make universal their national values. On the contrary, they think that their ideals of rationality, competition and acquisition are rooted in the individual the world over, and are therefore applicable to all. Any ambivalence between this explicit conjoin-ing of Americanization and globalization is resolved by the habitus of the CEO world:

> For all practical purposes, the sociocultural bubble that makes up the framework of their working experience eliminates these tensions . . . It is through the vocabular-ies of global speak that they are reconciled to any ambivalence they might experi-ence . . . They believe that they are responding in different ways to universal needs rooted in a conception of the individual as a rational, competitive and acquisitive social actor. (Davidson and Yates, 2002, p. 354)

Such a finding is replicated in the chapter on Germany and globalization by Kellner and Soeffner (2002). They find that the now habitual use of English business terms within industry and finance that have no direct translations into German is significant. The authors could of course make the point that it is a cultural reflection of the reality of economic neoliberalism. They actually imply that it is part of the process of Americanization. This aside, their finding that such English business terms have permeated from business elites to a wider class audience of young people is important. Kellner and Soeffner's (2002, pp. 142–4) suggestion is that a universal vocabulary of 'go for it'-type terms have entered the mental hard drives of young Germans, where they exist as 'event performance grooves'.

Such developments correspond most directly to a global Davos culture. Other researchers concentrate on how the influence of the faculty club has been taken up and institutionalized. Ann Bernstein (2002) documents how domestic and international organizations have succeeded in implementing smoking bans throughout South Africa as part of a lifestyle agenda – at the same time as the government has refused to take effective measures against the spread of HIV/AIDS. Inevitably, all the writers note the self-evident onset of McWorld aculturalization. One interesting finding, made by Tulasi Srinivas (2002) in his coverage of India, is that consumer culture is not just something being taken up by more affluent groups in a country where approximately a third of the population lives in poverty. He notes how globalization trickles down to the poor through, for example, the increasing use of shampoo rather than traditional oils and so on following heavy advertising campaigns.

Against these type of findings, a picture emerges that, as the title of the book suggests, globalization is producing as much heterogeneity as homogeneity. Without relying on any theoretical model derived from postmodernism, something that we will shortly come to, the writers tend to find that a number of countertrends are observable that at least offset the impact of unilinear cultural influences. A number of points can be made here. In relation to Hungary but with wider central European themes, János Kovács (2002) argues that there is no single model of globalization on offer. Indeed, the different Western artistic and political discourses that registered in Hungary both before and after 1989 are in some cases opposed. Moreover, there is no single central European or even Hungarian identity against which such cultural flows can be counterpoised. The evidence that Kovacs presents of changes in his society since 1989 do seem to support his initial claim that 'if homogenization is going to happen anywhere it's going to happen in Hungary'. Furthermore, he does not produce any evidence of outright rejection of Americanized forms of culture. Nevertheless, Kovács (2002) feels confident in talking of an 'eclectic reception of foreign cultural goods' and that 'bricolage seems to be the rule rather than the exception to it'. This point on how different external influences are being simultaneously incorporated into a national culture is made in relation to Taiwan. Hsin-Huang Michael Hsiao (2002) notes that in Taiwan since the early 1990s, besides a greater conspicuousness of American culture, there has been an infatuation with Japanese youth culture – Japan is the key regional player – through cartoons, videos and technology, with distinctly European inspirations. Simultaneously, there has been a rise in Taiwanese national identity in a repackaged form, in itself influenced by those external cultures.

As concerns the emergence of a McWorld global culture, specifically through the ubiquity of McDonald's food itself, Berger points out in the Introduction to *Many Globalizations* (2002, p. 7) that there is a distinction to be made between 'sacramental' and 'nonsacramental' consumption. Drawing on the fieldwork of the social anthropologist James Watson in China, he suggests that there should be no presumption that when people eat McDonald's food, they are necessarily forsaking their own culture, judging their traditional food as inferior, or, more directly, attempting to 'be like' young Americans. This may be the case initially, but the novelty of McDonald's quite quickly wears off and hence also the sacramental aspect to eating there – in part because it has become so commonplace, given the rapid spread of the restaurant chain.

This sort of finding, that there is no necessary self-conscious aspect to consumerism, is made by Özbudun and Keyman (2002) in relation to Turkey. The case is important as, according to a well-known thesis of Samuel Huntingdon, one of the book's editors, a cultural fault line exists between the West and the East, one that might be thought to lie in this near East country. The researchers find that contrasting political and religious identities among Turks – which are now more marked than when the research was undertaken – reveal themselves in television viewing and newspaper readership, but not in McDonald's or other fast-food consumption. Özbudun and Keyman conclude that modern business and tourist culture is in fact quite compatible with Turkish Islamicism. Coexistence is the rule of thumb, not replacement or rejection. In Japan, McDonald's has taken an increased share of the fast-food market over recent years, but it has also stimulated the growth of chains specializing in traditional food (Aoki, 2002). In India, McDonald's has not, as yet, been successful. Srinivas (2002, p. 97) states: 'The Indian consumer does not want standardization in food products.' He does, however, note the success of pizza restaurants.

The most striking juxtaposition of cultural globalization beside local nationalism is that related by Yunxiang Yan (2002). He argues that young Chinese people are more nationalist than ever before, to an extent that has on occasions alarmed the Communist Party, although nationalism is the only major ideological prop that the regime now has. However, this has not involved any kind of cultural rejection of America as such. Commenting on a leader of the student protests outside the American Embassy in Beijing in

April 1999 after the US bombing of the Chinese Embassy in Belgrade, who was wearing Nike sneakers and a Yankees baseball cap, Yan (2002, p. 20) says: 'I suddenly realized that at least for youths like Lin, there might actually be a truly global culture that can be enjoyed by people from different cultural backgrounds while they are politically nationalist at the same time.' When the authorities reacted to the bombing by removing NBA (the US National Basketball Association) replays from Chinese state television, students like Lin were apparently the most vociferous in calling for their continued showing. Investigations elsewhere of national cases reveal degrees of political/cultural ambivalence even where the group in question might be thought to have a particular agenda. For example, an essay by Stephen Epstein on Korean underground music finds that punks in the Seoul area draw on external music and clothing styles to create an identity that is neither hostile to all things American per se nor to Korean national identity, although with respect to the latter, it is generally opposed to educational ambition. Rather, the writer argues, it is a case of the use of the global in the agency of a particular national identity formation (Epstein, 2001).

The emphasis within the contributions to *Many Globalizations* is clearly on the range of external influences and their ambivalent receptions in national contexts. This sees a shift in emphasis away from the homogenizing trajectories of McWorld, Davos, faculty club and popular movements and one-dimensional impacts of acceptance, rejection or replacement. 'Coexistence' of cultures seems to come closest to capturing what is happening, although this summation does not quite seem to convey the messiness of the reality. In a sense, this is the view of globalization made by various writers whose understanding of the process can be termed 'cultural hybridity', a popular term in the 1990s, which we now consider.

Cultural Hybridity

The outlook of the cultural theorists who see globalization as giving rise to greater hybridity rather than homogeneity is informed by the kind of post-modernist theoretical slant touched on above in relation to Featherstone's important 1992 collection. Writers who favour this approach draw attention to the central role of migration and communication in the contemporary mixing, rather than standardization, of cultures. Probably the single most influential theorist of hybridity is Appadurai, a professional anthropologist who spent much of his academic career at the University of Chicago. His *Modernity at Large* (1996) is an account of culture itself, not simply a critique of globalization as homogenization. His widely quoted writings form the basis of the discussion of hybridity in this chapter.

Appadurai's (1992) initial contribution to the debate on the cultural consequences of globalization was made in Featherstone's edited compilation in a brilliant essay entitled 'Disjuncture and difference in the global world economy'. The thrust of the essay was to reject cultural homogenization in favour of what he termed 'indigenization', the process through which global cultural commodities are repatriated through the lens of the local culture in question. In light of this, Appadurai suggests that, and this is a criticism of cultural imperialism made by others, homogenization overlooks the agency of peoples in less developed countries, in depicting them as duped by Western films, TV and so on. *Modernity at Large* included this theme in a broader assessment of globalization and added the impact of mass migration. Understandably, given that the internet was only in its infancy at this time, there is no mention of its role in the transnational communication of migrants. In subsequent writings, certainly his *Fear of Small Numbers* (2006), he incorporates the internet into his depiction of globalization. Talking of the way in which globalization undermines a stable relationship between nation-states and peoples, Appadurai (2006, p. 24) says: 'Virulent nationalisms also thrive in the context of cyberspace, but they nevertheless complicate the solidity of ties between space, place and identity.' Appadurai mentions in the Introduction that the general intent of this recent book was to dwell on the negative side of globalization, something that critics suggested was absent in *Modernity at Large*. However, there is nothing in it to suggest that he has revised his opinion about the extent and impact of globalization, even in relation to his frankly extravagant claims about the demise of the nation-state, which we will shortly outline. Indeed, Appadurai (2006, p. 22) is quite prepared to refer to ours as a 'hyperglobalized world' and talks, for example, of 'the virtually complete loss of even the fiction of a national economy'.

Appadurai is candid that his disciplinary background in anthropology predisposes him to detect difference. So while acknowledging that globalization uses a variety of instruments of homogenization – armaments, language, clothing styles and so on – he thinks that the impact is not simply one of cultural imposition by dominant cultures that reflect hierarchies of power and wealth. In short, Appadurai (1996, p. 32) rejects the premise of Americanization: 'The new global economy has to be seen as a complex, overlapping, disjunctive order that cannot any longer be understood in terms of existing centre-periphery models.' Globalization, 'not the story of homogenisation', in fact sees a rupture of culture as a property of the nation-state – he places a hyphen between the two terms to emphasize the linkage, one now badly frayed. This is a recent development:

The theory of a break – or rupture – with its strong emphasis on electronic and mass migration, is necessarily a theory of the recent past (or the extended present) because it is only in the past two decades or so that media and migration have become so massively globalised, that is to say, active across large and irregular terrains. (Appadurai, 1996, p. 9)

Without producing any statistical evidence, Appadurai claims that migration flows are more intensive and extensive than at any other point in history. He does not deny that stable and homogeneous communities exist with traditional patterns of socialization. However, such stability is undermined through the 'woof of human motion, as more persons and groups deal with the realities of having to move or the fantasies of having to move' (p. 34). Crucially, migrants now have access to 'mediascapes', 'mass mediated imagaries' that enable a variety of connections external to where the individual or group comes to settle. Appadurai formally rejects a technological determinism to this, but suggests that the combination of migration and mass-mediated 'imagaries' compels the work of the social imagination to the extent that it becomes a social fact. Here his conception is presumably of a social reality born of globalization akin to the collective conscious of Durkheimian sociology. A network of micro-narratives of film, TV and music has been summoned up that allows 'modernity to be written more as a vernacular globalisation and less as a concession to large scale national and international policies' (p. 10). There has emerged a series of 'diasporic public spheres' (p. 22), outside the reach of the nation-state, that act as 'cultural laboratories of diversity' (p. 174).

Although the empirical evidence is slight, Appadurai's work is marked by memorable quotes. Capturing the micro- and macro-levels of this deterritorialized conception, he writes:

> Pakistani cabdrivers in Chicago listening to cassettes of sermons recorded in mosques in Pakistan or Iran create diasporic public spheres that confound theories that depend on the continued salience of the nation state as the key arbiter of important social change. (Appadurai, 1996, p. 4)

So, as media forms, communication flows and migrant streams slice open the borders of the state and disturb their national content, nations lose their bearings as their original identity is questioned. The resulting crisis of the state paradoxically leaves open the potential for a revival of ethnic nationalism, as groups make frantic quests for the exclusive cultural security of yesteryear. Appadurai's thinking here is reminiscent of Castells' understanding of the resurgence of identity as resistance. Ronald Nieven (2004, p. 41), another influential cultural theorist, captures the given predicament:

> World integration, or at least the process of delocalization associated with it, has made the question 'who are we?' more salient, more important for the expression of selfhood than it was for those who were once relatively unaffected by colonial or cultural domination.

On occasions, Appadurai goes further in actually questioning the future viability of nationalism altogether, certainly in the form it currently exists as an ideology associated with the state. Instead, what is likely to emerge is a set of deterritorialized communities and organizations (for example NGOs) besides companies, banks and so on with differing and conflicting outlooks and ideologies.

This projected culmination aside, and certainly the positive gloss on globalization as a 'cultural laboratory of diversity', there are strong similarities between Appadurai's thinking in respect of the role of migration and technology and Anderson's (1998b) thesis of long-distance nationalism. Anderson first gave extended consideration to the notion of long-distance nationalism in 1994 (Anderson, 1994) in an essay that was clearly influenced by the role of returning political émigrés from the USA to newly independent Eastern European countries and, in particular, the warring nations of the former Yugoslavia. Thoughts about exile, enforced and more voluntary, had appeared in an essay on nationalism written two years earlier, in which Benedict Anderson (1992, p. 9) had evoked, by way of example, the national imagining of a gastarbeiter from Greece sitting in a one-room apartment in an anonymous German town staring mournfully at a faded Lufthansa poster of the Parthenon: 'This Lufthansa Parthenon is transparently not a real memory for the melancholy worker. He has put it on his wall because he can read it as a sign for Greece – in his Stuttgart misery – for an "ethnicity" only Stuttgart has encouraged him to imagine.' This image was set within a wider appraisal of the historic relationship between migration from the late nineteenth century to the late twentieth. In an extended consideration on long-distance nationalism, drawing on the claim of Lord Acton (1909) that exile is the 'nursery of nationality', Anderson (1998b) further documented the psychological yearning of displacement and the political importance of organizations to nationalist movements in response to, in particular, the break-up of multinational empires.

The similarity to Appadurai is evident in Anderson's argument that despite this historic relation of the migrant to the home country, real and imagined, for the most part, immigrants have been absorbed into the country of settlement – certainly in so-called nations of immigration, primarily the Americas but also Australia and New Zealand – over the past 200 years. Now, however, the revolutions in communications, media and transportation that enable instantaneous contact with fellow nationals outside and within the country of origin allow the preservation of identity and sap the ability of the host state to compel immigrant integration. Technology has 'profoundly affected the subjective experience of migration'. In a passage that already appears slightly dated, among other examples, Benedict Anderson (1992, p. 68) states:

The Moroccan construction worker in Amsterdam can every night listen to Rabat's broadcasting services and has no difficulty in buying pirated cassettes of his country's favourite singers. The illegal alien, Yazuza-sponsored, Thai bartender in a Tokyo suburb shows his Thai comrades karaoke videotapes just made in Bangkok.

'Multiculturalism' and 'difference' may be celebrated in their own right in sections of societies like Britain, Australia and America, but understood in this way, such an ethos should be understood as enforced recognition that immigrants will retain primary interests and allegiances to polities and cultures outside the state in which they live. Benedict Anderson (1992, p. 72, emphases added) suggests that there has been a shift from 'say *American*-Armenian through *Armenian*-American'. Appadurai (1996, p. 172) concludes: 'The formula of hyphenation (as in Italian-Americans, Asian-Americans and African-Americans) is reaching the point of saturation, the right hand side of the hyphen can barely contain the unruliness of the left hand side.'

More concerned with the political consequences of this process, Anderson is more pessimistic than Appadurai about long-distance nationalisms. Appadurai (1996, p. 198) does note, for example, the role of diaspora Hindu organizations in funding groups that destroyed mosques in India in the 1990s, but somehow wants to counterpoise a long-distance patriotism against nationalism as a general development. As suggested, his general fascination is with migration as a 'laboratory of diversity' and the cultural fracturing of the nation-state this entails. Anderson, while no academic defender of states, sees long-distance nationalism as, for the most part, an irresponsible right-wing phenomenon that projects ethnic absolutes from afar without regard for their disruptive impact on the ground. Viewed in this way, the link between hybridity and fundamentalism is closer than to a 'world of difference' multi-culturalism. This alternative way of conceiving the political consequences of the contemporary cultural experience of migration – long-distance national-ism as ethnic cleansing and destruction 'back home' – should be considered a first possible criticism of understandings of globalization as hybridity as set out by Appadurai. However, it does not question the premise of the case. This rests on the assumption that migration is of a scale that is undermining the ethnic basis of nation-states.

The subject of migration is a massive one and cannot be given full coverage here. However, a number of relevant points can be made. First, there is a tendency in Appadurai to exaggerate the historic levels of ethnic homogene-ity that existed prior to the contemporary age of globalization, given the scale of earlier periods of migration. It would, for example, be an interesting if diffi-cult exercise to compare the immigrant make-up of the populations of New York and Chicago – the two cities where Appadurai has had academic posi-tions in recent years – in the decades after 1900 and 2000. Evidence from the age of migration in the period before 1914 indicates that there should be no automatic presumption that migration is currently proportionately higher in American cities. In New York and Chicago, as in other America cities, the scale of Hispanic immigration particularly has had great cultural import over the past 30 years. However, as one of the chroniclers of this population stream reveals, it is something with its own history, one that ebbed and flowed over the course of the twentieth century (Davis, 2001).

Second, and relatedly, Appadurai seems to take for granted that migration is now on a greater scale than ever before. There is some evidence for this and all the projections indicate that the intensity and extent of migration is likely to increase. However, it should be noted that the most authoritative estimates for numbers of immigrants – classed as those who live outside the country of their birth – are actually rather small: 3% of the world's population according to the most recent UN estimate (www.esa.un.org/migration). Of course, given the scale of illegal migration, it is likely that this figure is a serious underestimate. But even if the figure is, say, 5% and allowances are made for vast differences in scale within and between countries, one in twenty still represents a fairly small proportion of the world's population. Looked at in these terms, migration is perhaps a somewhat overrated topic, the more remarkable sociological phenomenon being for people to stay put. It is true that states struggle to control migration flows despite ever greater resources and technological sophistication devoted to doing so. But they are not power-less in the face of migration flows, and in richer economies, governments shape the form migration takes on behalf of those employers who actively favour immigrants for their hard work, skill and acceptance of low pay for the lowly jobs that domestic workers will not do.

Third, and this is actually a point that qualifies the one just made about migration's limited level, globalization is arguably motivating movement on a greater scale within nation-states rather than between them. Currently, the greatest peacetime internal migration in history is taking place within China from the country to the city – largely a population shift from the rural interior to the industrialized coast. No doubt this development is having various cultural consequences, but – leaving aside the fact that peasants from minor-ity ethnicities are among those who have made the trek – it is an intranational one. International migration itself is still predominantly regional rather than truly global, that is, within the Americas, within Europe and so on.

Fourth, there seems to be an irredeemably positive conception of migration in Appadurai's 1996 *Modernity at Large*. There is no mention of the exploita-tion, insecurity and acute loneliness that are part and parcel of migration for so many, something that is disproportionately experienced by people from poorer countries, given the overriding economic dimension of global migra-tion. Appadurai's discussion has no mention of class differences with respect to migration, although it surely should qualify his discussion in some measure – quite how, in cultural terms, is admittedly not fully clear. Compare the plight of, say, an elite, 23-year-old Indian web designer from Mumbai working in Silicon Valley, who has to hand the latest internet technology to contact family and travels home twice a year, with a 43-year-old illegal kitchen porter from Kerala living in New York City with an immediate and extended family in India who rely on his remittances earnings. The former no doubt mixes freely with his colleagues of numerous national backgrounds and, on the occasions he turns off his laptop, can enjoy the Californian good life. The latter probably depends more intimately on a few cultural and more strictly personal mementos he has with him. He uses his mobile to phone his wife and children regularly but is anxious not to talk for too long, given the cost of international phone calls. And in any case he reflects, on hitting the cancel button, what good is a call compared to playing with his children whom he now sees on his screen saver? What free time he has he spends with fellow immigrants from his native state in the cafés and parks near where he works in Brooklyn.

The latter scenario is, in fact, based partly on Biju from Kiran Desai's 2006 Booker Prize-winning novel, *The Inheritance of Loss*, a character whose travels emphasize the cultural limitations of migration. The boring day-to-day reality of immigrant life in America ultimately ends in ruin for Biju upon his return to India. Financial vicissitude, beside the drudgery of a 10-hour, 6-day working week in a meat-packing factory, is the context for Upton Sinclair's *The Jungle* (1949), a panoramic story of settlers in Chicago written a century earlier, an account that dispels any notion of migration as anything other than a grind. Ethnic identity and a cultural flux of, in particular, Eastern European peoples vividly colour this great novel – in which the principal theme is that of class – in the opening scene of a Lithuanian wedding.

To continue on this theme, the following passage from Dubravka Ugresic, the Croatian writer who was forced to leave Zagreb in the early 1990s as the then president, Franjo Tuđman, squeezed domestic criticism, is relevant to any impression that migration is a contented medium of permanent contact and cultural flux:

> Asylum seekers, emigrants, refugees, nomads, migrants, people who have been exiled and those seeking their papers – all of them annoy the communities where they end up. Civilized places never admit this, of course. They pound their chests with their multiculturalism, working in earnest on projects for support and integration . . . All to keep from smashing their heads against the hard truth: newcomers irritate the local majority . . . Literature tends to show the romantic side of exile. In reality, people live in exile in submerged trauma. (Ugresic, 2007, p. 16)

Leaving aside whether or not such trauma was more keenly felt now or in the past, the reference to Sinclair's *The Jungle* alerts us to a fifth point, the fact that there is reason for thinking that the cultures of migrants were more strongly preserved in the past than is the case today precisely because of the lack of global communication technologies. Immigrants to the US in the nineteenth and twentieth centuries, while for the most part intent on becoming good Americans, set about creating stable community organizations, above all churches, once they had found their feet precisely because they lacked the psychological security of instantaneous links to the old country. Such organizations had political ramifications, although for the most part of a more progressive, unificatory nationalist type than is perhaps the case today. Speaking of the late nineteenth and early twentieth centuries, Hobsbawm (1987, p. 154) notes:

> The greater migration of peoples and the more rapid development of cities and industry which threw together uprooted masses against each other, the greater the basis for national consciousness among the uprooted. Hence, in the new national movements exile was the main place for incubation. When the future President Masaryk signed the agreement which was to create a state uniting Czechs and Slovaks (Czechoslovakia) he did so in Pittsburgh, for the main basis of an organized Slovak nationalism was to be found in Pennsylvania rather than in Slovakia.

Similarly, early American Croat and Serb organizations of one type or another supported the establishment of a federated Yugoslav state. Long-distance nationalist affiliations were, moreover, a matter of life and death. For example, according to Padgett (1989, p. 17), most Serbian men of military age returned from America to the Balkans in 1914 to fight the Austrian armies.

At the level of individual communication, we can perhaps question whether the depth of the communication of migrants with those at home has been enhanced by modern technologies. In their classic sociological account of early twentieth-century immigrant life in America, Thomas and Znanieck (1927) describe how semi-literate Polish peasants would struggle with writing letters to their families back home, but would persevere, often with the help of a relatively well-educated member of the community like a priest, to produce minor narratives of their new lives. Perhaps such a process served to underline their existential distance from the villages of their youth in a way that is no longer so acute. However, it is quite possible that such communications contained more information and more heartfelt meaning than a hurried text, email or even a web cam chat.

Sixth, Appadurai's and Anderson's conception of cultural transmission is actually rather formal, something that allows the kinds of historical comparisons made above. The understanding is that immigrants draw upon cultural resources from their home country alone, although there is some suggestion that, once extracted, diasporic forms emerge in migrant contexts. By contrast, and this point is at variance to the point made about the isolation of immigrants, others emphasize how 'the global city' produces its own hybridity. Stephen Castles (2002) suggests that the extent of contemporary cultural intermingling subverts unilinear notions of long-distance nationalism. At issue here is the creation of cultural forms that are somehow more than the sum of their parts as their various named national strands are not presented and understood as the property of a particular group. Nederveen Pieterse (1995, p. 53) colourfully captures this cultural predicament in a oft-quoted remark, when he talks of 'Thai boxing by Moroccan girls in Amsterdam, Asian rap in London, Irish bagels and Chinese tacos'.

These criticisms largely leave untouched the central point of Appadurai and Anderson that nation-states no longer have the ability or even the will to try to integrate immigrant newcomers. In their estimation, this gives rise to globalization as heterogeneity rather than homogenization. Legal scholars who have recently approached this issue from a different angle lend some support for this kind of view. In *Beyond Citizenship: American Identity after Globalization*, Peter Spiro (2007) finds that immigrants choose to become US citizens at a surprisingly low rate. He argues that this is because they have little direct motivation for doing so as the actual benefits are slight. As Spiro (2007, p. 159) puts it: 'The real prize is legal residency, not citizenship. It's all about the green card, not the naturalisation certificate.' Recent US Supreme Court cases have failed to discriminate in favour of citizens over residents. In Britain, the 1998 European Human Rights Act makes such distinctions unlawful. Meanwhile, the hundreds of thousands of immigrants from EU accession countries who have entered the UK since 2005 have only the incentive of a vote in national elections for becoming British. Looked at in this way, a Pole living in Britain or America can retain their national passport, have instantaneous contact with fellow nationals at home and abroad, return to Warsaw regularly (weekend trips on easyJet if they live in the UK), while enjoying virtually all the entitlements – schools, health, benefits and so on – of the bona fide British and Americans with whom they live and work. The case therefore represents a strong challenge to traditional notions of national identity, which have historically assumed that residency, cultural identity and citizenship are congruent.

There are, however, several points that can be made in response to this. On the one hand, there are various hierarchies of nationality and education involved in the process. In the British case, there may be limited reason for EU nationals to acquire British citizenship, but this is not the case for nationals from outside Europe. Citizenship is something that is not simply an optional extra but a necessity for a Congolese asylum seeker granted temporary leave to remain in the UK, or a Filipino nurse who entered Britain through the now modified highly skilled migrants scheme. It represents a foothold through which they can secure not simply welfare and social security benefits but legal residency. On the other, it is not the case that nation-states have simply thrown up their hands in the face of global migration and given up the attempt to secure the cultural integration of newcomers. Certainly the under-taking is complex and the proposals about how they might do so appear comical to some. This was the case, for example, with the suggestion of Lord Goldsmith, the former British attorney general, to introduce a series of meas-ures to anchor Britishness among all citizens, not simply immigrants: a national holiday celebrating citizenship, a revival of the Treason Act of 1351 and the idea – mentioned only in passing – of ceremonies in which British youths would recite an oath of allegiance to the Queen.

More important than any state attempt at integration are the countless daily instances of banal nationalism. While they may hardly register in the consciousness of the adult immigrant, it is far less likely that they fail to impress their children. They will generally acquire the legal nationality of the host country automatically by virtue of birth and grow up with national and, in particular, local ties and identities. Of course, it is probable that they will have some cultural influences and affiliations from their parents, while their degree of integration may be limited by racial exclusion. Simultaneously, to return to the issue of homogenization, it is questionable how distinct the cultural commodities are – PlayStation, World Wrestling Entertainment, Nike and so on – that children pester their parents to buy them wherever they are. Nevertheless, the following remarks of Harris (1990, p. 17) on the national identity of the children of immigrants are instructive:

> Perhaps the child or the grandchild will invent a nostalgia, a personal explanation of current unhappiness, which will make of special significance the origin of the parent or grandparent. But these private fictions are rarely of much significance, nor do they affect most people – despite much American talk of 'roots'. Nor do they survive the passing of many generations. The ease of the shedding of national iden-tity is more impressive than its retention.

These remarks may appear at best misplaced, given the outrages of second-and even third-generation British Asian terrorists. Here, however, the cause was not directly that of long-distance Pakistani nationalism so much as global jihad in the face of a perceived war against Muslims. Moreover, the recent trials of the plotters have revealed that in some instances the individuals involved were remarkably well integrated into British society.

Cosmopolitanism

Like hybridity, cosmopolitanism has been seen as a positive development associated with globalization in recent years. At its most basic, 'cosmopoli-tanism' refers to belonging not to a single cultural form, like a nation, but to many parts or all of the world. The roots of cosmopolitanism go back to Plato and Ancient Greece. The concept was much discussed and generally endorsed in the eighteenth-century Enlightenment. For example, Kant counterpoised the 'national delusion' of superiority to 'world patriotism and local patriotism', both of which 'are required of the cosmopolitan', that is, a loyalty to one's locality and the wider world (Kleingeld, 2003). Perhaps his scathing comments on the capabilities of African people have prevented this eminent authority being quoted more widely on the matter. A second Enlightenment way of conceiving cosmopolitanism, found for instance in the great French *Encyclopédie* – the attempt started by Diderot and D'Alembert to collate and systematize all existing knowledge, the Wikipedia of the eighteenth century – was of a peripatetic individual or group. Subsequently this was identified as an altogether negative trait. Notoriously, both Hitler and Stalin denounced the Jews as 'rootless cosmopolitans'. Although present-day neo-Fascists no doubt rail against the anti-nationalism of cosmopolitanism, its contemporary academic discussants have, as one might expect, been far more positive about this perceived trajectory in recent years.

Most writings on cosmopolitanism over the past 15 years have been produced by Left liberal intellectuals who view it as sociological development, one that can take progressive politics beyond the palpable failure of proletarian internationalism of the mid-twentieth century and the relativist blind alleys of multiculturalism and identity politics of the 1990s. There is no single or overriding theory of cosmopolitanism that we might conveniently single out and discuss. Robin Cohen and Steven Vertovec (2002) list as many as six different strands. Here I condense them into three different approaches to the subject.

The first is that of an identified sociocultural condition as a product of globalization. Beck (2000. p. 96) refers to 'the empirical indicators of cosmopolitanism'. Presumably they might act as a sort of checklist in assessing how cosmopolitan a particular society is. This done, we could make comparative judgements and summations of the general level of cosmopolitanism. The list includes:

- the flow of cultural commodities
- the prevalence of dual citizenship
- the level of political intensities
- the political representation of minorities
- multilingual proficiency
- the degree of mobility
- the development of communication forms
- the incidence of involvement in transnational networks.

One can of course envisage how aspects of this inventory produce homogenization or hybridity in the light of the above discussion. For example, more and more people speak English as a global language, at the same time as migration produces multilingual contexts like schools.

Beck does not dwell on such matters but, as mentioned earlier, he suggests that 'the deterritorialized', cosmopolitan society that is now in the ascendant gives rise to greater individual and institutional – that is, collective and organizational – self-reflection and reflexivity. People can no longer take the values and mores of their own society to be dominant, but are forced into 'a learning process', in which one's own life is tested and ways of relating to others can be learned. The philosopher Kwame Appiah (2006, p. xx) suggests that the cosmopolitan condition is one of enforced recognition that 'A world in which communities are neatly hived off from one another no longer seems a serious option if indeed it ever was'. In the same vein, sociologist Stuart Hall (2002, pp. 26–7) says that there is now 'something artificial and absurd about the attempts to preserve and keep intact a single culture'. Beck implies that this form of cosmopolitanism is rather different from its more strident and programmatic Enlightenment precursor. However, the result is no less optimistic, one might even say utopian, than that of the eighteenth-century *philosophes* who envisaged a world governed by reason and based on science. Beck (2000, p. 100) suggests that a cosmopolitan society is where cosmopolitan values rate more highly than national ones, in which cosmopolitan parties, identities and institutions come to the fore and gain 'increasing power in relation to national and nationalist counter movements to the extent that they can assert themselves on a world wide scale'. As Enlightenment authorities were generally forthright in expressing their opposition to ecclesiastical dogma, so Beck clearly posits nationalism as being the 'enemy' – he uses the term – of cosmopolitanism.

A second variant of projected cosmopolitanism to emerge in the 1990s was of an emerging political project. Probably its foremost exponent is David Held through his cosmopolitan democracy thesis. Others have contributed to this Left liberal understanding of developments of global politics, notably Mary Kaldor (1995). The principal contention for our purposes is that nationalism is no longer a sustainable form of politics and economics. Held (1995) is careful not to suggest that national identities will wither away in the face of globalization. However, he suggests that planetary concerns over such things as the environment, poverty, equitable trade regimes and criminal justice, coupled with a myriad of ties and formal treaties – most dramatically realized in the regional institutional form of the EU – are producing a changed conception and remit for politics. Hitherto, the impetuses of political parties and movements have been towards national institutions of representation – councils, parliaments and so on. Now they have the opportunity – indeed are compelled – to make use through enhanced transportation and communication of extranational institutions to produce multi-level governance. Meanwhile, the dealings of states are increasingly informed by norms of cosmopolitanism, acceptable forms of behaviour, at home and abroad. It thus acts as a mediating discourse.

There is another slightly different variant to this form of cosmopolitanism. It is one that acknowledges the importance of the growth of international organizations, but stresses the importance of the growth of global civil society from below. In this, transnational organizations – NGOs like Amnesty International and Greenpeace – act as important organizational forms. The importance of both types of development, from above and below, are captured by Rainer Bauböck (2002, p. 123):

> For a cosmopolitan project it may be important to consider how cultural communities that are no longer confined within the boundaries of the state system might transform this system in the long run. If we accept Gellner's account of nation building as an attempt to make cultural and political boundaries coincide, then transnational cultural communities pose a quite significant challenge to the nation-state.

There is a third form of cosmopolitanism, which again is by no means opposed to either of the above, indeed, it is implicit within the thinking of Beck in particular. Its distinction lies in the emphasis placed on how individuals and groups develop a cosmopolitan attitude or disposition with a corresponding practice or competence. This stems from a set of multiple identifications, the gift of divergent cultural experiences, especially those associated with travel. This results in an 'orientation, a willingness to engage with the Other', in the estimation of Hannerz (1992, p. 239). In the view of Iyer (1997), cosmopolitans views their own lives with a certain worldliness.

There are various criticisms that can be made of cosmopolitanism, some of which are similar to the above points on hybridity. The understanding of cosmopolitan democracy does seem to be something that belongs to the measured optimism of the Left liberal intelligentsia of the 1990s. The notion that the room for manoeuvre of nation-states has been fundamentally altered by the slow creep of internationalism – tying down Gulliver – as a particular trend within the wider transformation of globalization, was dealt a heavy blow by the unabashed unilateralism of the Bush administrations from 2000 until February 2009. Arguably, however, the continuities of this American presidency with the more superficially internationalist period of the Clinton administration that preceded it were greater than the differences. At almost the end of the 2000s, it seems that democracy, freedom of speech and universal justice are actually in retreat across the world rather than in the ascendant. The Chinese Communist Party might have felt the need to hire PR consultants from London in the run-up to the 2008 Beijing Olympics, while Vladimir Putin may still claim that Russia is a 'managed democracy', but this does not amount to much. Meanwhile, on the two central issues of our times, trade and global warming, as debated through the WTO and the UN respectively, effective negotiation and agreement seem as distant as ever. Of course, cosmopolitan democracy may be a laudable aspiration, an ideal worth supporting. Unfortunately, however, that is all it really is. For all the short-comings of the realist approach in international relations, which emphasizes the autonomy of the state as a political actor, it appears closer to the current political mark (Takeshi, 2006). It is noticeable that while Held and McGrew (2007) seek to defend globalization from critics who have concluded that either it is an overrated concept or does not exist at all, they do so by refer-ence to the expansion of world markets and so on, not ongoing political developments.

A second criticism, one that should be applied to the sociological projec-tions of cosmopolitanism associated with writers like Beck, is that there is relatively little empirical research to substantiate the case. Beck does set a research agenda that might be tested but his actual writing contains few references or actual instances. At times, one rather feels that his is a work of futurology as much as sociology, or at least a rather optimistic sociology. One attempt to subject the issues just discussed to examination has been made by sociologists Michael Savage, Gaynor Bagnall and Brian Longhurst (2005) in a study based on interviews with the residents of three Manchester suburbs in the late 1990s. Their study, inevitably of a limited scale and location – no doubt their findings would have been rather different if their focus had been inner-city Manchester, certainly central London – does not examine issues of cultural homogenization and has little directly to say about hybridity.

Cosmopolitanism is considered an academic discourse within the broader study of globalization. Referring in particular to Beck as a theoretical point of departure, one of Savage et al.'s aims was to look at their respondents' degree of international contacts, connections and their resulting global awareness. Their general finding was that a little less than a quarter 'exhibited some kind of comparative frame of reference at some point in their narratives' (Savage et al., 2005, p. 191). This was chiefly due to kin who live outside Britain in English-speaking Commonwealth countries. 'What we find therefore is a population that do spread beyond national confines to embrace broader global contacts which are strongly orientated to former imperial colonies'. By contrast, Savage et al. found fairly few people who might be termed 'citizens of the world' through possessing a global outlook. Those who do were appar-ently products of turbulent life histories 'usually through having lived in different nations or having served in the armed forces overseas'. They were 'highly unusual vis-à-vis other local residents, and mostly out of step with their current surrounds'. In light of this, Savage et al. (2005, p. 202) conclude: 'Global reflexivity does not seep into people's lives because of the pervasive-ness and power of global idioms and cues, but depends on local and personal circumstances.' As indicated, insofar as they detected a global reflexivity, it was one 'shaped primarily by a white, English speaking, diaspora rather than by any far reaching cosmopolitanism'. The authors do not make the point directly but this of course reflects the continuing salience of an earlier phase of globalization, that is, empire.

The wider finding of Savage et al. is that the basis of much theorizing that hinges on an opposition between the global and the local, especially prevalent in Castells and Giddens, is suspect. Savage et al. (2005, p. 204) state that there is no evidence in 'half a million words of transcript' that people define their identity by drawing on this binary as one of contrast and opposition. Rather, they are aware of the connectivities in which their lives are located. As such, they recognized and expressed awareness of global influences within their immediate localities. This is very different from a conscious recognition of a set of global concerns that are set apart from the local and in some way challenge it. Hence the local versus cosmopolitan dichotomy just does not hold water. Insofar as there are wider horizons of consciousness, they are born of diaspora. While the concern of *Globalisation and Belonging* (Savage et al., 2005) is civic as opposed to national identity, this central finding has obvious implications for Beck's assertion that the cosmopolitan citizen stands in self-conscious opposition to the national.

A third criticism of cosmopolitanism – one which would actually apply to Savage et al.'s account – is that it fails to distinguish between transnationalism and cosmopolitanism. Caglar (2002) makes the point that transnational connections generally exist through ethnocultural groups. This in turn relates to the above discussion of long-distance nationalisms as being especially virulent ones. If the world is beset by them, as Anderson claims, it is far from becoming a place of greater toleration and mutual acceptance. Finally, cosmopolitan projections of global interconnections make little allowances for socioeconomic class. Again Beck is a particular culprit in this respect. Craig Calhoun argues that writings on cosmopolitanism are not really sociological at all, and their excessive optimism puts them at risk of being about ethics or simply wishful thinking. In respect of the emergence of cosmopolitan class factions, they are the ones that are at the forefront of global capitalism. In a passage that has echoes of Davidson and Yates's research on American CEOs, Calhoun (2002, p. 106) states:

> Cosmopolitanism – though not necessarily cosmopolitan democracy – is now largely the project of capitalism, and it flourishes in the top management of multinational corporations and even more in the consulting firms that serve them. Such cosmopolitanism often joins elites across national borders while ordinary people live in local communities. This is not simply because common folk are less sympathetic to diversity – a self serving notion of elites. It is also because the class structuring of public life excludes many workers and others.

In the face of this, Calhoun argues not for some form of cosmopolitan democracy, but a recognition that nationalism has a historic relationship to democracy and is not necessarily reactionary and exclusive. Therefore it is a vital sentiment to draw on the face of capitalist uniformity.

Conclusion

The conclusion to this chapter can only be disappointing for anybody looking for any kind of concise summation of globalization and national cultures. That could only be done by concentrating on one emergent trend to the exclusion of others and/or by caricaturing discrete national pasts as compared to an amorphous global present. But saying this does not mean that certain conclusions cannot be drawn from the above discussion. Difficult as the subject is to define, it is not without definite trends even if it seems that one cannot express one without immediately signalling its opposite if not equal. With further caveats about how the list is only indicative, not exhaustive, I suggest that there are several points to be made.

Globalization has indeed imparted a never previously experienced degree of cultural similarity. Global cultures may have existed before through conquest and empire but they were inevitably more geographically limited than is the case today. Never before have the populations of the world shared such a degree of common interests and consumer forms as relayed by technology and transportation across the planet. Such interests and products are necessarily neither peculiar nor exclusive to a particular group. This is captured by the term 'homogenization'. The form that cultural homogenization takes is not neutral but is strongly influenced by the world's most powerful and richest nation, the USA. To be more precise, it takes the form of American life as portrayed and conveyed by its media and entertainment conglomerates. It is one that encounters varying degrees of resentment and cynicism, but even in the regions where it encounters overt hostility – not just the Arab world, but also parts of South America, Asia and Europe – it has a widespread appeal. This development is captured by the term 'Americanization'.

These points are at odds with the postmodern penchant in cultural studies to portray globalization as fragmentation. Although, as implied, I think this trend has been exaggerated for interior theoretical reasons, we should note as a second conclusion that cultural globalization involves heterogeneity. Even in those studies made by researchers who are not intellectually predisposed to uncover variation, a picture of eclecticism emerges, in which the imposition of global cultures is moderated by national filters, resulting in varied outcomes. Simultaneously, the technological forms upon which global culture is disseminated are utilized by domestic actors – commercial, political and artistic – to further repackage forms of national culture. Among those writers who are predisposed to detect difference, a picture emerges in their mediations of a world of national cultures increasingly broken up, hybridized, by the impact of migrants who retain connections – personal, cultural and political – to national pasts by dint of modern communication technologies. In the more extreme version of this thesis, alternative cultures arise out of the maelstrom of migration and media. I noted a tendency to romanticize the plight of the migrant in some of this depiction, but there is no doubt that the quickening pace of migration is having an unsettling effect on national cultures.

This leads to another conclusion to be drawn from the above discussion. Qualifications about no 'golden ages' are particularly apt here. However, to return to Held's distinction that one should attempt to delineate between the impact of globalization on cultures and the context for the reception of culture, it seems that contemporary migration coupled with technological transformation are shifting the cultural ground underneath the feet of nations. Education, community and media within the state and civil society that, together with the family, act as the key agencies of national socialization now exist in a changed context. Globalization is serving to dilute ethnic and cultural population majorities in a way that confounds the historic assumptions of nationalists. This does not necessarily portend a future of domestic confusion, as long-distance nationalisms crisscross the world while states increasingly lack the political will or ultimately the national raison d'être to compel their populations to see themselves as fellow nationals. It is folly in all things to discount the continuing organizational power of the nation-state and the political chameleon that is nationalism. But it certainly does represent a changed cultural context. Here, as much as in relation to any other aspect of our subject, globalization has signalled an as yet undetermined challenge to nationalism.

Summary Points

- In considering the issues discussed in this chapter, it is important to bear two things in mind: global cultures are not historically new and national cultures are themselves composed of various influences.
- A much debated issue in the social sciences is whether globalization is serving to homogenize culture and thereby flatten the distinctive nature of national cultures.
- The proposition that culture is being homogenized looks at how American products and values are conveyed across the world by multinational companies.

- While aspects of this thesis are obviously true, writers have generally found it too simplistic as it assumes that people passively drop their own culture and 'buy into' a monolithic American one.
- The few studies that have actually examined this question have found that the process is more complex as aspects of older national cultures are vibrant and have actually been stimulated in some instances by foreign influences.
- A more influential thesis is that of heterogeneity. This thesis looks at how migration and media have served to fragment national cultures. Although overstating its case, it is true that the ethnic homogeneity of peoples is being undermined by the scale of contemporary migration.
- This argument is supplemented by a third subject considered, that of cosmopolitanism, which suggests that societies and peoples are forced to recognize that 'their way' is only one among many.

6

Nationalism, Globalization and Islam

Introduction

This chapter examines whether world religion, specifically Islam, can be considered a global force. The matter can be directly put at the outset: what evidence is there that radical currents of contemporary Islam, spurred by currents within globalization, are challenging nations and nationalism through the endeavour to form a world caliphate through a unified 'ummah', a single indivisible Muslim congregation? The question is rather crude as it concurs with a perception, found in Britain and elsewhere, that Muslims are a united people whose commitment to each other outweighs allegiance to the particular nation-state they are in, and who seek to impose their religion through an Islamic government and sharia law everywhere, whether they are the majority of the population or not. Even if one were to assume that Islam, given the authority of the Koran,[1] is relatively clear and unambiguous in its instruction to all believers, the reality is that there is anything but unity among Muslims. There is division within and between Muslim countries in the Middle East and Asia and among Muslim minorities elsewhere. Therefore the idea that there is a basic 'oneness' among all Muslims that overrides divisions of ethnicity, nationality and variant of faith (principally Shia and Sunni Islam) is nonsense. This point was made by various scholars in the 1990s responding to Huntington's well-known 'clash of civilizations' thesis (first made in 1993, and expanded in 1998). In it, Huntington argued not that Islam acted not so much as a global phenomenon, but as a regional one that ran up against the West in a world where, after the end of the Cold War, cultural conflict, rather than ideology or economics, is the greatest division facing humankind.

Consideration of whether or not Islam, as an organizing principle for humanity, poses a global challenge to nationalism assumes the existence of the threat, cultural and/or terrorist (one implicit in Huntingdon), that Muslims present wherever they are. It concurs therefore with perceptions post 9/11 that Muslims per se present a danger to Western and Asian societies and, in a fundamentalist guise, in countries in the Middle East and elsewhere where they are in the majority. Daniel Pipes (quoted in Milton-Edwards, 2004, p. 192), the right-wing American commentator, colourfully puts it thus:

> To me every fundamentalist Muslim, no matter how peaceable in his own behaviour, is part of a murderous movement and is thus, in some fashion, a foot soldier in the war that Bin Laden has launched against civilization. They are barbarians and must be treated as such.

This issue, Islam as threat, is not one that I address in this chapter. However, its latter stage, the key section, does deal with whether or not what the French writer Olivier Roy refers to as 'neofundamentalism' represents a global phenomenon.

The chapter first discusses the contention that Islam is incompatible with nations and nationalism. The chapter then looks in brief at historic issues of ethnic/national distinction within Muslim societies as they arose from the seventh century and, specifically, at the attitude of Islamic reformers in the nineteenth and twentieth centuries to nationalism, an aspect of the Muslim response to invading European powers. In the mid-twentieth century, nationalism, both in a pan-Arab guise and in local variants, was more powerful than Islam in the struggle for colonial independence. The subsequent phase of Middle Eastern and Asian history saw a definite Islamic reaction against the political pre-eminence that nationalism had taken in the Muslim world. The chapter notes the views of the principal figures who offered at some level a different model of organization for Muslims, one of Islamic states. The attempts over the past 40 years or so to build Islamic states, infuse religion into national liberation struggles, and, more generally, to reassert the centrality of Koranic teachings in all aspects of life can be grouped under the heading of 'Islamism'. Here I consider whether it has succeeded in displacing the centrality of nationalism in the Middle East in particular. My scepticism that it has leads to a final consideration, largely through the thesis of Roy (2004), that we are currently entering a new phase of a distinctly global Islam. Discussion concludes with a critical assessment of Roy's thesis through an examination of the pronouncements of the figurehead of al-Qaeda, Osama bin Laden.

I note definitions of terms as and when it is relevant to do so as the discussion develops. It is worth mentioning at the outset that I am of course aware that the Muslim world is not confined to the Middle East. In fact, a minority of Muslims live in that region of the world. However, as this chapter is based on the work of others and as there is a tendency to treat the three things – the Middle East as a region, the Arabs as a people and Islam as a religion – as one and the same thing, even when the author initially cautions against so doing, much of the following discussion is, in fact, about this area. Moreover, this is in some respects perfectly understandable, as the Middle East was the area in which Islam originated and, to this day, forms its locus, notwithstanding more numerous Muslim societies in Asia and the substantial size of the Muslim populations in parts of Europe.

Islam, Nations and Nationalism

There are various levels at which it has been suggested that Islam as a religious faith and therefore Muslims as people(s) are in some way at odds with nations and nationalism. Pieterse (2005, p. 83) states without qualification that: 'Islam is at odds with the modern state and nationalism, and thus it has been argued that it has no place to accommodate modern international relations.' Although Piertse does not adopt the sort of orientalist tone associated with, in particular, the writings on the Arab world of Bernard Lewis, his implication that Islam acts as an ideological impediment to modernity is similar. Piertse (2005, p. 86) also thinks that Islam is ambivalent about capitalism, a contention he makes without recognizing that there is as much criticism of mammon in the Bible as in the Koran. Conversely, there is a historic connection between Muslims and the expansion of trade from the time of Muhammad, himself a merchant. In our age, parts of the contemporary Islamic world, the United Arabs Emirates for example, are just as 'capitalist' as New York, London or Shanghai – perhaps more so (Bhatia, 2008).

A second view, put by Peter Mandaville (2007, p. 11) in an otherwise masterly overview of contemporary Islam and politics, is that nation-states and national identities did not historically gestate in the Middle East as they did in Europe. He does not posit an incompatibility between Islam as a religion and nationalism as a political ideology as such, but nevertheless suggests that nations did not evolve in an 'organic' fashion in the region, instead they have done so through imposition from above. Leaving aside liberalism and without dwelling further on market capitalism, the notion that modern national identity arose organically in Europe is mistaken. *Peasants into Frenchmen* (Weber, 1877) is the title of one of the most important books in the history of the study of nationalism, an encapsulation of how the French state imposed a common Gallic identity on its different social classes and disparate geographical regions. A case could be made for stronger historic national identities in the Arab world than in Europe, given a shared language derived from a common religion.

Such academic criticisms are rather different from a third argument, one made by Muslim authorities, that nationalism is contrary to Islam. As indicated above, such claims form part of the later discussion of Islamism. The line of reasoning is generally that the essential unity of Muslims that existed through and as an expression of an overriding administrative caliphate (latterly through the Ottoman Empire) was corrupted by the divisive influence of nationalism, part of the wider distortion of Muslim civilization visited upon them by Western Christian invaders and craven Muslim leaders. Speaking of early Islamic society, the Indian, then Pakistani scholar and politician Sayyid Abul A'la Mawdudi (1967, pp. 14–15) states: 'Differences on the basis of nationality, race and tribal conflicts did crop up now and again . . . But the idea that the Muslims of the world constitute one Amah remained intact.' Ruhollah Khomeini (1981, p. 332), the first leader of the Islamic Republic of Iran, 1979–89, expressed similar sentiments, although he saw fit to blame the Arabs for the loss of early Islamic unity:

> Unfortunately, true Islam lasted for only a brief period after its inception. First the Umayyads and the Abbasids inflicted all kinds of damage on Islam . . . Their rule was based on Arabism, the principle of promoting the Arabs over all other peoples, which was an aim fundamentally opposed to Islam and its desire to abolish nationality and unite all mankind in a single community, under the aegis of a state indifferent to the matter of race and colour.

In his book *Ummah or Nation* (1992), the Muslim scholar Abdullah al-Ahsan also depicts a lost unity, but suggests that it occurred in the twentieth century, in an account that argues that Islamic and national identities are incompatible. He says that their combination in a state – for the most part, he is concerned with Pakistan, a Muslim state established after the partition of India following independence from Britain in 1948 – that claims to be Islamic and simultaneously national gives rise to a wholesale identity crisis among Muslims. Thus: 'With the development of nationalism, and in particular the emergence of Muslim nation-states, the Muslims seem to have become somewhat confused about where their first loyalty lies – whether primary loyalty belongs to the ummah or to the nation-state' (al-Ahsan, 1992, p. 29).

Finally, it is worth mentioning the view of a contemporary writer, Graham Fuller (2003, p. 19), that the unity of the Muslim ummah makes for a post-national togetherness that is propitious to globalization. He thinks that it can act as a identity akin to feelings of regional unity among the peoples of Europe with the EU. The implication of his argument is that nationalisms and nation-states in the Middle East are less of an impediment to regionalization than elsewhere, as they are artificial entities, the nonorganic products of imperialism.

The Koran – the word of God to a believer as conveyed through his prophet Muhammad, and the word of Muhammad to a nonbeliever – contains some 64 references to the ummah, the community of believers. From the time of Muhammad to the late medieval period, the word carried quasi-ethnic connotations: the Muslims as distinct from the Franks and so on. Gerasikmos Makris (2007, pp. 45–53) points to ongoing ambivalence surrounding the term, a tension 'characterizing the dialectical relationship between the global vision of the worldwide imagined Community of Believers and the ways in which this translated in specific Islamic societies, informing and being informed by local idioms and world views'. Such a tension is given sharp illustration by his discussion of how in Islamist Sudan over the past 20 years, membership of the ummah has been an official means of classifying who possesses bona fide national identity and who does not. In this inventory, northern Arabs have qualified as properly Sudanese by dint of their inclusion within the fold of the historic ummah compared to second-class African Muslims who live in the south of the country. So in this case and others, far from acting as a pole of wider Muslim unity in contrast to the exclusiveness of nationalism, member-ship of the ummah can act as an axis of discrimination.

In methodological terms, general considerations on Islam being either compatible or incompatible with nationalism are altogether too vague. Rather, as Makris (2007, p. 1) suggests, a case by case, country by country approach is a more fruitful line of inquiry. His favoured method is to approach Islam not as an object, but as a 'discursive tradition, a movement within the flow of history' that becomes 'concretized at particular times'. For this reason, besides more substantive issues, he is sceptical of Gellner's influ-ential attempts to provide an interpretative understanding of Islam and national identity in the Middle East, based on a distinction he drew between local and literate traditions of Islam. Insofar as he does subscribe to an iden-tifiable method of understanding the relationship between nationalism and Islam in the Muslim world, it is one in which the state rulers draw upon reli-gious sentiment in nation-building – nationalisms imposed from above through authoritarian states. Makris (2007, pp. 48–51) refers to studies by Zubaida of Iraq and Syria that confirm such a political trajectory. In such cases, the state has acted as a 'zone of imagination', in which a recognition of, if not necessarily a loyalty to, the nation was imposed and ruthlessly enforced during the twentieth century.

Further examples could be taken from outside the Middle East. For example, in the former central Asian countries of Kazakhstan, Kyrgyzstan, Tajikistan, Turkmenistan, and Uzbekistan (collectively, the stans), Islam has been used to bolster authoritarian nationalisms since the break-up of the Soviet Union (Pottenger, 2005, p. 145). Of course, such an attempt to combine nationalism and Islam will be viewed by some as a cynical exercise in power politics. No doubt many Muslims took just this view of Saddam Hussein's attempt to present himself as an Arab Muslim leader in the traditions of Saladin in the latter period of his totalitarian rule of Iraq. However, the preva-lence of the fusion of religion with national identity in the Arab world and Asia means that abstract claims about Islam's incompatibility with nations and nationalism are meaningless in practical terms. Like other religions, Islam does posit a wider collective. Indeed, the Koran refers to a single community of believers, an ummah, united under Allah. However, in practice, it has not only been subject to the influence of the local and particular – traditions and ideologies, nationalism in recent history – but conjoins with them. Accordingly, contemplation of the related question of whether membership of a nation-state detracts from the primary Muslimness of a people is, again, a rather pointless question. As Makris (2007, p. 52) argues, nation-states are, in general terms, neither more nor less alien to Muslims than they are to any other wider groups of co-religionists.

Islam and Arab Nationalism

This said, it is true that direct consideration of the utility of nationalism, more specifically the nation-state and its compatibility with Islam, only occurred in the Muslim world with the intrusion of modern European imperialist powers from the late eighteenth century within a wider response to the Enlightenment. Specifically, the French invasion of Egypt in 1798 prompted an ongoing discourse in the Muslim world of a loss of unity in the face of external aggression. Egypt had been part of the Ottoman Empire since 1515. Naturally, not all the considerations were approving. The most important figure in nineteenth-century intellectual and political debate was Jamal al-Din al-Afghani (1838–97) who, while advocating an Islamic response to the challenges posed by European advancements in science and industry, was by no means critical of modern nationalism. The Egyptian Hassan al-Banna (1906–49), a key figure in the early twentieth century and founder of the Muslim Brotherhood, the single most important Islamic organization in history, seems at times to have wished to take the terms and concepts of nations and nationalism and use them for pan-Islamic purposes. For example, he stated that: 'The Horizon of the Islamic fatherland transcends the boundaries of geographical and blood nationalisms to create a nationalism of high principles, pure beliefs and the truths which God has made a source of light and guidance for the world at large' (quoted in al-Ahsan, 1992, p. 26). Roxanne Marcotte (2005, p. 77) suggests that al-Banna's vision of a revitalized Islam, as set out in his tract 'Our Mission', was one based on Muslims organizing and leading educational and charitable schools and foundations. In such a way, he thought it could act as a crucial modernizing force for a resurgent Egypt. Even Muhammad Abduh (1849–1905), regarded as the founder of Islamic modernism, and an authority who was more explicit in his rejection of nationalism for pan-Islamization in the face of Western imperialism, confessed to loving his country and its people. It is possible to identify a tradition of Islamic modernism or reformism to this day. Naturally enough, scholars within this school continue to deal with nations and nationalism, given their importance, the implications for Islam and so on. For example, one present-day figure of some importance, Syrian Shaykh Muhammad Sa'id Ramadan al-Buti, sometimes dismissed as an apologist for the Assad regime in Damascus, names nationalism as one of the pillars of the Islamic state together with culture, education and religion itself (Makris, 2007, p. 183).

In terms of its political importance, Islamic reformism was of less significance than Arab nationalism in the 1920 and 30s and it receded further in the immediate aftermath of the independence of Arab countries from European control after 1945. Arab nationalists attempted to build a movement across the region that brought together its peoples in a single overarching state form to enable the 'rebirth' of their civilization in the face of division and external interference. Its supporters, mainly comprising students, officers, middle-class civil servants, professionals and intellectuals, rarely rejected Islam outright. On the contrary, whether Christian or Muslim, its spokesmen identified Islam as an important means by which a common culture and language had permeated the Middle East to create a single Arab people. This was true, for example, of the Syrian writer and administrator Sati al-Husri (1879–1967; for the life of this exemplary figure, see Cleveland, 1971) and the Lebanese academic George Antonius (1891–1941), author of the influential *The Arab Awakening*, published in 1938. Some even tried to co-opt Islam in a socialist form of Arab nationalism, suggesting that the root of the problems of the Arab world originated through tyrannical leaders, supported by a corrupt 'ulema' (Muslim scholars trained in Islam and Islamic law). This had made them vulnerable to imperialist aggression and exploitation from Europeans, the materialistic invaders with whom they had cooperated. Ernest Dawn (2000, pp. 47–8) comments that this interwar discourse posited a return to 'true Islam, science and learning that would restore Arab unity and vigour, restore the Arab nation to its lost rightful position in world leadership'. The conception is similar to contemporary fundamentalist projections of a restoration of an supposed Islamic golden age. However, the use of Islam by Arabists in this era was in relation to how it fostered unity within a modernizing pan-nationalism, rather than a religious force and destination – an Islamic state of some form – in itself.[2]

As indicated, Arab nationalism aimed at some level, more or less explicitly, to create an overarching Arab state with a centralized government. A move in this direction was made in 1958 with the formation of the United Arab Republic between Egypt and Syria, with plans for the inclusion of Iraq and North Yemen. However, the project only lasted three years, foundering on disagreement wrought by attempted Egyptian domination. The formation of an intended regional political party, the Arab Socialist Baath Party, in Damascus some years earlier actually succeeded in supplying an ideology of authoritarian state-building in Syria and Iraq from 1963 on when the respective branches took power. In general, the period of the late 1940s through to the humiliating defeat of Egypt by Israel in the Six Day War of 1967 was characterized by, on the one hand, lofty declarations at Arab League meetings of the need for unity in the face of Zionism – the ideology of Jewish state-building – and, on the other hand, much jockeying for regional leadership between rival state leaders. The most important rivalry, increasingly evident from the early 1960s, was that between the socialist-tinged Arab nationalism of President Nasser in Egypt and a pan-Islamic message from the rulers of Saudi Arabia, made partly by exiled Egyptian 'imams' (leaders of a mosque or a community) who escaped state persecution in Cairo to take up academic positions in Mecca, Medina and elsewhere in the Kingdom of Saudi Arabia (KSA).

Meanwhile, nation-states entrenched themselves across the region as a whole. Ille Pappe (2006, p. 506) comments that: 'In the formal realms of life, in this period [the 1960s], Arab nationalism as a modern ideology slowly disintegrated into the local national ideologies.' This does not mean that Arab nationalism, perhaps better called 'Arabism', was by the early 1970s a completely spent force. Aziz Al-Azmeh (2000, p. 75) talks of the creation over recent decades, despite appearances, of a shared regional political culture through a cohesive pan-Arab intelligentsia and civil institutions that transcend Arab boundaries, 'which the efforts of the Baath parties or the Arab League combined could not accomplish'. At a popular level, he points to a collective Arab culture through the regional popularity of Egyptian soap opera. However, the more profound point is that Arab nationalism failed to achieve regional unity.

Islamism

Scholars generally agree that the period from 1967 onwards sees a marked political shift in the Muslim world away from progressive strains of nationalism, Arab or more local. As Giles Kepel (2004, p. 5), the French authority on the Muslim world, puts it: 'Barely a generation after many Muslim nations won their independence, the Islamic world entered a religious era that largely cancelled out the nationalist period which preceded it'. Abdel Salam Sidahmed and Anonshiravan Ehteshami (1995, p. 6) talk of the Six Day War between Israel and Egypt, followed by the death of President Nasser four years later, as a 'disaster, which shocked the credibility of Arab nationalist/ populist regimes and forces and sowed the seeds of discontent that later sprouted as Islamist forces'. They say this led to a 'permanent reverse' in post-independence Middle East history characterized by 'slogans of liberation, development, and socialism'. Thereafter, although other populist regimes thrived in the region (in Iraq, Syria, Libya and Algeria), with similar structures and discourses, the tide was permanently reversed. The only possible problem with such analysis is that it implies that Islam had somehow been absent in the previous period when obviously this was not the case. Rather, it had not been at the centre of the political stage. The point is that the secular forms of nationalism as ideologies were vulnerable to attack by Islamic activists in a region of strong traditional religion, as nationalism was susceptible to being identified as a foreign imposter (Bruce, 2003). In the place of Arab nationalism, a new sociopolitical force was 'maturing rapidly – namely, Islamism' (Sidahmed and Ehteshami, 1995, p. 89).

'Islamism', or the more cumbersome 'Islamicism', is the term favoured by most academic observers to describe the trend. Others prefer 'political Islam', 'radical Islam' or 'Islamic fundamentalism'. 'Islamism' seems to have the advantage of being rather less controversial than the alternatives, especially Islamic fundamentalism, but conveying a projection of the essential relevance of Islam to all aspects of life.

Islamism should not be considered a revival of Islam so much as a selective reinterpretation and reassertion of its centrality, a point made by Fred Halliday (1994, p. 93). Most commentators stress the importance of politics to Islamism – the movement that has taken centre stage in the Muslim world since 1967. Thus Azza Karam (2005, p. 5), in making a preference for 'Islamism' over 'Islamic fundamentalism', says that it refers to a 'continuum of movements which have a quintessentially political agenda, revolving around Islamizing [rendering more Islamic] the structures of governance and the overall society'. Makris (2007, p. 193) refers to Islamicism as 'a particular form of Islamic assertiveness with clearly visible political traits and sometimes explosive methods'.

Clearly, the buildings of parties, clandestine and open, with a religious agenda, the attempt to take state power to implement sharia law and so on are political acts. My reservation with this stress is that it omits other developments in the Muslim world that have taken place over the past 40 years. Although they need not detain us in themselves, I am referring to cultural, business, media and consumer practices and innovations that fall within a wider emphasis on the centrality of Islam. Take the rise in the numbers of women wearing headscarves (the hijab) and the veil (the niqab) in Asia, the Middle East and Europe. Certainly this is part of a political agenda and one to be rigorously enforced, in the estimation of many its supporters, by the state as well as by ordinary Muslims. As Issam al-Arayan, an Egyptian doctor who was one of the main theorists of the extremist group Jamaat, put it: 'When the numbers of female students wearing the veil are high, we may take it as a sign of resistance to Western civilization and advent of iltizam, the strict observance of Islamic laws' (quoted in Kepel, 2002, p. 82). However, unless one were to believe that it is just a political gesture and/or an act of a male coercion, the wearing of the veil by Muslim women has to be understood as part of a wider religious and cultural movement. I would also place the international rise of Islamic banking – financial services that attempt to observe the prohibition in the Koran of interest or 'usury' being charged by lenders – and charitable and community work within this wider Islamist tendency in recent history. Once again such things cannot be neatly separated from politics. The credibility acquired by Islamic political parties, through their economic, welfare and educational capacities, has been crucial to their rise in the face of corrupt and indolent states and political elites. Hamas among Palestinian Muslims and Hezbollah with Shia Muslims in the Lebanon, the latter constituting a state within a state, are prime examples of this. But the point stands that to identify everything associated with the reassertion of Islam as 'political' is too restrictive.

The central claim above, that Islamism as a political movement involved an ostensible rejection of nationalism, specifically Arab nationalism, is, of course, a political one. What formal attitude have Islamists had, broadly, to nationalism in recent history? Here it is legitimate to note the following observations on nationalism of Sayyid Qutb (1906–66) and Mawdudi (1903–79), mentioned above. Their thinking is indicative of the more radical end of Islamism. If a figure like Sati al-Husri, with his idealistic vision of an inclusive pan-Arab state, was a figure who exemplified the previous era, the vision of Qutb and Mawdudi is more formally indicative of recent history – although they actually formulated and propounded their thinking on the subject in the mid-twentieth century when they were out of step with the times.

As indicated above, opposition to nationalism as a foreign ideology, imported into the Muslim world, is part of a wider Islamist rejection of Western values. Mawdudi's (1992, p. 13) calls for Islamic universalism should be seen in the context of his view that: 'Western civilization strikes at the very roots of that concept of ethics and culture which is the base of Islamic civilization . . . Islam and western civilization are like two boats sailing in totally opposite directions.' He counterpoised the sovereignty of the nation-state, as a centralized entity representing a nation, with the idea of 'Islamic sovereignty'. This is an ambiguous concept as, in practice, it allowed his role in Jamaat-e-Islami, a Pakistani, as opposed to a universalist, political party, committed to complete Islamicization of the country at the expense of any secular notions of nationhood.

Since 2001, Qutb has been presented as a sort of ideological mastermind to al-Qaeda.[3] In actual fact, his writings have a more mystical flavour than Wahhabism, the literalist school of Muhammad ibn Abd-al-Wahhab (1703–92), ideologue to both the contemporary Saudi Arabian religious establishment and Osama bin Laden and his followers. Furthermore, on at least some occasions, Qutb cautioned against the use of violence lest it sepa-

rated the perpetrators from ordinary Muslims. Leaving this aside, his opposition to nationalism was part of a more extensive condemnation of the West,
a place of 'jahiliyya' – unIslamic ignorance. Important to his thinking was a
two-year visit to America at the end of the 1940s. Mandaville (2007, p. 77)
comments that while he recognized the material achievements of American
society: 'He [Qutb] felt that these had been achieved at an unacceptable cost.
His account of American culture focused on what he saw as the devastating
erosion of capitalist individualism on the moral character of that society.' In
particular, Qutb was critical of the 'animalistic mixing' of the sexes (Calvert,
2000). Although initially sympathetic to the overthrow of the pro-British
Egyptian monarchy by Abdul Nasser and his Free Officers Movement in
1952, Qutb was subsequently rounded up and imprisoned in 1954 in a crack-
down on Islamic activists critical of the new regime. In jail, where he was
tortured and eventually executed in 1966, he wrote his most well-known
book, *Milestones*.

In *Milestones* (1985), he contrasts 'dar-ul-Islam', understood not as a territory but a 'homeland where faith rules and sharia of god holds sway', with
'dar-ul-Harb': 'any place where the Islamic sharia is not enforced and where
Islam is not dominant becomes the home of hostility'. There should be no
concessions to nationality within dar-ul-Islam whatsoever:

> Islam is not a few words, pronounced by the tongue, or birth in a country called
> Islamic, or inheritance from a Muslim father . . . The homeland of the Muslim, in
> which he lives and which he defends, is not a piece of land; the nationality of the
> Muslim, by which he is identified, is not the nationality determined by a govern-
> ment; the family of the Muslim, in which he finds solace and which he defends, is
> not blood relationships; the flag of the Muslim, which he celebrates and for which
> he is thankful to God, is not military victory . . . The fatherland is that place where
> the Islamic faith, the Islamic way of life, and the sharia of God is dominant; only this
> meaning of 'fatherland' is worthy of the human being. Similarly, 'nationality'
> means belief and a way of life, and only this relationship is worthy of man's dignity.
> (Qutb, 1985, p. 123)

This abstract ideal of Qutb can, at one level, serve as a starting point for any
evaluation for the actual political record of Islamists vis-à-vis nationalism
after 1967 and the dimming of Arab nationalism.

It would, however, be unfair to judge the actual record of Islamists against
this abstraction as inevitably their record will be found wanting, given the
reality of a political terrain dominated by nation-states, unfinished national
liberation struggles and Western imperialism. Nevertheless, we can point to
a series of events in recent history that have been taken to indicate the
upward surge of Islamism, in distinction to nationalism, beside the less
overtly political, more cultural and business developments mentioned above.

The first was the Iranian Revolution of 1979, successfully establishing an Islamic state under Ayatollah Khomeini and, at least for a time, championing Islamic movements against existing regimes across the Muslim world, while railing against American imperialism. Second, with the immediate qualification that it did not receive fulsome support from Iran, the successful mujahedeen (fundamentalist Muslim guerrillas) opposition to the Soviet occupation of Afghanistan from 1980 that achieved, with substantial US backing, the effective defeat and withdrawal of the Red Army in 1989. After the toppling of the Soviet successor government of President Najibullah in 1992, there were a series of Islamic governments, culminating in that of the Taliban between 1996 and the American invasion of autumn 2001. The role of the Afghanistan wars over the past 30 years has been seen as crucial to the rise of Islamism. In military terms, it drew together an internationalist band of Islamic fighters in the 1980s, who subsequently sought to take their struggle elsewhere. Ideologically, it produced a captive audience of Afghan boys and young men who were subject to an educational curriculum consisting solely of Koranic study in the 'madrassas' (religious schools) in the refugee camps along the Pakistani border. A further Islamist state success has been the governments in Sudan since 1989, notwithstanding the shift in emphasis since the removal of the internationalist ideologue Hassan al-Turabi from power in 1999 by President Omar al-Bashir.

During the 1990s, violent campaigns were conducted by Jamaat al-Islamiyya in Egypt and the Islamic Salvation Front (FIS) in Algeria. The same decade witnessed the rise of Islamic movements in Bosnia and Chechnya, in the context of civil war and external occupation respectively. From its foundation in 1987 partly from the Muslim Brotherhood, the Palestinian Islamic political party Hamas has grown in popular support within the West Bank and the Gaza Strip. In January 2006, it replaced Fatah, the main faction of the Palestinian Liberation Organization (PLO), as the largest political party in the legislature of the Palestinian Authority. To the north in the Lebanon, Hezbollah, the Shia Muslim organization, has entrenched its power base and extended its political support, despite the best attempts of the Israeli army to dislodge it over the summer of 2006. Recent history has seen the emergence of al-Qaeda as an international Islamic terrorist network, committed to taking jihad, holy war, to the Western enemy and overthrowing 'apostate' Muslim governments. As is well known, the organization is capable of executing attacks as spectacular as those of 9/11 in America in 2001. Meanwhile, the past decade has seen the success in local and national elections of Islamic political parties in a variety of countries across Asia, the Middle and Near East and Africa. The government of the Justice and Development Party in contemporary Turkey would be an important instance of this.

Besides these political events, it is also legitimate to identify the transnational Muslim reactions against acts that were considered blasphemy against the Prophet Muhammad as indicative of the rise of Islamism. Muslims world-wide protested against the publication of Salman Rushdie's novel *The Satanic Verses* in 1989. Anxious to try to renew his credentials as an international Islamist, Ayatollah Khomeini, the then political leader of Iran, famously pronounced a 'fatwa', an injunction for all Muslims to seek to kill, on Rushdie. More recently, the publication in a Danish newspaper in 2005 of a cartoon of Muhammad, deemed insulting by many Muslims, provoked protests across Europe, the Middle East and Asia. Some crowds in Muslim countries ransacked and burnt Western embassies and tried to kill their staff.

It should be obvious that these developments should not be considered as some sort of coherent and united movement. On the contrary, several of them were in themselves divisive for Islamists. For example, the Taliban government in Afghanistan was condemned for its barbarism by some leading Islamic figures. The murderous campaign of Jamaat al-Islamiyya against tourists visiting Egypt alienated a large section of its domestic support, while the indiscriminate violence of FIS (notwithstanding controversy over the role of the Algerian army in some of the worst atrocities) led to widespread revulsion in Algeria and beyond. Nevertheless, they exist as events in what can be considered within the overarching rise of Islamism in recent decades.

There is debate among scholars as to what extent Islamism should be considered a success or not. It is not our concern to enter into it in detail here, suffice it to mention that Kepel (2002), a commentator who, as revealed above, sees a marked turn in the political orientation of the region from the early 1970s away from nationalism, thinks that political Islam has been more or less a complete failure. Although it is possible to detect a slightly different tone from this line in his most recent book, *The War for Muslim Minds: Islam and the West* (2004), Kepel (2004, p. 72) claims that since 1979 no Sunni political movement has come close to replicating the mass mobilization of the 'Shia unrest that caused bazaar merchants and disinherited underclass to overthrow the shah of Iran in 1979'. He thinks that with the exception of Afghanistan under the Taliban, which in itself did not present a replicable model for an Islamic state and society, their attempts to take state power across the Muslim world have led to disappointment over the past 20 years due to the strength of existing states and/or a failure to win the hearts and minds of local populations.

Seen in this light, the 9/11 attacks on America, intended to 'rouse Muslims across the world in solidarity against the American offensive and sweep Islamists to power in Muslim countries', represented not so much the high watermark of political Islam but a signal of its demise (Kepel, 2002, p. 4). As Kepel (p. 375) puts it: 'In spite of what many commentators contended in its immediate aftermath, the attack on the United States was a desperate symbol of isolation, fragmentation and decline of the Islamist movement, not a sign of its strength and irrepressible might.' Moreover, far from the act triggering a mass uprising among Muslims, it led to catastrophe for Islamists in Afghanistan and then in Iraq. More generally, Kepel considers that the advantages of terrorism – 'its suddenness, its use of surprise and its anonymity – are also its greatest weaknesses when the time comes to reap the political dividends' (p. 16). Thus, violence 'has proven to be a death trap for Islamists as a whole, precluding any capacity to hold and mobilize the range of constituencies they need to seize power' (p. 376).

Mandaville (2007) takes issue with the starkness of Kepel's sort of 'death of Islamism' argument. He points to an emerging political pragmatism of Islamists across the Muslim world as, where possible, they generally now participate in elections and, when elected, parliaments. He suggests that their recent commitment to constitutional arrangements and recognition of ruling establishments was learnt the hard way through the failure of violence to achieve anything other than brutal state repression in the 1990s. Mandaville (2007, p. 146) suggests that the electoral support of Islamist parties is not due primarily to any popular belief that the full implementation of sharia law will solve everything, but to their reputation as a relatively honest alternative to the status quo, based on their civic activity. Egypt serves as a good example of Mandaville's argument, where the Muslim Brotherhood continues to grow in size and influence within the national parliament – constitutionally, opposition parties cannot hold a majority of the seats anyway – despite the fact that it is officially banned. That Islamic parties are capable of being democratic – as opposed to having no truck with any opposition party and a secular constitution – would appear to be evidenced by the behaviour in power of the ruling Justice and Development Party in Turkey. Although the matter is complex and hinges on the actions and attitude of the Israeli government, it is possible that Hamas, widely condemned as a terrorist organization, may come to recognize the state of Israel in return for a genuine political settlement. However, whatever the implications of current events for the longer term orientation of Islamic political parties, it is the case that Kepel and Mandaville appear to agree. Kepel (2002, p. 359) states: 'In Turkey, as in Jordan or Egypt, the devout middle class is now looking for an acceptable form of access to the system, a modus vivendi with the regimes in place and with the secular bourgeoisie.'

A rather different sort of analysis is provided by another French authority on Islam, Olivier Roy. In Roy's (1994) view, Islamism has never actually superseded nationalism despite pretences to the contrary. He points out that Islamic political parties have only succeeded in gaining substantial support in the Muslim world insofar as they have adapted the issues of nation to an Islamic agenda. With typical boldness, Roy (2004, p. 70) contends that: 'Islam is never a strategic factor. The religious dimension always contributes to more basic ethnic and national factors, even if it provides afterwards a discourse of legitimation and mobilisation.' Islamic organizations are actually themselves the product of their local environments: 'Despite their claim to be supranational most Islamist movements are shaped by national particularities' (p. 62). Roy thinks that the abstract quality of Islamist claims that their struggle is a universal one against apostate and 'kafir' (nonbeliever) states just does not square with the reality that they and their opponents are actually 'rooted in history'.

The only qualification that Roy makes to this analysis is that of the Islamic opposition to the ruling classes of Saudi Arabia and Pakistan. Roy (2004, p. 66) attributes 'the scarcity of Islamo-nationalists' in those countries to the difficulty in defining them as nation-states. Both regimes tend to justify themselves by 'pretending to herald a transnational Muslim identity'. As a result, the political complexion of Islamists is shaped by their opposition to that claim. Therefore, in the KSA, they take issue not first and foremost with the monarchy for its misadministration of the Saudi nation-state, but with its principal claim to be the valid custodians of the holy mosques of Mecca and Medina. Important as these exceptions are, Roy (2004, p. 44) is quite sure that the 'key to understanding the contemporary territorial struggle is nationalism and ethnicity, not religion'. To this end, he identifies Chechen and Palestinian movements as instances of 'classic modern liberation struggles'. He does not spend any time discussing the 'national' nature of the Iranian revolution; although the country is important in his analysis for other reasons we will shortly look at.

Others have made the point that, in crucial respects, the Iranian revolution conformed to a wider pattern of national identity and interest trumping an internationalist message. Sami Zubaida (2004) notes that article fifteen of the revolutionary constitution stipulated that only somebody of Iranian nationality could be president, with the result that Jalaloddin Farsi, a long-time disciple of Khomeini, could not stand in the election of 1980 because his mother was Afghan. Despite the Shia Muslim basis to national identity, Iranian religious minorities – Christians, Jews, Zoroastrians – were granted certain citizenship rights as Iranians, short of standing for office. The nationalization of the revolution became more entrenched as war with Iraq, launched with American approval by Saddam Hussein in September 1980, dragged on and the called-for Islamic revolution across the Muslim world failed to occur. Zubaida (2004, p. 416) continues:

> The war with Iraq sharpened the sense of national identity of the revolution as Iranian and Shi'i against a hostile Arab (predominately Sunni) world. Khomeini and the other leaders spoke frequently of the Muslim nation of Iran. The Iranian nation, in their discourse, was the vanguard of the Islamic revolution of the world. The direction of the revolutionary propaganda and subversion to other parts of the region, notably Syria and Lebanon, followed the logic of Iranian national interest. The analogy drawn by many observers is that of Russia and communism: internationalist rhetoric and nationalist foreign policy, the logic of 'socialism in one country'. In Iran, too, the failure of the rest of the Muslim world to follow the path

of revolution (on Islamic terms) and the hostilities of enemies lead to a retrenchment of the Islamic Republic as a national project, which fits with the older forms
of Iranian nationalism. Predictably, with the waning of the initial revolutionary
flush and rhetoric, the Islamic republic is routinised into a national state like the
others, with a distinct Iranian identity in religion, culture and politics.

If this then was the fate of Islamism in the one instance where its proponents
effectively succeeded in taking state power, it remains to be considered if the
current era of globalization is producing a worldwide movement that is
succeeding, directly or indirectly, in superseding the power of nationalism. In
doing this, discussion concentrates on Roy's original and at times quite brilliant writings. First, however, we consider the general ways in which scholars have depicted the impact of globalization on Muslims.

The Threat and Opportunity of Globalization to Muslims

The following is not intended as a comprehensive overview of this matter.
However, we can identify a number of points that observers have made,
admittedly some times rather off the cuff. The first is that globalization presents, broadly, a threat to Muslims. There are a number of points here. Several
scholars have emphasized that accentuated global inequality will impact
disproportionately on Muslims, swelling a resentment that produces a violent
reaction. The premise is that as a population aggregate, Muslims in Europe,
the Middle East and Asia predominately belong to the less well off of the
world's population. In this vein, Beverley Milton-Edwards (2004, p. 83) states:
'Global economic visions have enriched the Western countries to a far greater
extent than those of Muslim countries.' She also claims, rather bizarrely: 'In
this respect Islamists represent one strand of the anti-global movement that
tends to be more commonly associated with long haired environmental
protestors rather than bearded Muslim ones.' Others stress that globalization,
understood as the advance of markets and its attendant neoliberal ideology,
has brought social disruption and dislocation within the Muslim world.
Akbar Ahmed (2007, p. 66), in a rare break from self-aggrandizement in his
book, *Journey Into Islam*, says: 'With advancing globalization, Muslim culture
and religion may again be entering a period of crisis, not unlike that faced by
the Muslim community in 1857 under the prospect of British-ruled India.'
Similarly, Kepel (2002, p. 370) suggests: 'As the twenty-first century dawned,
this dilution of Islamist ideology within a global market economy took place
in an environment that was very different from that of the previous decades.'
Issues of injustice and external intrusion are no doubt key to the perception

of some Muslims that globalization, in respect to economic trends and American imperial might, is a distinctly Western phenomenon designed to inflict further suffering upon them.

A second, and not necessarily contradictory point, is that globalization, this time understood in relation to communication technology and migration, is actually leading to the further spread of Islam. On the one hand, this refers to the intensification of Islam within its historic areas. For example, Greg Fealy (2005, p. 156) points to the role upon their return home of Indonesian and Malaysian migrant workers, influenced by Wahhabi Islam while in Saudi Arabia, in what he terms the 'Islamic revival' in those countries over the past 30 years. On the other hand, there has been the relatively recent formation of large-scale Muslim populations within geographic areas, principally in Europe, outside its core zones of the Middle East, Asia and parts of Africa. In fact, academics who study Muslims in Europe tend now to refer to the phenomenon not as a migrant, diasporic or 'transplanted' grouping, but an established one, given that much of its composition, certainly in France, Britain and Germany, consists of the children and grandchildren of migrants who came from North Africa and Asia in the post-1945 era. In the estimation of Pieterse (2005), cultural theorist of globalization, European Muslims of various nationalities now form part of a wider transnational ummah whose communication links and thus self-consciousness have been aided by global-ization. The political accompaniment of intensification and enlargement – feelings and perceptions of Islamic solidarity – is heightened through the perceived war on Muslims being waged by the West, understood as prima-rily the USA.

In the estimation of some, notably Dale Eickelman and James Piscatori (1996) and Roy (2004), the upshot of such developments, together with the impact of transnational Muslim organizations, is the 'decentring' of the Muslim world. Roy suggests that the ability of Muslim activists outside the Middle East to set up websites and make quasi-religious, political judgements – without a formal Islamic education – and in that way communicate with other Muslims worldwide bypasses the traditional authority exercised by the Islamic clergy, the ulema. Conversely, others have pointed out that the tradi-tional ulema have responded with websites and, more importantly, satellite TV channels of their own, while the most important development has been the dissemination of Wahhabi interpretations of Islam by dint of the enor-mous wealth behind its Saudi proponents – the single most important agency of what Makris (2007, p. 247) refers to as 'orthodoxy production'. The moti-vation is not just to proselytize. As mentioned above, the intention of the Saudi religious and political establishment in promoting Wahhabism in the 1960s was to counter Egyptian regional influence. In the 1980s, they sought to counter Iran's endeavours to speak for Muslims. More recently, the political purpose of Wahhabism has been to pre-empt the threat of al-Qaeda to the

Saudi ruling class from Muslims in the kingdom and beyond, with a form of Islam that is strict but highly politically conservative.

Third, and relating indirectly to both market ideology and the decentring of Islam, there has been a rise in Islamic consumerism. On the one hand, this consists of a whole range of products and services, notionally associated with Islam, for the Muslim consumer with sufficient cash or credit. Companies specializing in Islamic holiday resorts in Turkey and elsewhere would be an example of contemporary commercial religiosity (that which is excessively or sentimentally religious) as the obvious intention of the experience is not religion but pleasure. On the other hand, a Muslim – or a Christian, a Jew and so on – can, if they wish, seek the guidance of Koranic interpretation directly from an infinite variety of media sources without having to rely on the word of the imam of the local mosque or reading the holy book themselves. In practice, certain figures wield authority in this respect, giving them almost celebrity status. Sheikh Yusuf Al-Qaradawi, the Egyptian-born Muslim preacher, is probably the best example of this type of development. He conducts a weekly phone-in programme on the Qatar-based Al Jazeera TV station, in which he pronounces on a variety of topics, many of a lifestyle sort. Al-Qaradawi is particularly popular with the aspirant but would-be pious middle classes across the Gulf and wider Arab world, who seek Islamic guidance and approval in their individual choices for themselves and their families.

Finally, observers have pointed to the 'global nature' of al-Qaeda. In doing this, they have possibly been too keen in pointing out a paradox, as al-Qaeda is generally cast, not least because of its close relationship with the Taliban regime in Afghanistan, as set upon turning the clock back to a golden age of Islamic simplicity, one unsullied by the evils of modernity. There are a number of given aspects of 'the global' in al-Qaeda. Al-Qaeda is not a hierarchical and structured organization but rather a loose conglomeration or 'network' of cells with the spiritual figure of Osama bin Laden at its head. In this way, it has been suggested that it has the capability to appear, fade away and re-emerge without being vulnerable to government agencies' efforts to break the organization's lines of command through intercepting its terrorist operations, bombing its bases and assassinating its leaders (Kepel, 2004, p. 120). In 2009, eight years on from 9/11, such analysis seems somewhat misplaced, as al-Qaeda has failed to mount another terrorist attack on the mainland of its enemy, the USA. Insofar as it is true, the lack of an authoritative command structure within the organization has resulted in its 'poor performance' in Iraq. The murderous campaign of al-Qaeda against Shia Muslims, organized by Abu Musab al-Zarqawi until his death in 2006, apparently contrary to the wishes of bin Laden, only alienated local support. More recently, Ayman al-Zawahiri, the group's second in command, has complained of poor recruitment and internal communication between its bases in Iraq and outside.[4]

Leaving its possible inadequacies aside, this organizational versatility is thought to be furthered by its cosmopolitan personnel. Here the evidence suggests that most of its activists post 9/11 have been drawn from first-generation to third-generation European migrants who have drifted from the social margins towards extremist interpretations of Islam in recent years. As Marc Sageman (2006, p. 128) puts it, speaking of the young men drawn to al-Qaeda: 'The common themes in these trajectories were loneliness, alienation, marginalization, underemployment and exclusion from the highest status in the new or original society. Although the future terrorists were not religious, they drifted to mosques for companionship.' Others have emphasized the modern lifestyle of the terrorist, one quite incompatible with the Islam they espouse. Kepel (2004, p. 107) says, for example, that the 9/11 hijackers, themselves Saudi nationals, spent the night before their fateful day watching pay per view pornography in their hotel rooms.

The use of the internet and mobile phones for communication, websites and satellite TV for propaganda, and numerous accounts and layered investments – much of the money derived from bin Laden's construction wealth – to finance itself do clearly make al-Qaeda a distinctly global player. Whatever the instrumentality of its use of technology, this clearly puts the organization at odds with a vision of an Islamic future akin to the social simplicity of the time of the Prophet Muhammad. Kepel (2004, p. 112) contrasts their murky image with al-Qaeda's reality:

> True, Bin Laden and Zawahiri had been buyers at the bankrupt Soviet bazaar, where nuclear warheads and other dirty weapons were on offer at yard-sale prices; they also had suspicious friends in Baghdad and Tehran. But they were first and foremost children of an unlikely marriage between Wahhabism and Silicon Valley, which Zawahiri had visited in the early 1990s. They were heirs not only to jihad and the ummah but also the electronic revolution and American-style globalization. Despite their beards and the soap opera costumes they donned for Arab television audiences, they had ambitions and interests in common with hackers and cosmopolitan boys everywhere.

From these general themes of the relationship between globalization and Islam, we now consider the particular contribution of Roy to understanding the issue.

Roy and Global Neofundamentalism

We saw above how Roy, professor of religion at l'Ecole Practique des Hautes Etudes in Paris, is convinced that Islamism – the reassertion and politicization of Islam that took place in the Middle East after the perceived failure of Arab nationalism in the mid-twentieth century – signally failed in its attempt to trump the issues of nation with religious ones. Roy (2004, p. 83) argues that: 'By the late 1990s most of the Islamist movements had become more nationalist than Islamist. Their field of action is now largely limited to their own country.' It is not altogether clear if what Roy terms 'neofundamentalism' has similarly failed to supersede the issues of nation. It is safe to assume that he thinks it has not succeeded in doing so, inasmuch as he identifies nationalism as the continuing principal motivating force in the Muslim world as elsewhere. However, on another, not necessarily more profound but rather different level, he appears to view neofundamentalism as distinct from an ideology concerned with the state like Islamism and nationalism. As we will discuss, he thinks that it gels with an individualism wrought by globalization. The following discussion is derived mainly from his book *Globalised Islam* (Roy, 2004).

Although erudite, Roy's writings in general, and this book in particular, are marked by a series of iconoclastic claims seemingly designed not to baffle and frustrate the reader, as appears the case within, for example, some schools of French philosophy. However, some of his arguments appear counterintuitive to the point of being provocative. For example, one suspects that Roy intends a typical sentence in *Globalised Islam* (p. 3), such as, 'Islam is experiencing secularization, but in the name of fundamentalism', to lead at least to initial puzzlement. This said, Roy's depiction, as recently as 2000, of the main orientations of European Muslims was fairly conventional. Writing in 2000, Roy simply drew a contrast between a vocal fundamentalist school of thought that is attempting 'to build an unreconstructed community by preaching to individuals, and trying to address the real concerns of individuals who lost most of their community link', and 'the silent majority of the believers, who found their way on the basis of compromises, adaptations and makeshift ideology' (Roy, 2000, p. 5).

In *Globalised Islam*, Roy makes a sweeping link – it is not accompanied by any analysis of contemporary Christian movements in the USA or elsewhere – in the compatibility between globalization and neofundamentalist, both Christian and Muslim:

> Globalisation can be accommodated through a liberal reformist view of Islam, a charismatic and spiritual approach (like the Christian evangelical movements), or a neofundamentalist stress on sharia (laws) and ibadat (rituals). All of these approaches are based on individual reformulation of personal religiosity (even if it leads to a reaffirmation of the role of community). What the last two approaches share in common is that they reject any theological or philosophical dimension in favour of devotion (ibadat). Fundamentalism is synonymous with westernisation and above all is also (but not exclusively) a tool of westernisation. (Roy, 2004, p. 26)

This projection has led to criticism that the roots and orientation of contemporary Christian orthodoxy, certainly that which emanates from US churches, are interwoven with a far more strident individualism, derived from free-market ideology and the American dream (Makris, 2007, pp. 196–7). In fact, Roy (2004) claims that individual Muslims, even when seemingly far removed from the actual reality of the ummah while engrossed in the dark recesses of the World Wide Web, always maintain in their mind some notional psychological link to a physical community of believers. In other words, the individual religious journey for the neofundamentalist Muslim always takes place in relation to the collective body of the fellow faithful. However, the key similarity for Roy (2004, p. 34) between contemporary fundamentalisms, whether Christian or Muslim, is a common degree of individual, consumer-like choice, something that is expressed by his reference to 'supermarkets of faith'.

Roy does not really distinguish the terms 'neofundamentalist Muslim' from the 'global Muslim', such is the given affinity between globalization and neofundamentalism in his discussion. In fact, the terms appear rather interchangeable and in themselves elastic. Islamic neofundamentalism, as a specific form of fundamentalism (variants are not delineated), is spreading from 'Pakistan's madrassas to Islamic bookshops in Paris or mosques in London, via hundreds of websites ... It thrives in very different and even opposing contexts, from former Muslim Brothers to the Tablighi Jama'at and Wahhabis' (Roy, 2004, p. 232). Global Muslims consist of those who are settled permanently in mainly Western states and those within Muslim majority countries who 'distance themselves from a given Muslim culture and stress their belonging to a universal ummah, whether in a purely quietist way or through political action' (Roy, 2004, p. xi). They are, irrespective of what term they are described by, not part of a formal organization or precise school of thought, but part of a wider 'trend, a state of mind, a dogmatic relationship to the fundamentals of the religion' (p. 3).

Roy does not provide any extended discussion or even a definition of globalization, but it is clear from his discussion that key in its relationship to religion are matters discussed in Chapter 5 – deterritorialization and cultural homogenization, or, perhaps more accurately put, the evisceration of historic cultures. He also points to the way in which neofundamentalists use a discourse of identity and human rights taken from the West against imperialism and reaffirm their Islam by purifying it. Roy (2004, p. 23) suggests that this understanding – that neofundamentalists use Western discourse against the West – reveals how hatred of America as the great Satan is compatible with the same people forming a lengthening queue for visas outside the US consulate in Tehran. There is another explanation, of course. It is that those who go through the ritual of burning the Stars and Stripes outside Iranian mosques on a Friday are not actually the same people who seek US visas. Quite possibly those Iranians who want to emigrate seek not the reformulation of their Islamic identity in the West, but escape from the conservatism and lack of opportunity of the now moth-eaten autocracy of the ayatollahs. However, perhaps the two things are not incompatible and it is certainly true that London in particular has acted as a magnet for numerous radical Islamic activists from the Middle East and North Africa in recent years. Well-known cases like Sheikh Abu Hamza al-Masri, preacher at the Finsbury Park mosque in north London, indicate that they are scarcely complimentary about their host societies upon arrival.

The principal consequence of the contemporary phase of globalization has been its cultural impact. Roy acknowledges that previous forms of globalization have influenced the orientation of Islam, but he suggests that the present one differs in the extent of the external effect of technology and language. Crucially, in its given disregard for local and traditional cultures, contemporary globalization has given the neofundamentalists an opportunity to 'start over' through an imagined return to a pure Islamic society, one unsullied by the perversions of contemporary Western and Muslim societies. Roy claims that neofundamentalists are not interested in counterpoising an authentic Muslim culture to those that exist in America, Europe, Asia, the Middle East and elsewhere. Rather, they favour an original one that is based solely on their literal interpretation of the Koran without the influence of local histories and traditions, Islamic or otherwise. In consequence, they reject both the materialism of Western culture and particular customs within the Muslim world, for example Sufi traditions within Islam. As Roy (2004, p. 25) puts it:

> Globalisation is a good opportunity to dissociate Islam from any given culture and to provide a model that could work beyond any culture . . . Fundamentalism is both a product and an agent of globalisation, because it acknowledges without nostalgia the loss of pristine cultures, and sees as positive the opportunity to build a universal religious identity, delinked from any specific culture, including the Western one perceived as corrupt and decadent – a constant topic of fundamentalism literature. But maybe this last twist is the real victory of westernisation.

It is a commonplace of the social sciences that reference to 'culture' only makes any sense – given that there is a plurality of them – when there are 'cultures'. If there was a single universal human way of doing things, the term would cease to be of much use. Roy suggests that globalization has provided neofundamentalists with an opportunity to go beyond cultural diversity by enabling them to conceive and impose a truly world religion that is identical wherever it is found. In this, one can see the similarity between a given Western form of globalization and a neofundamentalist one; the difference is that one seeks the universalism of Disney and McDonald's, the other the veil and the mosque.

In seeking a new religious culture, neofundamentalists apparently dispense with centuries of Koranic interpretation, the riches of Islamic learning, a reverence for particular Muslim civilizations and, most importantly, the legitimacy of scholars and imams for religious-minded laypersons. Here Roy mentions several Muslim preachers now in jail, some with backgrounds in drugs and petty crime, others converts from Christianity, who attracted groups of followers through their fiery rhetoric at particular London mosques in the 1990s. More recently, the growth in internet use has lent itself to the attempt by hitherto marginal figures in the Western Muslim world to bypass the authority, one based on years of formal study, of established imams.[5] After all, it is not that difficult for an individual with a little IT knowledge to set up a website and make all kinds of claims allegedly based on the Koran. Although Roy does not make the point, even this is not required, given the ready-made web formats of social networking sites like Facebook and MySpace. Although the website of Hizb ut-Tahrir (www.hizb.org.uk), another organization Roy discusses, cannot be said to jettison traditional Islamic learning, it does devote a certain amount of space to criticizing the perceived conservatism of some British Muslim organizations.

If, in Roy's estimation, globalization provides a tabula rasa upon which neofundamentalists can conceive an immaculate notion of Islam, there are other motivations for neofundamentalism. Drawing on earlier analysis and using a historical frame of reference that he generally eschews in an emphasis on the originality of contemporary globalization, Roy suggests that neofundamentalism has arisen from the exhaustion of Islamism as a political project. Particularly important in this was the failure of the Iranian revolution to realize the hopes of its supporters: 'The Islamic revolution in Iran has been, in my opinion, one of the key factors in secularisation: who in Iran, apart from a cabal of conservatives (or fanatical secularists), can speak of the growing influence of religion in society' (Mandaville, 2007, pp. 334–5)? One can perhaps see that a disdain for religion, resulting in secularization, stems from the contamination it has experienced through the Iranian government being composed of Muslim clergy and all political acts allegedly having a religious dimension. This would be the case even if politicians were themselves free of corruption, which is certainly not the case in Iran. The logical escape from this reality for the individual Muslim in Iran would be in a religious orientation that valorizes a decontaminated Islam of everyday life, one that concerns itself with the five pillars of the faith and is self-consciously distanced from the sleaze and graft of state power. This, in part, is something Roy associates with a neofundamentalism as it applies to the quietism of Wahhabism (a Sunni form, therefore not something found in Shia Iran), a following in Islam that for the most part does not intrude into politics but concerns itself with the individual and community attaining a routine in which everything accords with the Koran and the Hadith (a body of traditions relating to Muhammad).

However, Roy suggests that neofundamentalism, like Islamism, also contributes to the same contemporary predicament: religiosity, an excess of religion and, crucially, its overextension into all areas of life. This results in the paradox of greater secularization as religion ceases to be embedded within a traditional culture and is thus emptied of meaning. Roy (2004, p. 40) suggests that neofundamentalists and Islamists are the unwitting agents of globalization and secularization:

> The real secularists are the Islamicists and neofundamentalists, because they want to bridge the gap between religion and a secularised society by exacerbating the religious dimension, overstretching it to the extent that it cannot become a habitus by being embedded in a real culture. This overstretching of religion, after a period of paroxysmal parousia (for example, the Islamic revolution of Iran, or any given jihad), necessarily leads to a new schism: politics is the new dimension of any religious state, and the death of any jihad waged out of a concrete strategy, nation or social fabric. What resurfaces is politics, as in the case of Iran, but also religion as a multifaceted practice, hence the heterogeneous dimension of Islamic revivalism. Redefining Islam as a 'pure' religion turns it into a mere religion and leaves politics to work alone. Islam is experiencing secularisation, but in the name of fundamentalism.

Elsewhere, however, Roy (2004, p. 25) suggests that neofundamentalism should not be bracketed with Islamism, but is something that belongs to a post-Islamist age – our conjuncture, in which there is a reaction to the cynicism that political Islam produced. It is one that seeks 'beyond or beneath politics, autonomous spaces and means of expression, feeding contradictory and burgeoning forms of religiosity'. A post-Islamist age is thus not one in which there is a decline of religion per se, but rather one that sees the expression of the crisis of the relationship between religion and politics as well as 'the trend toward fragmentation of religious identity and authority, a blossoming of new and different forms of religiosity that might be antagonistic toward each other, and paradoxically a blurring of the lines between Christian and Muslim religiosity (not dogmas, of course)' (Roy, 2004, p. 3).

Al-Qaeda, clearly not a quietist movement, is one form of this new religiosity. We noted above how observers have stressed the global dimensions of this loose-knit terrorist organization. In his discussion of al-Qaeda in *Globalised Islam*, Roy places emphasis on its ability to find terrorist recruits in some European countries from among the ranks of alienated Muslim youth. He suggests that even if the bombers hail from the Arab world, they have no tangible connections with it and are not linked to or used by any Middle Eastern state, intelligence service or radical movement, as had been the case with the militants of the 1980s. In fact, he suggests that they reject any identity other than that of being Muslim. Roy (2004, p. 274) quotes Khaled Kelkal, the first French Islamic radical to carry out a terrorist action in France, in an interview shortly before his initial attack: 'I am not French, I am not an Arab, I am a Muslim.'

Writing before the rise of mainly sectarian violence in Iraq in 2004, Roy depicts al-Qaeda not so much as a cause, born out of the grievances within the Muslim world, but as a 'pathological consequence of the globalisation of the Muslim world', a manifestation of 'deterritorialised, supranational Islamic networks that operate specifically in the West and at the periphery of the Middle East' (Roy, 2004, p. 303). They form part of a wider pool of would-be militant jihadists who:

> Fight at the frontier to protect a centre where they have no place. They fight not to protect a territory but to re-create a community. They are besieged in a fortress they do not inhabit. This empty fortress syndrome is related to the pathological dimension of their jihad. (Roy, 2004, p. 289)

Elsewhere, he speaks of the young French Muslims as people enacting the Israeli–Palestinian conflict through attacks on Jewish targets as a sort of 'cowboys-and-Indians game for a local audience, one having little or no connection with the real world'. In an informal survey, Roy (2004, p. 45) notes that none of those involved could name a single town in Palestine or had any connections to mosques or Islamic organizations.

In comparative terms, Roy (2004, p. 43) thinks that al-Qaeda's terrorism belongs to a 'Western tradition of individual and pessimistic revolt for an elusive ideal world'. Unlike the 'usual' terrorists – the IRA, the PLO, the Tamil Tigers and even the more fundamentalist ETA – there can be no room for negotiations with bin Laden as his aim is not political but 'simply to destroy Babylon'. In Roy's estimation, and again contrary to general opinion, bin Laden is outside the tradition of jihad, holy war. That is because jihad, as a holy war, 'has always been instrumentalised for political and strategic purposes, by state actors or would be actors'. Roy (2004, p. 56) suggests that among al-Qaeda recruits:

> There is a strange mix of deep personal pessimism and collective millenarianism optimism among this type of terrorist; they do not trust the people they are fighting for (they are indifferent to killing Muslims), they are sure to die, and as political scientist Farhad Khosrokhavar pointed out in the case of the Iranian martyrs of the Iran-Iraq War, they know that even if they succeed, the future society will not match the ideals for which they are fighting.

Clearly, Roy is not particularly impressed with al-Qaeda, describing it as more like a sect or mafia than a professional underground organization, and comparing it negatively to the Communist Internationals of the twentieth century, with their mass parties, affiliated trade unions, women's bodies, cultural and social clubs and intellectual fellow travellers. The quest of neofundamentalists to rebuild the ummah on the ruins of vanishing cultures is their weakness – 'a by-product of globalisation'. As for the calls of Hizb ut-Tahrir for a global caliphate, Roy (2004, p. 238) is rather contemptuous, as the conception is 'not a real geographical entity and has no territorial or sociological roots'. Its advocates try to cover the futility of their task by stressing that a new caliphate is urgently needed. But the strategy 'lacks a concrete basis of a territorial, ethnic or economic type on which to build such a community'. According to Roy (2004, p. 30), the wider predicament facing neofundamentalism is that of 'an imaginary escape from political deadlock, even to the bloody nightmare of Al Qaeda'. Thus, the quietist neofundamentalist response consists of 'shunning integration into Western societies by playing on the set of religious and sociological tools [that is, adopting a discourse of identity and difference] available on the Western market'. The more dramatic one, that of al-Qaeda, valorizes mindless violence in itself.

Osama bin Laden, a Global Muslim?

Roy makes a distinctive contribution to coverage of al-Qaeda. It is one that chimes with a growing consensus that the threat posed by Islamic terrorism in recent years has been exaggerated to justify the 'war on terror' of the Bush administrations and their political allies. However, is his analysis of neofundamentalism as a global phenomenon correct? Certainly I think he provides great insight into the present direction of a conspicuous minority of Muslims (for a wider critique of Roy and Kepel, see Mamdani, 2005). However, it is not our intention here to try to provide an overarching critique of *Globalised Islam*. Rather, I want to finish this chapter by considering whether al-Qaeda as a key form of neofundamentalism marks a new political departure, one that sets it apart from nationalism as an ideology and practice. In doing so, I draw on an edited collection of the statements of Osama bin Laden, *Messages to the World* (2005), made through websites and satellite TV channels since the early 1990s. It should be said that bin Laden is not, of course, the entirety of al-Qaeda – in itself a somewhat inchoate organization as already discussed – and therefore one should exercise caution in assuming that everything he says is representative of all terrorists, especially those in the West. However, his pronouncements, as much as his frugal lifestyle, in contrast to the gluttony of the Muslim leaders he castigates, clearly do strike a chord with many Muslims across the world, including those who disagree with al-Qaeda's violence. In that sense, it is legitimate to suggest that what he has to say has a wider importance. The following is not intended as a comprehensive examination of the kind of Islam that motivates bin Laden and his followers, but rather some pertinent points, given the case made by Roy.

The first is that bin Laden seems aware of the ill-defined nature of his ultimate ambition, to the extent that he does not spend much time outlining it. Bin Laden (2005, p. 121) rejects any suggestion that he and al-Qaeda are cut off from the wider mass of Muslims, but one detects a slightly plaintive tone here: 'I assure you that we are part of this ummah, that our goal is the victory of the ummah.' He claims that al-Qaeda is simply part of the Muslim struggle against 'the global crusaders' (p. 108), but he gives no outline of what the victory of the ummah against the enemy will bring. We saw above how both Islamist and academic critics claim that an organization that relies on violence will necessarily be distanced from those whom it purports to represent. Bruce Lawrence suggests that the necessarily secretive, quite literally hidden, nature of al-Qaeda gives bin Laden a mystique for supporters and enemies alike, but that his vision is a narrow and self-limiting one that can have 'little appeal for the great mass of believers, who need more than scriptural dictates, poetic transports, or binary prescriptions to chart their everyday lives, whether individuals or as collective members of a community, local or national' (bin Laden, 2005, p. xxii). On occasions, notably after the 9/11 attacks, bin Laden has referred to the loss to Muslims of the end of a caliphate with the fall of the Ottoman Empire in 1922. However, Lawrence points out that there is no priority or even urgency given to restoring the caliphate today. He comments that (bin Laden, 2005, p. xxii): 'Bin Laden seems at some level to recognize the futility of a quest for restitution. He sets no positive political horizon for his struggle. Instead, he vows that *jihad* will continue until "we meet God and get his blessing!"' A perpetual struggle without a clearly defined goal is unlikely to find a broader constituency.

If, on this level, bin Laden seems an aloof figure, he is relatively direct on the immediate goals of Muslims in the Arab world. This is because he actually has clear territorial objectives. They are highly unlikely to be achieved in the present circumstances, but are not in themselves of an abstract and intangible nature. His first and most important preoccupation is the removal of the American military bases and all their personnel from Saudi Arabia and the wider Arabian Peninsula – interestingly, he makes no direct criticism of the regimes of the UAE, even though they are even more hedonistic than the Saudi ruling class. It is worth noting that bin Laden first rose to prominence after the Iraqi invasion of Kuwait in August 1990, when it seemed that Saddam Hussein was about to launch his armies south into Saudi Arabia. This prompted bin Laden to offer the Saudi monarchy the use of veteran Afghani fighters, al-Qaeda ('the base' in Arabic) as it had become known, to repel the Iraqis along the desert border.[6] The proposal was rejected by the then ruler King Fahd, quite possibly for political as well as military reasons, in favour of a massive American military build-up. Bin Laden's role in the welter of criticism of Fahd and his palace stooges, including initially from parts of the religious establishment, for inviting in the US infidel set him on a collision with the monarchy, who attempted to silence him. In April 1991, bin Laden left for Afghanistan and then Sudan, never to return, the Saudi government revoking his citizenship three years later.

On the continued presence, as bin Laden terms it, the 'occupation', of Americans in the kingdom – 'the cornerstone of the Islamic world' – he is quite clear. It is 'The greatest disaster to befall the Muslims since the death of the Prophet Muhammad'. Bin Laden's (2005, p. 25) injunction to his fellow Saudis is: 'Expel the Polytheists from the Arabian peninsula.' Elsewhere, he asks 'brother Muslims' rhetorically if it makes any sense for '*our* country . . . [to be] the biggest purchaser of weapons from America in the world and America's biggest trading partner in the region' (bin Laden, 2005, p. 29, emphasis added). Bin Laden's criticism of the religious justifications made by sections of the Saudi religious establishment for the influx of American troops, the enlargement of US bases and so on after the Iraqi invasion of Kuwait is as strident as that directed towards the royal family. In fact, it seems to disgust him more because of the relationship of the ulema to the ummah. He accused bin Baz, the chief Saudi mufti, of 'excusing this terrible act, which insulted the pride and sullied the honour of our ummah, as well as polluting its holy places' (bin Laden, 2005, p. 7). In a general address to 'the honourable scholars of the Arabian peninsula and Saudi Arabia in particular' in the mid-1990s, he seems to blame them for the general predicament of Saudi Muslims:

> You are all aware of the degree of degradation and corruption to which our Islamic ummah has sunk, in its government and in the feebleness and cowardice of many of its scholars in the face of its enemies, as well as in its internal divisions. This is because of their neglect of religion and weakness of faith, which allowed the enemy to attack. The enemy invaded the land of our ummah, violated her honor, shed her blood and occupied her sanctuaries. (bin Laden, 2005, p. 14)

If removing Americans from Arabia is bin Laden's priority, the creation of an Islamic Palestine appears a secondary objective. Bin Laden has been criticized from within the Muslim world for neglecting the Palestinian question, something he seems a little sensitive about. Whatever the history and genuineness of his commitment to the Palestinians, bin Laden (2005, p. 9) thinks that Muslims have a 'legal duty . . . [to] wage jihad for the sake of God and to motivate our ummah to jihad so that Palestine may be completely liberated and returned to Islamic sovereignty'. Within this, bin Laden (2005, p. 61) places particular emphasis on the liberation of the al-Aqsa Mosque and the Holy Mosque in Jerusalem 'from the grip of the Americans and their allies'.

How are these objectives to be achieved? Quite simply, by killing Americans – all Americans, not just military personnel or those in the Arab world: 'Every American is our enemy, whether he fights directly or whether he pays taxes.' He claims categorically – and completely erroneously – that Muslims hate Americans, Jews and Christians as 'part of our belief and our religion'. His hatred and animosity has been with him for as 'long as I can remember', he feels it as a warlike torment (bin Laden, 2005, pp. 70, 87).

It is these kinds of statements and their realization, through terrorism, which lead writers like Roy to suggest that bin Laden's quest is the destruction of Babylon – that place where jahiliyya (unIslamic ignorance) exists, everywhere. Others suggest that the very existence of al-Qaeda means a war without end. There are two things to be said here, neither of which should be taken to suggest any kind of excuse for bin Laden's and al-Qaeda's murderous undertakings. First, he places his hatred as a defensive reaction to American killings of ordinary Muslims in their occupation of Muslim lands. In line with virtually every nationalist and ethnic offensive, he claims that the action is defensively motivated. With justification, bin Laden (2005, p. 141) states that innocent Muslims are the victims of American aggression: 'We ourselves are the victims of murder and massacres. We are only defending ourselves against the United States. This is a defensive jihad to protect our land and people.' Speaking in the 1990s, he states that the slaughter of Muslims is taking place in Palestine, Iraq, Somalia, Western Sudan, Kashmir, the Philippines, Bosnia, Chechnya and Assam (p. 153). If he were writing today, he might substitute Afghanistan for Bosnia.[7] If only, he says, the Americans would 'live and let live' as Muslims wish. Responding to the suggestion that al-Qaeda actions are not motivated defensively against a particular aggressor, bin Laden (2005, p. 238) asks sardonically: 'Perhaps you can tell us why we did not attack Sweden, for example?'

Second, he has stated that if American killings and occupation cease, then peaceful co-existence between Muslims and the Christian world is possible. He suggests, moreover, that models are available from Islam's past that demonstrate this is possible:

> If we look back at our history, we will find there were many types of dealings between the Muslim nation and the other nations in peacetime and wartime, including treaties and matters to do with commerce. So it is not a new thing that we need to create. Rather, it already exists. (bin Laden, 2005, p. 46)

If this is credible, it is worth noting that bin Laden is no more extreme in his outlook than the Harvard scholar, Samuel Huntington. Indeed, bin Laden (2005, p. 124) has gone out of his way to endorse Huntington's 'clash of civilizations' thesis: 'I say that there is no doubt about this. It is a very clear matter, proven in the Qur'an and the traditions of the Prophet.' As for oil, bin Laden suggests its price should be set by market laws of supply and demand. He seems to have no objection to its sale to the West but thinks that the price of oil is set artificially low by the Saudi regime, not an equal trading partner but a 'US agent' (p. 46). His insistence on the strict demarcation of geographic boundaries separating Muslims from Christians according to Islamic law means, he says, that it is wrong for Muslims to 'stay long in the land of the infidels' (p. 140).

Finally, it is worth noting that in one interview, bin Laden is at pains to point out that all his five wives have been Arabs, not Afghans. Presumably he had the opportunity to marry Afghan women had he wished during the 20-odd years that he has lived there. About his native Saudi Arabia, bin Laden (2005, p. 248) is wistful: 'I miss my country greatly, and have long been absent from it.' However, 'this is easy to endure because it is for the sake of God'.

Taking these things together, bin Laden and al-Qaeda appear as rather more conventional political animals than Roy suggests. Their principal aims are essentially territorial and, if accomplished, it is possible to imagine that some of sort of understanding between East and West might be established. As this would have to involve the complete destruction of the state of Israel and the removal of all Christians from Muslims lands, it is, to say the least, difficult to conceive. However, the political intent is not of an ephemeral or utopian (or perhaps dystopian) bloody war without end in itself. This is not to say that bin Laden is simply a nationalist, as his religious agenda does make him distinct. But it is true that the continuities in his outlook with the priorities of nationalism are more pronounced than might be thought. More importantly, perhaps inevitably, there is no attempt to dismiss issues of land and people for God and sharia, as was the case with Qutb, quoted above, rather, the two conjoin. What differentiates bin Laden and al-Qaeda from nationalist-type organizations is their exclusive use of violence, something that, as has been pointed out, gives them the power to shock, but a far more profound weakness.

These points do not apply so directly to new directions taken by neofundamentalists in the West. Given the diffuse nature of this subject, it is difficult to make any firm points. But even here there is reason for thinking that national issues are rather more entrenched than a writer like Roy seems to suggest. A cursory glance at the British website of Hizb ut-Tahrir (www.hizb.org.uk) reveals a preoccupation with political issues in Pakistan. Most of the organization's activists are of Pakistani origin.

Conclusion

This chapter has considered whether Islam is succeeding in overcoming divisions of nations and nationalism. We first considered whether or not Islam is intrinsically opposed to nations and nationalism because of its insistence on a single, indivisible ummah. The argument was that there have always been distinctions of identity within the wider body of Muslim believers. Since the advent of nationalism in the Middle East through the influence of and in reaction to European imperialism in the nineteenth century, nationalism has combined with Islam to produce distinct identities. Especially important in this process has been the use of a Muslim guise by authoritarian leaders in the twentieth century in their state-building programmes. In general terms, there should be recognition of the dialectical tension between the universalism of Islam and its particular application within states, but this does not amount to a direct contradiction.

Second, we saw that thinkers in the Muslim world struggled with this tension in their efforts to formulate a regional and religious response to the self-evident superiority of European military and industrial power in the nineteenth and early twentieth centuries. However, the discourse of Islamic modernism, one that continues to this day, was less prominent than that of Arab nationalism in the independence struggles of Muslim peoples in the mid-twentieth century. Arab nationalism pragmatically drew upon Islam in projections of an essential historic unity of the people of the geographic region as a whole.

Arab nationalism signally failed in its goal of regional integration. Out of the disappointment there arose a renewed emphasis on the political importance of Islam, in a movement known as 'Islamism'. In its more radical ideological formulations, especially those of the Egyptian thinker Qutb, Islamists rejected nationalism altogether as alien to the Muslim emphasis on a community defined solely by togetherness of believers. Recent history has been punctuated by a series of events that demonstrate the importance of Islamism. However, it is questionable whether the movement has succeeded. Leading authorities, notably Kepel, suggest that it has not made the breakthroughs anticipated; the contemporary detour into al-Qaeda's terrorism reveals its exhaustion. There is some reason to think that this is too stark a conclusion, given an emerging Islamist political pragmatism in parts of the Muslim world. The key point is that there is little reason to believe that it has successfully overcome the power of nationalism as something that both motivates and divides Muslims.

With this in mind, we turned finally to the important and original contribution of Roy in understanding a possible global direction for contemporary Islam. He argues that nationalism remains, in contrast to the hopes of some Islamists, the principal political force in the Middle East as elsewhere. However, he does impute that global Islam is something different, a qualitatively new phenomenon that departs from previous political models. That is because global Islam chimes with the tendency of globalization to deracinate pre-existing cultures. In this way, it gives neofundamentalists the opportunity to reformulate an original and therefore pure religious identity. In doing so, its advocates bypass the traditional structures and figures of scriptural authority. The most dramatic expression of this development, al-Qaeda-linked terrorists, is indicative of the wider path of neofundamentalism: they are cut off from durable organizational structures and mass support.

There is much of interest within Roy's thesis. However, a brief examination revealed that the outlook of the world's most famous neofundamentalist, Osama bin Laden, is more preoccupied with mundane matters of territory than elusive evocations of a global caliphate. He speaks much of the time as a Saudi addressing fellow Wahhabi Muslims over the given insult to their faith of Americans residing in the land of the prophet. Certainly he appeals to a wider Muslim constituency when dealing with Palestinian matters, but at all times there appears to be a Saudi parochialism to his outlook. In other words, he speaks first and foremost as a Saudi to other Saudis. What sets him apart are not his political objectives but the reliance of al-Qaeda on random acts of violence to fulfil the injunction to kill Westerners in general and Americans in particular. This is noteworthy in itself, but it does not mean that al-Qaeda has replaced a nationalist agenda with a global one. There is greater continuity between al-Qaeda and the imperatives of nationalism than Roy acknowledges. Therefore, this form of globalization, that of radical Islam, has only partially succeeded in superseding the power and political coordinates of nations and nationalism.

Summary Points

- There is no intrinsic unity among Muslims any more than there is unity among peoples of other faiths.
- While there is a tension between the universalism of the Muslim ummah and the division of Muslims peoples within nation-states, claims that Islam is somehow just 'against' nations and nationalism are wrong.
- With European expansion into the Middle East and Asia from the eighteenth century on, nationalism was one of the issues that thinkers in the Muslim world were forced to confront.
- In the twentieth century, the most important response to European imperialism was Arab nationalism: a movement intended to unite Arabs in a single federal regional state.
- From the 1960s onwards, the perceived failure of Arab nationalism stimulated a reaction throughout the Middle East and parts of Asia known as 'Islamism'.
- Islamists wanted to replace existing states with an explicitly Muslim government committed to implementing Islamic law, a radical aim that was only really achieved in Iran in 1979.

- Nowhere has the goal of a wider spiritual unity among Muslims replaced the territorial imperatives of nations and nationalism.
- More recently, however, some scholars have argued, notably Roy, that globalization has given rise to Islamic fundamentalism.
- Rather than Islamic fundamentalism being opposed to globalization, Roy thinks that it is part of it, especially in respect to its universalism. Roy's thesis makes telling points, but does not seem to square with the imperatives of Osama bin Laden and al-Qaeda.
- Bin Laden is in fact preoccupied with expelling the American infidels from the land of the prophet, Saudi Arabia, and accepts that the world is divided by regional religions rather than being ripe for a global caliphate, that is, Islamic government.

Conclusion

The intention here is not to try to meld the various findings of the previous chapters into a seamless overview and thus present a definitive answer to the question: Which force is the greater, nationalism or globalization? As suggested in the Introduction, we are, however, probably stuck with this form of discussion, as binaries present manageable alternatives when understanding complex phenomena. And, as in certain respects, it is quite legitimate to ask which force seems to be emerging the stronger, I do make such assessments here. However, the risk is that a balance ledger (spreadsheet in global speak) approach serves to flatten the ambiguous picture that has emerged in the various discussions. That would be quite contrary to the subject of nationalism and globalization. From the outset, I have attempted to present the central issue as one of paradox, of opposite things being true at the same time, of contradiction. The relationship of contradictory forces is known as a 'dialectical process' in the philosophy of the social sciences. The association of the term 'dialectics' with Marxism probably accounts for it being less common in academic usage than it was in the past. But labelling the relationship between nationalism and globalization as dialectical is only a starting point, it is not in itself revealing. So what conclusions can be drawn in light of the foregoing discussion of theory, economics, small advanced nations, culture and religion (Islam)?

The first is that the theoretical understanding of the place of nations and nationalism in human history critically influences whether or not one believes that globalization as an ongoing process will have any bearing on the central role they currently play. If one assumes that nationalisms provide cultural storerooms of meaning, derived from history, that anchor collective and individual identity, it is unlikely that the flow of currencies, images and words from elsewhere will have much impact on attachment and belonging. If, by contrast, it can be shown that those cultural storerooms were only built and filled relatively recently by the intersection of various modern forces, there is reason to think they can more readily be emptied and their objects of attachment replaced by new forms. However, I suggested that the debate between ethnosymbolists and modernists in the origination and nature of nationalism cannot be solved by repeating the well-worn, and now frankly rather boring, claims and counterclaims. Instead, it is more interesting to note that ethnosymbolists – whatever the affinities of their position with the romantic philosophy of Herder in which nations are timeless affairs of the heart – recognize that nationalism is not a constant in human history but undergoes historical change. In this respect, the recent work of Hutchinson (2005) on the long-term stimulus that globalization has given to nationalism, through taking and propagating one of its forms while inciting reaction against it, represents an advance. Simultaneously, a careful appreciation of the thoughts of Hobsbawm (not dissimilar to Castells' (1997) theorizing on how globalization arouses resistance identities) on the way that the inequalities within capitalism can fire nationalist causes in the short term is of interest to all students of the subject.

Nevertheless, it is certainly true that Hobsbawm is sceptical of the long-term viability of nationalism. This is because Hobsbawm (1992) claims that the time of nationalism as an ideology of state unification and building is past. It played this role in the nineteenth and twentieth centuries, but it is no longer a credible structure to undertake development in a global economic world. Now this claim is rather different from the fanciful notions that the nation-state, as McCrone put it, is going out of fashion, or that the nation-state has reached its end in a borderless world, as Ohmae claimed. However, perhaps even Hobsbawm's thesis was influenced to some degree by neoliberalism, the doctrine of the primacy of markets and the redundancy of states that has taken an almost theological hold over the world in the past 30 years. It is surprising that a Marxist historian should have made such an assessment, as he knows better than most that Marx foresaw that capitalism proceeds through a series of evermore dramatic crises. Later writers in the Marxist tradition like Nicolai Bukharin (1888–1938) pointed out that it relies on the intervention of the state in such periods (2003).

The final part of this book has been written as global capitalism has plunged into its most severe crisis since the 1930s, prompting governments to inject unprecedented capital sums into ailing financial and industrial companies. In Great Britain, the hitherto fiscal discipline of both Conservative and Labour governments has been replaced by a series of measures to try to boost the economy as it falls into recession – 'breathtakingly crass Keynesianism' according to the German finance minister, Peer Steinbruck. Some commentators speculate that the world recession may prove to be the most disastrous and far-reaching in history. What is notable at the present time is how the finest academic and business economists are unable to predict what is likely to happen to markets on a day-to-day basis, let alone in years to come. What we can say with certainty is that the fallacy that markets are self-regulating is not going to return for some considerable time. The economic role of governments, always crucial, has, through necessity, been brought centre stage.

Will this lead to a reverse in globalization and a spur to economic nationalism? I doubt this for two reasons. First, as we saw towards the end of Chapter 3, the process is so far advanced that its reversal on a scale that took place in the early 1930s, when nearly a third of trade was wiped out, would amount not to recession but to economic Armageddon. Second, there are currently no ideological alternatives to free-market capitalism – a system that, as Marx again correctly foresaw, is inherently global – as there previously were. In the 1930s, it was the political Right, committed to economic development from within, that chiefly benefited, with the exception of the USA and Scandinavia. There, interventionist economic measures to stimulate growth were adopted that derived from, or at least were redolent of, the British economist John Maynard Keynes. Keynes, as we saw, was himself drawn to economic nationalism more markedly than List in the nineteenth century. Keynesianism, in the period of the Second World War and after, existed as another twentieth-century ideology, besides Fascism, to reject the unfettered working of the market – a variant, admittedly far less pronounced, of economic nationalism. A third to do so was Communism, in reality a form of nationalism rather than working-class internationalism, which legitimated party-controlled states to manage economies.

Such were the scale of the disasters of Fascism and Communism in the twentieth century that it is difficult, although by no means impossible, to imagine their ideological return. Inevitably, there is much talk of the return of Keynes at present, but what is significant is that the use of measures that he broadly advocated – government investment to stimulate demand and so on – has been made to sustain globalization, not, as he favoured, to scale it down. In Britain and America, more public money has been given to financial capitalism to try to revive stock markets, the most globalized parts of the world economy, than to domestic industries. The crisis has not even produced a gathering of voices urging greater individual prudence. Instead, the message seems to be that consumers should do their bit to help the economy by borrowing yet more money, despite the general understanding that record levels of debt precipitated the crash. In sum, although the whole crazed experiment of neoliberalism has ended in disaster, the world still carries on as if it is the only show in town. In ideological terms, it still is. Thus economic nationalism, although of greater relevance than at any time over the past 30 years, lacks a credible partner like socialism, Fascism or even Keynesianism with which to combine to force an extensive political reorientation.

The second conclusion to draw concerns the fate of smaller nations in advanced democracies. The argument we looked at in Chapter 4 is that globalization is aiding the quests of Catalonia in Spain, Quebec in Canada and Scotland in Great Britain for greater degrees of independence. In large part this is because, according to their academic advocates, regional and global markets have taken the sting out of independence. If market access is assured whether or not a particular region is part of a larger state, and therefore its economic viability is not really at issue, this presents an advance in its quest for greater separation from its larger neighbour. This argument is taken a stage further by some writers (Keating) through the suggestion that minority nationalisms are no longer so oriented to the issue of the state. In any event,

Scotland et al. are 'free trade' or 'global nationalisms'. This argument again has surely received something of a setback in the context of recession and the renewed role of central governments. But it is perhaps true, although not certain or even irreversible, that a momentum has been established towards ever greater autonomy, perhaps independence – something that inevitably does involve the issue of state(s). Simultaneously, one has to ask if the end point envisaged – whatever it is exactly and it is not articulated in the various academic accounts looked at – is likely to stir sufficient passions to make the wrench of actual state secession. In the case of Scottish nationalism, perhaps the SNP is partially succeeding in making independence seem almost mundane and somehow inevitable – an unremarkable aspect of respectable politics. But the very arguments about globalization on which the move is in part predicated (undermined by current events as mentioned) serve also to make the prospect of going it alone as a nation less exciting and therefore less likely to receive fulsome popular support. Globalization has possibly impoverished nationalism in these cases. In other cases, national liberation through state independence remains as pressing as ever for the peoples involved.

What of culture, nationalism and globalization? Again the balance was mixed. On the one hand, there is no denying the homogenization of capitalism, indeed, the point is obvious. Such influences sit beside the normalcy of national cultures, something that nation-states continue to maintain and further. On the other hand, globalization does entail heterogeneity. Particularly interesting here is the way in which migration flows are disturbing the ethnic compositions of nations. This was always somewhat mythical in nationalist discourse. The point is that with globalization, it is becoming increasingly obvious that nations do not contain discrete cultures based on a stable population group. Now this may trigger anti-immigrant campaigns designed to restore ethnic and cultural purity – particularly in times of recession. Simultaneously, notions of a cultural free market are misplaced as some migrant groups jealously seek to preserve their original identities through long-distance nationalisms. It is wrong to romanticize migration. However, this vector of globalization, greater migration, is not something that can be easily reversed. It was markedly so in the interwar period when nationalism and recession much reduced migration's push and pull factors. But the process is now so massive and widespread that it is difficult to see a serious decline in migrant numbers. Indeed, the tendency of migrants to flow from economically poorer parts of the world to richer economies will probably accelerate because, as usual, poorer peoples suffer disproportionately from capitalist crisis and are compelled to seek a better living elsewhere.

Our conclusion in relation to any proposition that religion, specifically Islam, empowered by global media and communication and made more extensive by migration, is serving to circumvent nations and nationalism through its quest for a global caliphate can be fairly emphatic: there is no evidence for this. The account of Roy, who seems at times to suggest this, actually confirms – in discussion of the failure of Islamism over the past 30 years – that in the Muslim world, nationalism remains the principal motivational force. There is much of interest in what he has to say about neofundamentalism as a form of globalization. However, any supposition that Islamic neofundamentalism presents a new point of political departure should be set beside an examination of the outlook of the world's number one Muslim neofundamentalist, Osama bin Laden. I did not suggest that bin Laden is, in reality, a nationalist in Islamic clothing, because he is not. His religious objectives should be taken seriously in their own right. However, I did argue that his preoccupation with the issue of the occupation of territory, specifically that of his homeland Saudi Arabia, does make his aim closer to a nationalist than observers generally envisage. It is his terrorist methods not his ideology that is distinct; no nationalist group relies exclusively on violence.

Is there anything else in globalization that is leading to a changed nationalism? Quite possibly, but this book has not attempted a complete overview even if this were possible. Only once has it mentioned global warming. It is difficult to predict what effects global warming will have on nations and nationalism in centuries to come when, in all likelihood, peoples are forced to move as parts of the earth become uninhabitable. Perhaps by then they will have succeeded in arriving at some form of political organization that enables genuine cooperation. However, the present indicators are hardly promising in this respect. Younger readers will probably not remember Stanley Kubrick's 1964 Cold War, black comedy *Dr Strangelove* starring Peter Sellars. A well-known scene sees the US military chiefs at the Pentagon arguing furiously in their nuclear air raid shelter, as they wait for Russian retaliation for the nuclear strike they have launched, over how the 'commies' will have the advantage when they crawl out of their bunker into the smoking ruins of the world. Well, the comparison is not exact but perhaps there are parallels with the row that broke out recently between the US, Russian and Canadian nation-states over who should have control of the oil reserves at the South Pole, which are becoming extractable as the ice thins (http://archives. chicagotribune.com/2007/jun/10/news/chi-arctic_bdjun10). In the finest traditions of nationalism, the Russians planted their national flag in the melting wastes to proclaim as theirs the very resource whose burning, in a global world driven by profit, is endangering the future of us all.

Notes

Chapter 1

1   Gellner was, however, highly sceptical of the view that intellectuals (or the state) had imposed nationalism from above during the era termed 'official nationalism' in the late nineteenth century by duping the masses with false consciousness.

Chapter 2

1   Even a figure like Charles Montesquieu (1990, p. 213), the eighteenth-century authority on geographically determined national character, thought that with general progress, its influence would decline.
2   It should be pointed out that there other passages in Herder's diffuse writings where he is more ambivalent over imperial conquest. On occasions, with non-European peoples, he said that it was both positive and inevitable.
3   For an overview to a conference on the work of Anthony Smith first published in the journal *Nations and Nationalism*, see Guibernau and Hutchinson (2004).

Chapter 3

1   Friedman's (2000, p. 251) response to criticism of the theory is of interest and indicates that his 'McPeace' proposition was a little tongue in cheek: 'I was both amazed and amused by how much the Golden Arches Theory had gotten around and how intensely certain people wanted to prove it wrong. They were mostly realists and out-of-work Cold Warriors who insisted that politics, and the never-ending struggle between nation-states, were the immutable defining feature of international affairs, and they were professionally and psychologically threatened by the idea that globalization and economic integration might actually influence geopolitics in some very new and fundamental ways.'
2   Gilpin's treatment of nationalism, one in which it is conflated with

mercantilism as a statist approach rather than a force in its own right, is in his *The Political Economy of International Relations* (1987, Ch. 2).

3 It was as late as 1973 that President Nixon declared 'We are all Keynsians now'.

4 If this was the culture of mid-twentieth-century Ireland, economically it continued to be completely tied to Britain (see O'Day, 2000, pp. 26–8).

5 The OECD is a body based in Paris that represents states formerly committed to democracy and market freedom. Of its 30 members, 27 are described by the World Bank as being high income economies, the remaining three as being of upper middle income level. All statistics quoted are from the 'economic globalisation' section of the *OECD Factbook 2007*.

6 It is also true that James (2001, pp. 210–24) is sceptical that national governments now have the popular support and credibility to undertake the massive task of reversing globalization. He argues that the contemporary neoliberal consensus, enforced by the strong arm of Washington, is more resilient than the ephemeral commitment to internationalism in the 1920s, which quickly dissolved as the backlash against liberal cosmopolitanism that had started in the late nineteenth century gathered renewed momentum with the steep recession after 1929.

7 There are some signs that international business is headed in the same sort of direction, although both sides would doubtless deny it. Under the direction of its CEO Terry Leahy, Tesco, a supermarket sometimes identified as a globalization behemoth, has recently committed to reducing the volume of its produce flown into the UK by air to under 2% of total sales.

8 See the WTO trade profile page at stat.wto.org/TariffProfile/WSDB TariffPFView.aspx?Language=E&Country=E25,BR,CN,IN,JP,US,RU.

9 For the extent of the US military presence around the privatized oilfields that will remain for the long haul, see Holt (2007).

Chapter 4

1 Major beneficiaries were wealthy Croat foreign passport holders, generally Canadian and American, who had funded the HDZ war effort. In some cases, they also reaped political benefits through positions in government.

2 Jim Sillar's – former deputy leader of the Scottish National Party – complaint comes to mind of the Scots as 'ninety minute patriots', that is, those who are confident in waving the flag and singing the song at Hampden, but are content to leave their national allegiances behind as they exit the football stadium, rather than taking them on to the polling booth – not least in Glasgow Govan where he lost his parliamentary seat in 1992.

3 This is true of two of the writers' general books on the subject: McCrone (1998) and Guibernau (1996).
4 Symbols of a possible proto-European identity have been adopted by 16 EU member states in the new revised constitution. The fact that Britain is not one of them is unlikely to appease those critics who think that a federalist threat remains constant.
5 'SNP accuses Labour over euro' (3 January 2002) www.snp.org/press-releases/2002/news.82/view?searchterm=euro.
6 'Harvie on the progressive case for globalisation' (21 August 2007) http://scottishfutures.typepad.com/scottish_futures/2007/08/harvie-on-the-p.html.
7 'SNP snubbed as independence support slumps', www.telegraph.co.uk/news/main.jhtml?xml=/news/2007/10/31/nscots131.xml.
8 These lines were written while the SNP held its 2007 annual conference in Aviemore. Commentators remarked on how the debates that used to stir the passions and attract media attention on subjects such as whether or not the British monarch would continue to be the head of state in an independent Scotland have been replaced by day-to-day issues like health and education.
9 'Labour "shift" over independence' (3 November 2007) http://news.bbc.co.uk/1/hi/scotland/7075988.stm.
10 There are empirical studies that find that a European identity is emerging, but refrain from the claim that it is somehow eclipsing national identities (see Bruter, 2005).
11 'The Committee of the Regions – an introduction', http://www.cor.europa.eu/En/presentation/Role.htm.
12 It is worth mentioning that opinion polls in Ireland indicate that support for the new constitution is only 25% (http://news.bbc.co.uk/2/hi/europe/7079465.stm).

Chapter 5

1 Even within modernist accounts of nationalism, there is disagreement over the construction of culture. Gellner flatly rejected the 'invention of tradition' thesis, as it smacked of Marxist beliefs in ruling class indoctrination of the masses and proletarian false consciousness (see Magas, 1991).
2 Durkheim, for example, argued that state schools should be the guardians of national character par excellence, although admittedly his principal concern was national integration rather than distinctiveness – a point among others in a series of lectures at the Sorbonne, 1902–3, that formed the basis of his *Moral Education* (1968, p. 3).

3   For a wider consideration of contemporary French cinema, including levels of state subsidy, see Cowen (2004, Ch. 4).

Chapter 6

1   Steve Bruce (2003, p. 182) claims, for example: 'Islam is unusually theocratic ... In theory it permits no distinction between religion and other spheres of life.' Probably a better starting point is given by Gramsci (1982, p. 420): 'Every religion is in reality a multiplicity of distinct and contradictory religions.'

2   This said, with the possible exception of the Shah's Iran in the late 1960s and 70s, it is doubtful if the rulers/political elite of any Muslim country in the twentieth century attempted to formulate a nationalism that consciously rejected Islam. Even in the most extreme case, Attaturk's Turkey in the interwar period, there is reason to think that although Islamic symbolism was removed from state and civil society, the dominant nationalist discourse still relied upon a conception of the Turks as a Muslim people (see Anderson, 2008).

3   A BBC TV series shown in October 2004 compared Qutb to Leo Strauss, the German-born political philosopher who has come to be regarded as the intellectual grandfather of the 'neoconservatives'. 'Neoconservative' is a term given to the now discredited group of Washington-based intellectuals who exercised considerable influence over the foreign policy of George W. Bush after his election in 2000.

4   'Letters detail infighting over al Qaeda's Iraq mission', http://edition.cnn.com/2008/WORLD/meast/09/11/alqaeda.letters/index.html.

5   Mandaville (2007, p. 325) points out that internet use in the Middle East is actually fairly limited. Whether or not Roy is mindful of statistics on web access, the websites he examines are those of Western Muslims.

6   For details of bin Laden's 1990 meeting with the Saudi defence minister, see Kepel (2004, p. 181).

7   These lines were written during a sustained campaign in November 2008 of US air strikes on both sides of the Pakistan/Afghan border, killing numerous civilians as well as suspected local militants.

Bibliography

Abdelal, R. (2005) 'Nationalism and international political economy', in E. Helleiner and A. Pickel (eds) *Economic Nationalism in a Globalizing World* (Ithaca: Cornell University Press).

Acton, J.M. (1909) *The History of Freedom and Other Essays* (London: Macmillan).

Ahmed, A. (2007) *Journey into Islam: The Crisis of Globalization* (Washington DC: Brookings Institute).

Al-Ahsan, A. (1992) *Ummah or Nation: Identity Crisis in Contemporary Muslim Society* (Broughton Gifford, Wiltshire: Cromwell Press).

Al-Azmeh, A. (2000) 'Nationalism and the Arabs', in D. Hopwood (ed.) *Arab Nation and Nationalism* (Basingstoke: Palgrave – now Palgrave Macmillan).

Albrow, M. (1996) *The Global Age: State and Society Beyond Modernity* (Cambridge: Polity Press).

Alter, P. (1985) *Nationalism* (London: Edward Arnold).

Anderson, B. (1983) *Imagined Communities: Reflections on the Origin and Spread of Nationalism* (London: Verso).

Anderson, B. (1992) 'The new world disorder', *New Left Review*, **1**(193): 3–13.

Anderson, B. (1994) 'Exodus', *Critical Inquiry*, **20**: 314–327.

Anderson, B. (1998a) 'Nationality, identity and the logic of seriality', in B. Anderson, *The Spectre of Comparisons: Nationalism, Southeast Asia and the World* (London: Verso).

Anderson, B. (1998b) 'Long distance nationalism', in B. Anderson, *The Spectre of Comparisons: Nationalisms, Southeast Asia and the World* (London: Verso).

Anderson, P. (1992) 'Ferdinand Braudel and national identity', in P. Anderson, *A Zone of Engagement* (London: Verso).

Anderson, P. (1998) *The Origins of Postmodernity* (London: Verso).

Anderson, P. (2001) 'Scurrying towards Bethlehem', *New Left Review*, **2**(10): 5–30.

Anderson, P. (2007a) 'European hypocrisies', *London Review of Books*, **29**(18): 16.

Anderson, P (2007b) 'Jottings on the conjuncture', *New Left Review*, **2**(48): 5–37.

Anderson, P. (2008) 'Kemalism', *London Review of Books*, 11 September.

Aoki, T. (2002) 'Aspects of globalization in contemporary Japan', in P.L. Berger and S.P. Huntingdon (eds) *Many Globalizations: Cultural Diversity in the Contemporary World* (Oxford: Oxford University Press).

Appadurai, A. (1992) 'Disjuncture and difference in the global world economy', in M. Featherstone (ed.) *Global Culture: Nationalism, Globalization and Modernity* (London: Sage).

Appadurai, A. (1996) *Modernity at Large: Cultural Dimensions of Globalization* (Minneapolis: University of Minneapolis Press).

Appadurai, A. (2006) *Fear of Small Numbers: An Essay on the Geography of Anger* (Durham, NC: Duke University Press).

Appiah, K.A. (2006) *Cosmopolitanism: Ethics in a World of Strangers* (New York: W.W. Norton).

Archibugi, D. and Held, D. (eds) (1995) *Cosmopolitan Democracy: An Agenda for a New World Order* (Cambridge: Polity Press).

Arnold, M. (1978) *Culture and Anarchy* (Cambridge: Cambridge University Press).

Arrighi, G. (1994) *The Long Twentieth Century: Money, Power and the Origins of our Times* (London: Verso).

Barber, B. (1995) *Jihad vs. McWorld* (New York: Times Books).

Barnett, A., Held. D. and Henderson, C. (eds) (2005) *Debating Globalisation* (Cambridge: Polity Press).

Bauböck, R. (2002) 'Political community beyond the sovereign state, supranational federalism and transnational minorities', in R. Cohen and S. Vertovec (eds) *Conceiving Cosmopolitanism: Theory, Context and Practice* (Oxford: Oxford University Press).

Beattie, I.A. (2006) 'Review of Frieden, *Global Capitalism*', *Financial Times Weekend Magazine*, 8 April.

Bechhofer, F., McCrone, D., Kiely, R. and Stewart, R. (2001) 'A reply to Sam Pryke', *Sociology*, **35**: 200–9.

Beck, U. (2000) 'The cosmopolitanism perspective: sociology of the second age of modernity', *British Journal of Sociology*, **51**(1): 79–105.

Beck, U. and Sznaider, N. (2006) 'Unpacking cosmopolitanism for the social sciences: a research agenda', *British Journal of Sociology*, **57**(1): 1–23.

Bello, W. (2004) *Deglobalization: Ideas for a New World Economy*, 2nd edn (London: Zed Books).

Berger, P.L. (1997) 'Four faces of global culture', *The National Interest*, **49**: 23–9.

Berger, P.L. (2002) 'The cultural dynamics of globalization', in P.L. Berger and S.P. Huntingdon (eds) *Many Globalizations: Cultural Diversity in the Contemporary World* (Oxford: Oxford University Press).

Berger, P.L. and Huntington, S.P. (eds) (2002) *Many Globalizations: Cultural Diversity in the Contemporary World* (Oxford: Oxford University Press).

Berlin, I. (1976) *Vico and Herder: Two Studies in the History of Ideas* (London: Hogarth).

Berlin, I. (1991) 'Two concepts of nationalism: an interview with Isaiah Berlin', *New York Review of Books*, **38**: 19.

Bernstein, A. (2002) 'Globalization, culture and development: can South Africa be more than an offshoot of the West?', in P.L. Berger and S.P. Huntingdon (eds) *Many Globalizations: Cultural Diversity in the Contemporary World* (Oxford: Oxford University Press).

Bhatia, S. (2008) 'Recession Dubai style: 500 hundred chefs, 4,000 lobsters and Kylie', *Guardian*, 21 November.

Billig, M. (1995) *Banal Nationalism* (London: Sage).

Bin Laden, O. (2005) *Messages to the World: The Statements of Osama Bin Laden*, ed. B. Lawrence, trans. J. Howarth (London: Verso).

Bourdieu, P. (2002) *Firing B Against the Tyranny of the Market*, trans. L. Wacquant (London: Verso).

Breuilly, J. (1985) *Nationalism and the State* (Manchester: Manchester University Press).

Bruce, S. (2003) *Politics and Religion* (Cambridge: Polity Press).

Bruter, M. (2005) *Citizens of Europe* (Basingstoke: Palgrave Macmillan).

Bukharin, N. (2003) *Imperialism and the World Economy* (London: Bookmarks).

Burnell, P. (1986) *Economic Nationalism in the Third World* (Brighton: Harvester Press).

Caglar, A. (2002) 'Media corporatism and cosmopolitanism', in S. Vertovec and R. Cohen (eds) *Conceiving Cosmopolitanism* (Oxford: Oxford University Press).

Calhoun, C. (2002) 'The class consciousness of frequent travellers: towards a critique of actually existing cosmopolitanism', in S. Vertovec and R. Cohen (eds) *Conceiving Cosmopolitanism* (Oxford: Oxford University Press).

Callinicos, A. (2002) 'Marxism and global governance', in D. Held and A. McGrew (eds) *Governing Globalization* (Cambridge: Polity Press).

Calvert, J. (2000) '"The world is an undutiful boy!": Sayyid Qutb's American experience', *Islam and Christian–Muslim Relations*, **2**: 87–103.

Carr, E.H. (1941) *The Future of Nations: Independence or Interdependence?* (London: Kegan & Paul).

Carr, E.H. (1939) *The Twenty Years' Crisis, 1919–1939: An Introduction to the Study of International* Relations (London: Macmillan).

Castells, M. (1996) *The Information Age: The Rise of the Network Society*, vol. 1 (Oxford: Blackwell).

Castells, M. (2000) *The End of Millennium, The Information Age: Economy, Society and Culture*, vol. 3, 2nd edn (Oxford: Blackwell).

Castells, M. (2002a) *The Internet Galaxy: Reflections on the Internet, Business and Society* (Oxford: Oxford University Press).

Castles, S. (2002b) 'Migration and community formation under conditions of globalization', *International Migration Review*, **36**(4): 1143–68.

Castells, M. (2004) *The Power of Identity, The Information Age: Economy, Power and Identity*, vol. 2, 2nd edn (Oxford: Blackwell).

Castells, M. and Ince, M. (2003) *Conversations with Manuel Castells* (Cambridge: Polity Press).

Castles, S. and Miller, M. (2003) *The Age of Migration: International Population Movements in the Modern World*, 3rd edn (Basingstoke: Palgrave Macmillan).

Cheah, P. and Robbins, B. (eds) (1998) *Cosmopolitics: Thinking and Feeling beyond the Nation* (Minneapolis: University of Minneapolis Press).

Cleveland, W.L. (1971) *The Making of an Arab Nationalist: Ottomanism and Arabism in the Life and Thought of Sati' al-Husri* (Princeton, NJ: Princeton University Press).

Cohen, R. and Vertovec, S. (2002) 'Introduction: conceiving cosmopolitanism', in R. Cohen and S. Vertovec (eds) *Conceiving Cosmopolitanism: Theory, Context and Practice* (Oxford: Oxford University Press).

Cowen, T. (2004) *Creative Destruction: How Globalization is Changing the World's Culture* (Princeton, NJ: Princeton University Press).

Dabrowski, M., Gomulka, S. and Rostowski, J. (2000) 'Whence reform?: A critique of the Stiglitz perspective', http://siteresources.worldbank.org/INTDECINEQ/Resources/rostowski.pdf.

Davidson, J. and Yates, J. (2002) 'In the vanguard of globalization', in P.L. Berger and S.P. Huntingdon (eds) *Many Globalizations: Cultural Diversity in the Contemporary World* (Oxford: Oxford University Press).

Davis, M. (2001) *Magical Urbanism: Latinos Reinvent the US City* (London: Verso).

Dawn, C. (2000) 'The quality of Arab nationalism', in D. Hopwood (ed.) *Arab Nation and Nationalism* (Basingstoke: Macmillan – now Palgrave Macmillan).

Day, G. and Thompson, A. (2004) *Theorizing Nationalism* (Basingstoke: Palgrave Macmillan).

Desai, K. (2006) *The Inheritance of Loss* (London: Hamish Hamilton).

Deutsch, K. (1966) *Nationalism and Social Communication* (Cambridge, MA; MIT Press).

Devlin, K. (2007) 'SNP snubbed as support for independence slumps', *Daily Telegraph*, 1 November.

Durkheim, E. (1968) *Moral Education* (New York: Free Press).

Eickelman, D. and Piscatori, J. (1996) *Muslim Politics* (Princeton, NJ: Princeton University Press).

Engels, F. (1975) 'The Magyar struggle', in K. Marx and F. Engels *Collected Works*, vol. 8 (London: Lawrence & Wishart).

Epstein, S. (2001) 'Nationalism and globalization in Korean underground music', in R. Starrs (ed.) *Asian Nationalism in an Age of Globalization* (Richmond: Japan Library).

Ergang, R. (1931) *Herder and the Foundations of German Nationalism* (New York: Columbia University Press).

Fealy, G. (2005) 'Islamisation and politics in Southeast Asia: the contrasting cases of Malaysia and Indonesia', in N. Lahoud and A. Johns (eds) *Islam in World Politics* (Abingdon: Routledge).

Featherstone, M. (1992) 'Global culture: an introduction', in M. Featherstone (ed.) *Global Culture: Nationalism, Globalization and Modernity* (London: Sage).

Financial Times (2006) 'Empire strikes back as Tata bids for Corus', 21 October.

Frieden, J.A. (2005) *Global Capitalism: Its Rise and Fall in the Twentieth Century* (London: W.W. Norton).

Friedman, T. (2000) *The Lexus and the Olive Tree*, 2nd edn (London: HarperCollins).

Friedman, T. (2005) *The World is Flat: A Brief History of the Twenty-first Century* (New York: Picador).

Fuller, G.E. (2003) *The Future of Political Islam* (Basingstoke: Palgrave Macmillan).

Garnham, P. (2007) 'NY's share of foreign exchange trade slips as London dominates', *Financial Times*, 26 September.

Gellner, E. (1964) *Thought and Change* (London: Weidenfeld & Nicolson).

Gellner, E. (1973) 'Scale and nation', in E. Gellner, *Contemporary Thought and Politics* (London: Routledge & Kegan Paul).

Gellner, E. (1983) *Nations and Nationalism* (Oxford: Basil Blackwell).

Gellner, E. (1991) 'Nationalism in Eastern Europe', *New Left Review*, 1(189): 127–34.

Gellner, E. (1996) 'Do nations have navels', *Nations and Nationalism*, 2: 367–68.

Gellner, E. (1997) 'Reply to critics', *New Left Review*, 1(221): 82–118.

Giddens, A. (1990) *The Consequences of Modernity* (Stanford: Stanford University Press).

Gilesman, M. (1990) *Recognizing Islam, Religion and Society in the Modern Middle East* (London: IB Tauris).

Gilpin, R. (1987) *The Political Economy of International Relations* (Princeton, NJ: Princeton University Press).

Glenny, M. (1999) *The Balkans 1804–1999: Nationalism, War and the Great Powers* (London: Granta Books).

Gomes, L. (2003) *The Economics and Ideology of Free Trade* (London: Edward Elgar).

Gramsci, A. (1982) *Selections From Prison Notebooks* (London: Lawrence & Wishart).

Greenspan, A. (2004) *India and the IT Revolution: Networks of a Global Culture* (Basingstoke: Palgrave Macmillan).

Greenfeld, L. (2001) *The Spirit of Capitalism: Nationalism and Economic Growth* (Cambridge, MA: Harvard University Press).

Guardian (2006) 'The colonel's recipe for defeat', 2 February, p. 7.

Guibernau, M. (1996) *Nationalisms: The Nation-state and Nationalism in the Twentieth Century* (Cambridge: Polity Press).

Guibernau, M. (1999) *Nations without States: Political Communities in a Global Age* (Cambridge: Polity Press).

Guibernau, M. (2004) *Catalan Nationalism: Francoism, Transition and the Democracy* (London: Routledge).

Guibernau, M. and Hutchinson, J. (2004) *History and National Identity: Ethnosymbolism and its Critics* (Oxford: Basil Blackwell).

Hall, S. (2002) 'Political belonging in a world of multiple identities', in S. Vertovec and R. Cohen (eds) *Conceiving Cosmopolitanism* (Oxford: Oxford University Press).

Halliday, F. (1994) 'The politics of Islamic fundamentalism: Iran, Tunisia and the challenge to the secular state', in A. Ahmed and H. Donnan (eds) *Islam, Globlization and Postmodernity* (London: Routledge).

Hannerz, U. (1992) 'Cosmopolitans and locals', in M. Featherstone (ed.) *Global Culture: Nationalism, Globalization and Modernity* (London: Sage).

Hardt, M. and Negri, A. (2000) *Empire* (Cambridge, MA: Harvard University Press).

Harris, N. (1986) *The End of the Third World: Newly Industrializing Countries and the Decline of an Ideology* (London: Penguin).

Harris, N. (1990) *National Liberation* (London: IB Tauris).

Harris, N. (1991) 'A comment on national liberation', *International Socialism*, **53**: 82.

Harris, N. (1996) *The New Untouchables: Immigration and the New World Worker* (London: Penguin).

Harris, N. (2003) *The Return of Cosmopolitan Capital: Globalisation, the State and War* (London: IB Tauris).

Harvie, C. (2007) 'Drop the dead shark', *Guardian*, 17 August, www.guardian.co.uk/commentisfree/2007/aug/17/dropthedeadshark.

Hastings, A. (1997) *The Construction of Nationhood: Ethnicity, Religion and Nationalism* (Cambridge: Cambridge University Press).

Hayes, C. (1931) *The Historical Evolution of Modern Nationalism* (New York: Macmillan).

Hegel, F. (1994) *Philosophy of Mind* (Oxford: Oxford University Press).

Held, D. (1995) *Democracy and the New Global Order: From the Modern State to Cosmopolitan Governance* (Cambridge: Polity Press).

Held, D. (2005) *Debating Globalization* (Cambridge: Polity Press).

Held, D. and McGrew, A. (2007) 'Globalization at risk', in D. Held and A. McGrew (eds) *Globalization Theory: Approaches and Controversies* (Cambridge: Polity Press).

Held, D., McGrew, A., Goldblatt, D. and Perraton, J. (1999) *Global Transformations: Politics, Economics and Culture* (Cambridge: Polity Press).

Helleiner, E and Pickel, A. (eds) (2005) *Economic Nationalism in a Globalizing World* (Ithaca: Cornell University Press).

Hertz, N. (2001) 'A globalisation critic defends herself', *Prospect*, **66**.

Hertz, N. (2001) *The Silent Takeover: Global Capitalism and the Death of Democracy* (London: Heinemann).

Hetata, S. (1998) 'Dollarization, fragmentation and God', in F. Jameson and M. Miyoshi (eds) *The Cultures of Globalization* (Durham, NC: Duke University Press).

Hieronymi, O. (1980) *The New Economic Nationalism* (London: Macmillan).

Hirst, P. and Thompson, G. (1999) *Globalization in Question: The International Economy and the Possibilities of Governance*, 2nd edn (Cambridge; Polity Press).

Hobbes, T. (1962) *Leviathan (London: Oxford University Press).*

Hobsbawm, E. (1962) *The Age of Revolution 1789–1848* (London: New English Library).

Hobsbawm, E. (1975) *The Age of Capital 1848–1875* (London: Weidenfeld & Nicolson).

Hobsbawm, E. (1987) *The Age of Empire 1875–1914* (New York: Pantheon).

Hobsbawm, E. (1988) *The Age of Capital 1848–1875* (London: Cardinal).

Hobsbawm, E. (1992) *Nations and Nationalism Since 1780: Programme, Myth and Reality*, 2nd edn (Cambridge: Cambridge University Press).

Hobsbawm, E. (1994) *The Age of Extremes: The Short Twentieth Century 1914–1991* (London: Michael Joseph).

Hobsbawm, E. (2007) *Globalization, Democracy and Terrorism* (London: Little, Brown).

Hobsbawm, E. and Ranger, T. (eds) (1983) *The Invention of Tradition* (Cambridge: Cambridge University Press).

Holt, J. (2007) 'It's the oil', *London Review of Books*, 18 October.

Hroch, M. (1993) 'From national movement to the fully-formed nation', *New Left Review*, **1**(198): 3–20.

Hsiao, H.M. (2002) 'Coexistence and synthesis: cultural globalisation and localisation in contemporary Taiwan', in P.L. Berger and S.P. Huntingdon (eds) *Many Globalizations: Cultural Diversity in the Contemporary World* (Oxford: Oxford University Press).

Hussain, A. and Miller, W. (2006) *Multicultural Nationalism: Islamophobia, Anglophobia and Devolution* (Oxford: Oxford University Press).

Hutchinson, J. (2005) 'Nationalism and the clash of civilizations', in J. Hutchinson, *Nations as Zones of Conflict* (London: Sage).

Huntington, S. (1993) 'The clash of civilizations?', *Foreign Affairs*, **72**(3): 22–49.

Huntington, S. (1998) *The Clash of Civilizations and the Remaking of World Order* (London: Touchstone).

Iyer, P. (1997) 'The nowhere man', *Prospect*, Feb.

James, H. (2001) *The End of Globalization: Lessons from the Great Depression* (Cambridge, MA: Harvard University Press).

Jameson, F. (1998) 'Notes on globalization as a philosophical issue', in F. Jameson and M. Miyoshi (eds) *The Cultures of Globalization* (Durham, NC: Duke University Press).

Johnson, H. (ed.) (1968) *Economic Nationalism in Old and New States* (New York: Allen & Unwin).

Jones, C. (1987) *Internatio: The Rise and Fall of a Cosmopolitan Trading Class* (Brighton: Wheatsheaf).

Kahan, A. (1968) 'Nineteenth century European experiences with policies of economic nationalism', in H. Johnson (ed.) *Economic Nationalism in Old and New States* (New York: Allen & Unwin).

Kaldor, M. (1995) 'European institutions, nation states and nationalism', in M. Kaldor and D. Held (eds) *Cosmopolitan Democracy: An Agenda for a New World Order* (Cambridge: Polity Press).

Karam, A. (2005) 'Transnational political Islam and the USA: an introduction', in A. Karam (ed.) *Transnational Political Islam: Religion, Ideology and Power* (London: Pluto Press).

Keating, M. (2001) *Nations against the State: The New Politics of Nationalism in Quebec, Catalonia and Scotland*, 2nd edn (Basingstoke: Palgrave – now Palgrave Macmillan).

Keating, M. and Loughlin, J. (1997) *The Political Economy of Regionalism* (London: Frank Cass).

Keating, M. and McGarry, J. (eds) (2001) *Minority Nationalism and the Changing International Order* (Oxford: Oxford University Press).

Kellner, H. and Soeffner, H. (2002) 'Cultural globalization in Germany', in P.L. Berger and S.P. Huntingdon (eds) *Many Globalizations: Cultural Diversity in the Contemporary World* (Oxford: Oxford University Press).

Kepel, G. (2002) *Jihad: The Trail of Political Islam* (London: IB Tauris).

Kepel, G. (2004) *The War for Muslim Minds: Islam and the West* (Cambridge, MA: Harvard University Press).

Khomeini, R. (1981) *Islam and Revolution*, trans. H. Algar (London: Kegan and Paul).

Kleingeld, P. (2003) 'Kant's cosmopolitan patriotism', *Kant Studien*, **94**: 299–316.

Kohn, H. (1937) 'Twilight of nationalism', *American Scholar*, **6**: 259–70.

Kovács, J.M. (2002) 'Rival temptations and passive resistance', in P.L. Berger and S.P. Huntingdon (eds) *Many Globalizations: Cultural Diversity in the Contemporary World* (Oxford: Oxford University Press).

Krushna, P. (2005) *Trade Blocks, Economics and Politics* (Cambridge: Cambridge Press).

Kymlicka, W. (2001) 'Immigrant integration and minority nationalism', in M. Keating and J. McGarry (eds) *Minority Nationalism and the Changing International Order* (Oxford: Oxford University Press).

Laible, J. (2001) 'Nationalism and a critique of European integration: questions from Flemish parties', in M. Keating and J. McGarry (eds) *Minority Nationalism and the Changing International Order* (Oxford: Oxford University Press).

Larsen, P. (2007) 'Mathewson gives his backing to SNP', *Financial Times*, 16 March.

Lawrence, P. (2004) *Nationalism: History and Theory* (Harlow: Pearson Education).

Lawrence, R.Z. and Litan, R.E. (1986) *Saving Free-trade: A Pragmatic Approach* (Washington: Brookings Institute).

Leonard, M. (2005) *Why Europe Will Run the Twenty First Century* (London: Fourth Estate).

Lerner, D. (1958) *The Passing of Traditional Society* (Glencoe, IL: Free Press).

Levi-Faur, D. (1997) 'Friedrich List and political economy of the nation-state', *Review of International Political Economy*, **4**(1): 154–78.

List, F. (1909) *The National System of Political Economy*, trans. S. Lloyd (London: Longman).

Llobera, J. (2005) *Foundations of National Identity: From Catalonia to Europe* (New York: Berghahn Books).

McCall, C. (1999) *Identity in Northern Ireland: Communities, Politics and Change* (Basingstoke: Palgrave Macmillan).

McCrone, D. (1998) *The Sociology of Nationalism: Tomorrow's Ancestors* (London: Routledge).

McCrone, D. (2001) *Understanding Scotland: The Sociology of a Stateless Nation*, 2nd edn (London: Routledge).

McCrone, D., Kendrick, S. and Straw, P. (1989) *The Making of Scotland: Nation, Culture and Social Change* (Edinburgh: Edinburgh University Press).

McInnes, J. (2004) 'Catalonia is not Scotland', *Scottish Affairs*, **47**: 135–55.

McInnes, J. (2006) 'Castells' Catalan routes: nationalism and the sociology of identity', *British Journal of Sociology*, **57**(4): 677–98.

McLuhan, M. (1962) *The Gutenberg Man: The Making of Typographic Man* (London: Routledge).

Magas, B. (1991) 'Nationalism and politics in Eastern Europe: a response to Ernest Gellner', *New Left Review*, **1**(190): 138–44.

Makris, G.P. (2007) *Islam in the Middle East: A Living Tradition* (Oxford: Basil Blackwell).

Mamdani, M. (2005) 'Whither political Islam?', *Foreign Affairs*, **84**(1): 148–55.

Mandaville, P. (2007) *Global Political Islam* (London: Routledge).

Mangan, J. (1986) '"The grit of our forefathers": invented traditions, imperialism and popular culture', in J. McKenzie (ed.) *Imperialism and Popular Culture* (Manchester: Manchester University Press).

Marcotte, R.D. (2005) 'Identity, power and the Islamist discourse on women', in N. Lahoud and A.H. Johns (eds) *Islam in World Politics* (Abingdon: Routledge).

Marx, K. (1973) *Grundrisse* (Harmondsworth: Penguin).

Marx, K. (1976) *Capital*, vol. 1 (Harmondsworth: Penguin).

Marx, K. and Engels, F. (1998) *The Communist Manifesto* (London: Verso).

Mawdudi, S. (1967) *Unity of the Muslim World* (Lahore: Islamic Publications).

Mawdudi, S. (1992) *West versus Islam* (New Delhi: International Islamic Publishers).

Mill, J.S. (1882) *Considerations on Representative Government* (London: Longmans).

Milton-Edwards, B. (2004) *Islam and Politics in the Contemporary World* (Cambridge: Polity Press).

Montesquieu, C. (1990) *Selected Political Writings*, ed. and trans. M. Richter (Indianapolis: Hackett).

Munck, R. (1985) *The Difficult Dialogue: Marxism and Nationalism* (London: Zed Books).

Nairn, T. (1993) 'Demonising nationalism', *London Review of Books*, 25 February.

Nairn, T. (2007) 'Union on the rocks', *New Left Review*, **2**: 117–32.

Nairn, T. and James, P. (2005) *Global Matrix: Nationalism, Globalism and State Terrorism* (London: Pluto Press).

Nakano, T. (2004) 'Theorising economic nationalism', *Nations and Nationalism*, **10**: 211–29.

Nieven, R. (2004) *A World Beyond Difference: Cultural Identity in an Age of Globalization* (Oxford: Blackwell).

Noam, E. (1991) *Television in Europe* (Oxford: Oxford University Press).

O'Day, A. (2000) 'Nationalism and the economic question in twentieth century Ireland', in A. Teichova, H. Matis and J. Patek (eds) *Economic Change and the National Question in Twentieth-century Europe* (Cambridge: Cambridge University Press).

OECD (2007) *OECD Factbook 2007: Economic, Environmental and Social Statistics*, www.source.OECD.org/factbook.

Ohmae, K. (1990) *The Borderless World: Power and Strategy in the Global Marketplace* (London: HarperCollins).

Ohmae, K. (1996) *The End of the Nation-state: The Rise of Regional Economies* (London: HarperCollins).

Özbudun, E. and Keyman, E.F. (2002) 'Cultural globalization in Turkey', in P.L. Berger and S.P. Huntingdon (eds) *Many Globalizations: Cultural Diversity in the Contemporary World* (Oxford: Oxford University Press).

Özkirimli, U (2005) *Contemporary Debates on Nationalism: A Critical Engagement* (Basingstoke: Palgrave Macmillan).

Padgett, D. (1989) *Settlers and Sojourners: A Study of Serbian Adaptation in Milwaukee, Wisconsin* (New York: AMS Press).

Pappe, I. (2006) 'Arab nationalism', in G. Delanty and K. Kumar (eds) *The Sage Handbook of Nations and Nationalism* (London: Sage).

Pieterse, J.N. (1995) 'Globalization as hybridization', in M. Featherstone, S. Lash and R. Robertson (eds) *Global Modernities* (London: Sage).

Pieterse, J.N. (2005) 'Islam: an alternative globalism and reflections on the Netherlands', in A. Karam (ed.) *Transnational Political Islam: Religion, Ideology and Power* (London: Pluto Press).

Pollock, A.M. and Price, D. (2000) 'Rewriting the regulations: how the World Trade Organization could accelerate privatisation in health-care systems', *Lancet*, **356**: 1995–2000.

Porter, B. (2000) *When Nationalism Began to Hate: Imagining Modern Politics in Nineteenth-century Poland* (Oxford: Oxford University Press).

Pottenger, J.R. (2005) 'Islam and ideology in Central Asia', in N. Lahoud and A.H. Johns (eds) *Islam in World Politics* (Abingdon: Routledge).

Prebisch, R. (1950) *The Economic Development of Latin America and its Principal Problems* (New York: United Nations Department of Economic Affairs).

Pryke, S. (2002) 'Review of David McCrone', *Sociology*, **13**: 571–2.

Qutb, S. (1985) *Milestones* (Damascus: Dar Al-Ilm).

Reid, H. (2007) 'Scotland's nationalists can afford to relax', *Financial Times*, 7 October.

Rifkin, J. (2004) *The European Dream: How Europe's Vision of the Future is Quietly Eclipsing the American Dream* (Cambridge: Polity Press).

Ritzer, G. (2008) *The McDonaldization of Society*, 5th edn (Thousand Oaks, CA: Pine Forge Press).

Robbins, L. (1961) *The Theory of Economic Policy in English Classical Economic Policy* (London: Macmillan).

Robertson, R. (1992) *Globalization: Social Theory and Global Culture* (London: Sage).

Rocker, R. (1937) *Nationalism and Culture* (Los Angeles, CA: Rocker Publications).

Rose, J. (1916) *Nationality as a Factor in Modern History* (London: Rivingtons).

Rosenberg, J. (2001) *The Follies of Globalization Theory* (London: Verso).

Rosenberg, J. (2005) 'Globalization theory: a post mortem', *International Politics*, **42**(1): 65.

Rosenthal, M. (1986) *The Character Factory: Baden-Powell and the Origins of the Boy Scout Movement* (New York: Pantheon Books).

Rostow, W. (1960) *Stages of Economic Growth: A Non-Communist Manifesto* (Cambridge: Cambridge University Press).

Roy, O. (1994) *The Failure of Political Islam* (London: IB Tauris).

Roy, O. (2000) 'Muslims in Europe: from ethnic identity to religious recasting', *ISIM Newsletter*, **5**(1): 29.

Roy, O. (2004) *Globalised Islam: The Search for a New Ummah* (London: Hurst).

Sageman, M. (2006) 'Islam and Al Quada', in A. Pedahzur (ed.) *Root Causes of Suicide Terrorism: The Globalization of Martydom* (London: Routledge).

Savage, M., Bagnall, G. and Longhurst, B. (2005) *Globalization and Belonging* (London: Sage).

Schafaeddin, M. (2000) 'What did Frederick (sic) List actually say? Some clarifications on the infant industry argument', www.unctad.org/en/docs/dp_149.en.pdf.

Seton-Watson, H. (1977) *Nations and States: An Enquiry into the Origins of Nations and the Politics of Nationalism* (London: Methuen).

Sidahmed, A.S. and Ehteshami, A. (1995) 'Introduction', in A.S. Sidahmed and A. Ehteshami (eds) *Islamic Fundamentalism* (Oxford: Westview Press).

Sinclair, U. (1949) *The Jungle* (London: T. Werner Laurie).

Skidelsky, R. (1992) *John Maynard Keynes*, vol. 2, *The Economist as Saviour 1920–1937* (Basingstoke: Macmillan – now Palgrave Macmillan).

Smith, A.D. (1986) *The Ethnic Origins of Nations* (Oxford: Basil Blackwell).

Smith, A.D. (1991) *National Identity* (London: Penguin).

Smith, A.D. (1992) 'Nationalism and the historians', *International Journal of Comparative Sociology*, **33**(1): 58–80.

Smith, A.D. (1995) *Nations and Nationalism in a Global Era* (Cambridge: Polity Press).

Smith, A.D. (1998) *Nationalism and Modernism: A Critical Survey of Recent Theories of Nations and Nationalism* (London: Routledge).

Smith, D.M. (1994) *Mazzini* (New Haven: Yale University Press).

Soros, G. (2002) *On Globalization* (New York: Public Affairs).

Spencer, H. (1885) *The Man v. the State* (London: William Northgate).

Spiro, P. (2007) *Beyond Citizenship: American Identity after Globalization* (Oxford: Oxford University Press).

Srinivas, T. (2002) 'The Indian case of globalization', in P.L. Berger and S.P. Huntingdon (eds) *Many Globalizations: Cultural Diversity in the Contemporary World* (Oxford: Oxford University Press).

Stephens, P. (2007) 'How Salmond sweetens the snake oil', *Financial Times*, 16 April.

Stiglitz, J. (2000) *Globalisation and its Discontents* (Basingstoke: Palgrave – now Palgrave Macmillan).

Takeshi, N. (2006) 'A critique of Held's cosmopolitan democracy', *Contemporary Political Theory*, **5**: 33–51.

Thomas, W.I. and Znanieck, F. (1927) *The Polish Peasant in Europe and America* (New York: Knopf).

Tomlinson, J. (2007) 'Globalization and cultural analysis', in D. Held and A. McGrew (eds) *Globalization Theory: Approaches and Controversies* (Cambridge: Polity Press).

Travis, A. (2008) 'How to feel more British: oath of allegiance and a special day', *Guardian*, 12 March.

Tsygankov, A. (2005) 'The return of Eurasia', in E. Helleiner and A. Pickel (eds) *Economic Nationalism in a Globalizing World* (Ithaca: Cornell University Press).

Ugresic, D. (2007) *Nobody's Home* (London: Telegram).

Urry, J. (2000) *Sociology Beyond Societies: Mobilities for the Twenty-first Century* (London: Routledge).

Urry, J. (2003) *Global Complexity* (Cambridge: Polity Press).

Wallace, W. (1997) 'The springs of integration', in P. Anderson and P. Gowan (eds) *The Question of Europe* (London: Verso).

Weber, E. (1976) *Peasants into Frenchmen: The Modernization of Rural France 1870–1914* (London: Chatto & Windus).

Weber, M. (1930) *The Protestant Ethic and the Spirit of Capitalism*, trans. T. Parsons (London: Allen & Unwin).

Weber, M. (1948) *From Max Weber*, ed. and intro. by H.H. Gerth and C. Wright Mills (London: Routledge).

Weinberg, I. (1969) 'The problem of the convergence of industrial societies: a critical look at the state of a theory', *Comparative Studies in Society and History*, **11**(1): 1–15.

Wheen, F. (2000) *Karl Marx* (London: Fourth Estate).

Wolf, M. (2001) 'Infantile Leftist', *Prospect*, **65**.

Wolf, M. (2004) *Why Globalization Works* (New Haven: Yale University Press).

Yan, Y. (2002) 'Managed globalization: state power and cultural transition in China', in P.L. Berger and S.P. Huntingdon (eds) *Many Globalizations: Cultural Diversity in the Contemporary World* (Oxford: Oxford University Press).

Yudice, G. (2003) *The Expediency of Culture* (Durham, NC: Duke University Press).

Zangwill, I. (1917) *The Principle of Nationalities* (London: Watts).

Zubaida, S. (2004) 'Islam and nationalism: continuities and contradictions', *Nations and Nationalism*, **10**: 407–20.

Index